Hjalmar Johansen, Hans Lien Braekstad

**With Nansen in the North**

A Record of the Fram Expedition in 1893-96

Hjalmar Johansen, Hans Lien Braekstad

**With Nansen in the North**
*A Record of the Fram Expedition in 1893-96*

ISBN/EAN: 9783337187934

Printed in Europe, USA, Canada, Australia, Japan

Cover: Foto ©Andreas Hilbeck / pixelio.de

More available books at **www.hansebooks.com**

# WITH NANSEN IN THE NORTH

A Record of the *Fram* Expedition
in 1893-96

BY HJALMAR JOHANSEN

LIEUTENANT IN THE NORWEGIAN ARMY

TRANSLATED FROM THE NORWEGIAN
BY H. L. BRÆKSTAD

GEORGE N. MORANG

PUBLISHER AND IMPORTER

Toronto, Canada

# Contents

### CHAPTER I

The Equipment of the Expedition—Its Start—The Voyage along the Coast—Farewell to Norway . . . . . . . . .   1

### CHAPTER II

The First Ice—Arrival at Khabarova—Meeting with Trontheim—Arrival of the Dogs—Life among the Samoyedes—Christofersen Leaves us—Excursion on Yalmal—The last Human Beings we saw   10

### CHAPTER III

A Heavy Sea—Sverdrup Island—A Reindeer Hunt—The First Bear—A Stiff Pull—Firing with Kerosene . . . . . .   20

### CHAPTER IV

Death among the Dogs—Taimur Island—Cape Butterless—The Northernmost Point of the Old World—A Walrus Hunt—To the North . . . . . . . . . . . .   28

### CHAPTER V

Open Water—Unwelcome Guests—Fast in the Ice—Warping—The Northern Lights . . . . . . . . .   34

### CHAPTER VI

First Day of Rest—Surprised by Bears—The Dogs are let Loose—Ice Pressure—A Hunt in the Dark . . . . . .   40

### CHAPTER VII

More Bears—The Power of Baking Powder—"Johansen's Friend"—Electric Light—Shooting Competition . . . . . .   50

## CONTENTS

### CHAPTER VIII
Foot-races on the Ice—More about the Dogs—The Northern Lights—Adulterated Beer—Ice Pressure—Peder Attacked by a Bear . 57

### CHAPTER IX
Deep Soundings—The Bear and the Trap—Christmas and New Year—The Drift—Our State of Health—Walrus. . . . . 69

### CHAPTER X
Changes in the Ice—Trying the Dogs with the Sledges—The Return of the Sun—A Ski-tour in 60° below Zero—An Eclipse of the Sun—Unsuccessful Bear-hunting—Spring . . . . . 79

### CHAPTER XI
Summer Excursion on the Ice—Midsummer Day—"Suggen" and "Caiaphas"—The Drift . . . . . . . . . 92

### CHAPTER XII
Snow-blindness—More Dogs—Mistaking a Dog for a Bear—A Real Bear—A Retrospect—Nansen Asks Me if I will Accompany Him to the Pole . . . . . . . . . . . 105

### CHAPTER XIII
Nansen's Lecture—Fitting out the Sledge Expedition—Christmas and New Year Once More—Our Worst Pressures . . . . 120

### CHAPTER XIV
Beating the World's Record—The Depôt on the Big Hummock—The Second Arctic Night—More about the Equipment of the Sledge Expedition . . . . . . . . . . . 134

### CHAPTER XV
The Departure—We Make Two Starts—I Act as Snow-plough—Sun Festival and Celebration on Passing the Eighty-fourth Degree . 147

### CHAPTER XVI
Off at Last—The Fight Across the Ice to 86° 14'—Farthest North . 157

# CONTENTS

### CHAPTER XVII

The Norwegian Flag in the Farthest North—On the Way Home—Our Watches Stop—In the Kingdom of Great Silence—Tracks of Foxes—Mild Weather . . . . . . . . . . 171

### CHAPTER XVIII

More Lanes—Summer Weather—Another "Seventeenth of May"—A Whale—Where in all the World is Land? . . . . . 180

### CHAPTER XIX

More Ridges and Lanes—The First Bird and Seal—Whitsuntide—Fish—Still no Land—Short Commons—The First Ferry—A Lucky Shot . . . . . . . . . . . 192

### CHAPTER XX

"Longing Camp"—St. John's Eve Illuminations—Three Bears—A Long Sleep—The White Cloud-bank—Land!—In a Bear's Clutches . . . . . . . . . . . 207

### CHAPTER XXI

Farewell to the Drift-ice—"Suggen" and "Caiaphas" must Die—Under Sail at Last—What Land is this?—Attacked by Walrus—The Fog Lifts—We Cut our Sledges Adrift—A Snowless Land—Drift-ice Again—Plenty of Bears and Walruses . . . . 227

### CHAPTER XXII

Obliged to Winter—Our "Den"—Hunting the Walrus—Adrift Again—A Hard Struggle for Land—Awakened by Bears—Hunting Bears in the Kayak—An Inquisitive Walrus—Birds and Foxes—Our Implements—The "Hut" . . . . . . . . 248

### CHAPTER XXIII

An Uninvited Guest in our Hut—Walrus in Abundance—The "Water Bear"—Two Motherless Ones—The "Lean Bear"—We Change our Quarters—The First Night in the Hut . . . . . 261

### CHAPTER XXIV

Life in the Hut—Our Domestic Animals—Fox Traps, but no Foxes—A Kayak Adrift—Open Water—Christmas Once More . . 275

## CHAPTER XXV

The New Year — The Sun Reappears — Spring — Running Short of Blubber — The Bear which Wanted to Get into the Hut — Preparing to Start Again — The Land of the Ice-bear . . . 290

## CHAPTER XXVI

Farewell to the Hut—Across the Ice-field on Ski—Weather-bound for Fourteen Days—Open Water—Sailing on the Ice and at Sea—Where are We?—A Swim for Life . . . . . . 306

## CHAPTER XXVII

Hunting Young Walruses—A Walrus Cuts a Hole in Nansen's Kayak—We hear Dogs Barking—Nansen does not Return from his Reconnoitring—Six Strangers on the Ice—The Norwegian Flag Hoisted—Soap and Civilization . . . . . . . 318

## CHAPTER XXVIII

English Hospitality—A New Life—Post from Norway—Visit from a Bear—Excursions—Waiting for the Ship—Home-sick . . . 327

## CHAPTER XXIX

The *Windward* Arrives—Farewell to Franz Josef Land—The Last of the Ice—Norwegian Soil under our Feet—*Otaria*—The *Fram* has Arrived—We Meet our Comrades Again—Andrée—A Month of Festivities . . . . . . . . . . 334

*Photo by]* [LANCASTER.
DR. FRIDTJOF NANSEN.
*With Nansen in the North.]* *[Page 1.*

# CHAPTER I

*The Equipment of the Expedition—Its Start—The Voyage along the Coast—Farewell to Norway*

IT was in the spring of 1893 that we who were to share through good and ill the fortunes of the *Fram* began to assemble in Christiania. We came from different parts of Norway, and as we were strangers to one another, we scanned each other's faces with not a little curiosity. We were all, of course, absolutely confident as to the success of the expedition, and were most cordial in our greetings, wishing each other a successful journey to the Pole. With regard, however, to the time which the journey would take, opinions were divided. Those of us who had never been to the Arctic regions before naturally listened eagerly to the talk of the more experienced about pack-ice and ice-floes.

The expedition consisted of the following members:—

|  | Born |
|---|---|
| Dr. Fridtjof Nansen, chief of the expedition | 1861 |
| Otto Sverdrup, commander | 1855 |
| Sigurd Scott-Hansen, lieutenant in the Norwegian Navy, who undertook the meteorological, astronomical, and magnetic observations | 1868 |
| Henrik G. Blessing, doctor and botanist | 1866 |
| Theodore C. Jacobsen, mate | 1855 |
| Anton Amundsen, chief engineer | 1853 |
| Adolf Juell, steward and cook | 1860 |
| Lars Petterson, second engineer | 1860 |

Peder Hendriksen, harpooner . . . . 1859
Bernhard Nordahl, electrician . . . . 1862
Ivar Mogstad, general hand . . . . 1856
Bernt Bentsen, general hand, who joined the expedition at Tromsö . . . . . 1860

The thirteenth member of the expedition was myself; I engaged to go as stoker, as no other post could be found for me when I applied. My duties as stoker lasted only two months—until we entered the ice. After that I acted as meteorological assistant.

For two months before our departure we had a busy time, and the nearer the day approached the greater was the activity which we displayed. Men from the Akers Engineering Works were to be seen all over the ship. There were mechanics, joiners, carpenters, riggers, and stevedores. Juell and I were busy on the little island of Tjuveholmen, examining and making lists of the provisions. These were afterwards stowed away with the greatest care and order in the main-hold, the fore-hold, and the holds on both sides aft the cabin. In the bows, between the beams and the knees, lay Peder Hendriksen stowing dog-biscuits until the sweat ran down his cheeks. A cargo of these biscuits arrived from London when the ship was almost full, and I remember Dr. Nansen telling me what a start it gave him when, on coming on board one morning, he saw the deck covered with cases of them. Room had to be found for as many as we could stow away. It was really wonderful what that ship held; and she was not empty, either, when we got home. Indeed, we could very well have gone off on a new expedition with what remained.

We prepared a kind of plan of the various rows of boxes, so that we should easily be able to find the sort of provisions that might be wanted from time to time after we had got among the ice. The coal was stowed in the lower hold and in the bunkers on either side of the engine-room, while the paraffin oil was kept in large iron tanks in the lower hold, in the 'tween decks, and on the upper deck. A large quantity of the oil was kerosene. This was to be used as firing for the boilers, being sprinkled over the burning coals in the form of a spray by means of a steam-jet apparatus.

Most of the provisions were stowed away in the main-hold, every corner of which was utilized. If the boxes could not be got in between the knees, the space was filled up with firewood, which would always come in useful. Of good food there was plenty on board the *Fram*—preserved meats from Norway, Denmark, America, and Australia, such as pork cutlets, forced-meat balls, roast and corned beef, roast and corned mutton, rabbits, breakfast bacon, which we called "hymn books," various kinds of pemmican, cod roe, minced fish, mackerel, dried and grated fish, fish-meal, dried and tinned vegetables, jams and marmalades, rice, chocolate, cocoa, oatmeal, Indian meal, white and rye bread, flour, sugar, coffee, lime-juice, Knorr's soups, etc., etc. Everything was of the best quality that could be procured.

Dr. Nansen had the entire control of the vessel's equipment. He superintended everything and personally assured himself that all, both as regards the *Fram* and her provisioning, was exactly as he wanted it to be and satisfactory in every respect. Our chief knew the importance of a thorough equipment, and had spent many years in mastering every detail relating to such expeditions. Captain Sverdrup assisted him faithfully in all his work. This officer went about the ship, silent and quiet, noting everything, and speaking but little, but getting all the more work done on that account.

At last the day arrived when we were ready to

weigh anchor. It was the 24th of June, 1893. The day was dull and grey, but we did not feel at all depressed. We were in high spirits at having at length reached the point at which our journey was to begin. A large number of people had assembled to see us depart, but it took some little time before we could actually start. There was always something wanting at the last moment. I remember, for instance, that we waited in vain for the supply of ice for the steward, and had at last to go without it. "We shall have plenty of it later on," said the cook. Just before we weighed anchor, Nansen arrived alongside in the petroleum launch from his house at Lysaker, and soon afterwards the *Fram* glided quietly and majestically down the fjord, accompanied by a swarm of steamers and sailing craft, which sent us on our way with music and cheering. We could hardly feel that we deserved all this cheering, for we had as yet done nothing—we were only just going to begin.

We knew that we should have each and all to do our best if the confidence of those jubilant people in us was not to be disappointed. There were those among them, no doubt, who believed that we should never come back again.

At Horten, we took on board powder and signalling guns, and at Rekvik—where the wharf of Mr. Colin Archer, the builder of the *Fram*, is situated — we shipped our long-boats. Mr. Archer and his family came on board and remained with us while the *Fram* proceeded up the bay towards Laurvik and made a tour round the harbour, the people cheering and flags flying all the time. When Mr. Archer left the ship we fired our first salute, this time in honour of the builder of the *Fram*. As he stepped into the boat he said he was sure he would see the *Fram* again. That man knew what the ship could do.

Later in the day the sea became somewhat rough and the ship began to roll. This soon produced the first symptoms of sea-sickness in several of us. The engine worked admirably, and we were making about twenty-two miles in the watch. This was not much, but then we were deeply laden. Things were very lively on board. We were all in excellent spirits. We joked and chaffed each other early and late, but especially at meal-times, when most of us were together. Then the conversation usually turned upon what we were going to do when we reached the Pole. Nansen gave us a little music, and the cook was in a bad temper because we had such enormous appetites. "The coffee," he declared, "won't last beyond Tromsö." In the meantime we were advancing slowly but surely towards our goal.

On the night of the 28th of June we experienced very bad weather. The sea was not very high, but the round build of the *Fram* caused her to roll heavily. The waves washed constantly over her fore-deck; and on passing Lindesnæs, the most southerly promontory of Norway, we were obliged to throw overboard a number of empty paraffin-barrels and other deck cargo. The davits in which the long-boats hung creaked loudly.

I was in the engine-room with Petterson. It was not the most pleasant of places, being very close and confined, and it was not an easy task to act as stoker during such rolling. It would have been more agreeable if I had not been upset by sea-sickness at the same time.

On the evening of the 28th we anchored at Egersund, on the south-western coast of Norway. Next day we steamed past the Jæderen in smooth water, and, with the aid of sails, we made good progress.

On the 30th of June we began using the "Primus"

(a Swedish heating apparatus), instead of making a fire in the galley, which place the cook described as being only fit for Old Nick.

At Bergen we were magnificently *fêted*. Here we received our supply of Törfisk (dried codfish), which is an excellent article of food for men as well as for the dogs.

On the afternoon of the 2nd of July the fog obliged

THE *FRAM* AT ANCHOR.

us to anchor in the neighbourhood of Stadt, the well-known promontory on the west coast of Norway. Here we had our first opportunity on our voyage of obtaining some shooting. This time it was wild ducks.

On the 5th of July Sverdrup came on board at Bejan on the Throndhjem Fjord. A younger brother of his left the ship here. Scott-Hansen had hitherto acted as the *Fram's* captain.

On the 7th we anchored at Rörvik, on the island of Vigten, and were busily employed in re-stowing our coals and provisions. During the trip along the coast I lived mostly in the "Grand," as we called it.

NANSEN AND SVERDRUP ON THE BRIDGE.

We had both a "Gravesen"[1] and a "Grand"[1] on board. They consisted of the two long-boats, which, with the help of reindeer skins and sleeping-bags, we

[1] Two well-known restaurants in Christiania.

had fitted up as pleasant sleeping berths for the light summer nights.

Wherever we arrived we found that the people took the greatest interest in the expedition. We used to ask ourselves where all the people came from. We could see nothing but bare mountains, here and there covered with green patches, along the shore; yet we had no sooner stopped than we had a crowd of boats

VISITORS TO THE *FRAM*.

filled with people round about us. At one point, however, we passed a fisherman who was evidently a little behind the times. He hailed us and asked—

"Where are you from?"

"Christiania," we answered.

"What's your cargo?"

"Provisions and coal."

"Where are you bound for?"

"The Polar ice—the North Pole!" was our answer.

He evidently thought we were not in our right minds.

On the 12th of July we arrived in Tromsö. It snowed and hailed as if it had been the middle of winter. Here we were joined by Bernt Bentsen, who was to go with us as far as Khabarova as an extra hand, but on our arrival there he was engaged for the rest of the voyage.

At Tromsö Amundsen was severely injured through some coals falling upon him while he was at work in one of the bunkers. He received a big gaping wound in his head, but he did not seem to mind it much. He had his hair cut and washed, and the wound was then dressed and sewn up. He went about his work with his head enveloped in bandages the whole time, until we got fixed in the ice.

A coasting vessel laden with coals for the *Fram* had preceded us, and was to meet us at Khabarova. At Vardö the ship's bottom was examined by divers and cleared of mussels and weeds. At this our last place of call before leaving Norway, the inhabitants gave evidence of their great interest in our expedition by entertaining us to a sumptuous banquet.

On the 20th of July, at four o'clock in the morning, we steered out of the harbour and bade Norway farewell. I went up into the crow's-nest to have a last look at the land. It was hard to say when we should see it again.

## CHAPTER II

*The First Ice—Arrival at Khabarova—Meeting with Trontheim—Arrival of the Dogs—Life among the Samoyedes—Christofersen leaves us—Excursion on Yalmal—The last Human Beings we saw*

ON the 24th of July we celebrated the first birthday on board. It was Scott-Hansen's, and was kept up with great festivity. We had marmalade for breakfast and special dishes for dinner, followed by speeches.

Next day we sighted Goose Land, on Novaya Zemlya. We expected to reach it in the course of the day, but we were overtaken by fog and every trace of land disappeared. We had to keep off the coast while steering our course along it under sail and steam.

Kvik, Nansen's dog, which we had brought with us from Christiania, was, of course, a general favourite on board. It was a cross between a Newfoundland and Eskimo dog, and was very fond of anything made of leather. It devoured almost everything it got hold of—sailmakers' gloves, old shoes, clothes, paper, waterproofs, etc. It was not quite so bad, however, as the dog the American North Pole expedition had on board the *Polaris*. That dog used to eat door-handles!

It was on the 27th of July that we made our first acquaintance with the ice. We soon had it on both sides of us, but with much bumping against the icefloes we forced our way through them in the direction of the Yugor Strait. The engine-room was not now so warm as before. One day we had some trouble down there; a pipe burst and the pump was not in order; but things were soon put right again and no stoppage of the vessel took place.

It was a fortunate thing that we were well provisioned, for we boys on board the *Fram* had mighty good appetites. Each meal was a small *fête* in its way, and was seasoned with many a merry jest. Bentsen, in particular, had an inexhaustible fund of stories. He had always something fresh to tell us, and was never at a loss for some amusing tale. But it was only during the long polar night that he was really appreciated as he deserved to be.

It was a beautiful sight to see the midnight sun on the horizon looming blood-red over the surface of the water strewn with innumerable ice-floes, while the sky shone blue in the far distance. The *Fram* wended her way onward, readily answering her helm, but advancing slowly and heavily whenever it was necessary to ram through the ice; but with her we could ram without fear. She was now in her element, but under such conditions the man at the helm had a difficult task before him. Here the drift-ice did not always consist of nice, flat, decent floes, but assumed all kinds of shapes and forms. Jagged and cracked, grey, white, and dark, came drifting past us. Some were even covered with soil, others with fresh water, and all were heavy, slow, and deep in the water.

On the 29th of July, at half-past six in the evening we anchored off Khabarova. Here the person who had been commissioned to buy up dogs for the expedition in Siberia came on board. His name was Trontheim. His father was a Norwegian, and his mother a Russian from Riga, where he was born. He could speak German, and acted as our interpreter with the

Samoyedes. We learnt from him that the Kara Sea had been ice-free since the 4th of July, so that we might just as well have been here a little earlier. As soon as we had anchored we were boarded by the Samoyedes. They were dressed in clothes made of reindeer skins; most of them were ugly specimens of humanity, and all were dirty and ill-favoured. But the Russian traders who live here are fine-looking fellows, dressed in their long coats of reindeer skin and with their peculiar caps of reincalf skin. In the summer they stop at Khabarova, bartering their goods with the Samoyedes for various kinds of skins and furs. The Samoyede is very fond of spirits and tobacco, and when he knows they are to be got will often travel long distances with his reindeer or dogs. The traders have learned to turn this to advantage, and by the end of the summer, when they return home to dispose of their skins, they have generally done a most profitable business. The following summer they again return. The Samoyedes came on board to see Dr. Blessing and to benefit by his " healing wisdom." Some were troubled with festered hands, others with deafness. It is not at all unlikely that while these people were on board in the doctor's cabin, and their fur coats were left lying on the cabin floor, they were kind enough to present us with a good supply of vermin for the expedition; for soon after leaving Khabarova we noticed that we had companions of this sort on board, companions with whom we had no particular desire to travel.

There were ten Russians and thirty-five Samoyedes at Khabarova. They had no less than two churches there, one old and one new. On the 1st of August they celebrated a religious festival. Scott-Hansen, Mogstad, and I went ashore in the evening when the ceremony was over. There had been a service in both churches during the day. It appeared that there is a new and an old sect; but as the old sect had no priest just then, it had to pay two roubles to the priest of the new sect for a short service in the old church. As long as this lasted they crossed themselves and were most devout. But in the evening their religious zeal seemed to have disappeared entirely. Every man and woman was quite drunk. Several Samoyedes from the plains had arrived to take part in the celebration. We saw two of them who were driving like madmen with five reindeer among the tents. Outside one of the tents we saw a number of young foxes tied to small stakes driven into the ground. The two Samoyedes drove right amongst these foxes, whereupon a woman came screaming out of the tent, picked up the foxes, and carried them inside. We could not ascertain what they were going to do with these animals. Several of the Samoyedes were fighting, but they did not strike one another; they merely strove to tear the clothes off each other's bodies. Some amused themselves with a kind of skittles. The pins were pegs stuck into the ground, and at these they threw a piece of wood. Scott-Hansen looked into a tent and saw in a corner a strange-looking bundle of rags. He was rather taken aback when he saw the bundle begin to move and the face of an old woman appeared among the rags. She was completely drunk, and had rolled herself up into a bundle.

Trontheim and some of the Russians were several times obliged to interfere and keep them in order. Nor did the dogs seem to like all this noise. While we were going to the place where they were tied up a drunken Samoyede accompanied us. He wanted to show us that it was not with him that the dogs were angry, but with us. He courageously went up to one of the smooth-haired, white dogs, with upstanding ears, and wanted to pat it; but the dog snarled and snapped at him, and finally seized hold of one of the Samoyede's mittens, which hung and dangled at the end of his coat-sleeves, and held on to it with its teeth. This certainly did not help to convince us as to the dog's friendship for the Samoyede, but it undoubtedly convinced the Samoyede that dogs' teeth can easily find their way through fur mittens.

During these days we were busy cleaning the boilers and shifting the coals. Petterson and I were inside the boiler chipping off the salt which had been deposited on its sides. There was not much space for moving about inside the boiler. When we wanted to turn round we had to pull ourselves out and then crawl in again on the other side.

We looked a pretty sight when we had finished. The dirtiest of the Samoyedes would have looked clean in comparison with us. Nansen thought we ought to be immortalised, so he took a photograph of us.

Nansen, Sverdrup, and Peder Hendriksen—also called "Smallboy"—set out one day in the petroleum launch to investigate the state of the ice in the Kara Sea. They found plenty of ice; but along the coast there was a channel of open water. They shot a number of birds and one seal. As they were returning to the ship the engine got out of order, so that they had to make use of the oars.

While at Khabarova we put up an electric bell apparatus between the crow's-nest and the engine-room, so that the engineer might be in direct communication with the man aloft. We also got ready the apparatus for firing under the boiler with kerosene. The coaster with our coals was now anxiously expected. We began to fear she would never turn up.

On the 3rd of August we were ready, and the dogs were then brought on board. Trontheim was presented with King Oscar's gold medal of merit in recognition of the satisfactory manner in which he had performed his task. Nansen's secretary, Christofersen, also left us here. We should have been greatly pleased if he could have remained and accompanied us on the

Pilot.        Scott Hansen.        Petterson.
AT ANCHOR.

expedition. It was a solemn moment when he took leave of us and stepped into the boat with our letters for Norway. He had been supplied from the *Fram* with provisions for his journey. Afterwards we often thought of Christofersen, as he set off for the Samoyede camp in his white reindeer coat which he had bought of Trontheim, and with his rifle and otherwise scanty outfit. In all likelihood he would have many an adventure to go through before he returned home. On our return to Norway we learned that a day or two after our departure the coaster arrived—too late for us, however—and Trontheim and Christofersen returned in her to Vardö.

On the last day of our stay at Khabarova Bernt Bentsen was finally engaged to go on with the expedition. That boy did not take long to make up his mind! The weather was foggy as, late in the night, we weighed anchor. Nansen preceded the *Fram* in the petroleum launch to take soundings. On this occasion Nansen was in great danger of being seriously burnt. Some of the petroleum was spilt in the boat and caught fire. There had always been something wrong with that launch ever since we began to use it on the Christiania fjord. We passed safely through the Yugor Strait. The firing with kerosene under the boiler had not been successful. So much steam was required to blow the oil into the furnace that it became a question whether anything in particular was gained by it.

On Sunday, the 6th of August, on account of the fog, we made fast to an ice-floe close to the Yalmal coast. The quiet of Sunday reigned on board. We were all comfortably seated in the saloon, while the dynamo worked away steadily. Nansen, Scott-Hansen, Blessing, Hendriksen and I went ashore for a stroll. Near the beach, where we landed, the water was so shallow that we had to get out and wade, dragging the boat after us for a long way. Those of us who had sea-boots on had to carry the others on our backs both from and to the boat.

Scott-Hansen and I started off after ducks and

managed to shoot a few. While thus occupied we strayed away from the others. Near one of the small lakes, of which so many are to be found here, we discovered traces of a Samoyede encampment. While walking along and looking cautiously around us, for the night was somewhat dark, we suddenly saw a tent in the distance, probably a Samoyede tent, as we thought. We approached it warily to avoid being attacked by the dogs which, we presumed, would be sure to be about. But as we came nearer we found it was our comrades, who had taken some tarpaulins and oars from the boat and made a tent, inside of which they had made themselves comfortable. We found some driftwood, with the help of which we made some excellent coffee. This, along with a pipe of tobacco, we greatly enjoyed. We returned to the ship early in the morning.

On the 8th of August a boat with two Samoyedes came rowing out to the *Fram*. They kept near the stern of the ship. They were evidently afraid of leaving their boat, or perhaps they were afraid of being unable to get back to the shore again, on account of the ice. One of them was an old man with a grey beard, and the other quite young. We gave them some food, upon which they pointed towards land, evidently indicating thereby that there were more of them there. Bentsen, who was on the after-deck, threw down some biscuits to them, which they seized greedily. The young man at once tried his teeth upon them. There were some dog-biscuits among them, but they made no difference. Bentsen then took a match-box from his pocket and struck a match. The two Samoyedes looked up at the flame with open mouths. Bentsen threw the box down into the boat to them. The young Samoyede at once seized it and struck a match. He looked smilingly at the flame and then blew it out, after which

C

he carefully put the burnt-out match back into the box.
He evidently intended using it another time. In their
gratitude they made Bentsen a present of a pair of boots
made of reindeer skin. Soon afterwards we saw them
rowing towards the land in their wretched boat.

As we were obliged, by the state of the ice, to remain
in the same place, several of us went ashore in order to
see something of this little-known country, and meet
with some of the Samoyedes and barter with them.
The party consisted of Nansen, Sverdrup, Mogstad,
Blessing and myself. Blessing at once began gathering
plants on the desert plain, and I joined him. The other
three caught sight of some figures in the distance. They
were, no doubt, Samoyedes, but they appeared to be
frightened, and took to their heels. Our comrades
beckoned to them, but they ran still faster, and soon
disappeared from sight altogether. After having gathered some plants and shot some birds, Blessing and I
returned to the boat, up to which the water had now
risen. We took the tarpaulin from the boat and made a
kind of tent, which formed a good shelter for the night
after the others had returned, as it began raining and
blowing somewhat sharply. We went on, however,
telling stories and yarns until we fell asleep from sheer
fatigue. Sverdrup never enjoyed himself so much as on
such excursions. As soon as there was sufficient driftwood to make a good fire, and he could get the coffeekettle to boil, and our pipes were lighted, he was happy,
even though the shelter against wind and rain was not
of the best.

Early next morning we packed up and started for the
ship with the wind right against us, so that at first we
did not make much progress. When, therefore, late in
the forenoon, we got on board and could put on some
dry clothes and eat some food, these comforts were all
the more welcome. The observations made on this

occasion showed that the coast-line at this part of the country had been laid down in the chart about thirty-five miles too far west.

OFF THE COAST OF NORDLAND.

# CHAPTER III

*A Heavy Sea—Sverdrup Island—A Reindeer Hunt—The First Bear—A Stiff Pull—Firing with Kerosene*

DURING the following days the ice was loose, and we made good progress under sail and steam. Petterson and I, who usually kept watch together in the engine-room, now observed that our hair had grown inordinately long, so we set to work and cut each other's hair as closely as ever we could.

On the 12th of August the engine was stopped, and we used sails only. To the great joy of all of us we got on famously, for we wanted to save our coals as much as possible, since we expected them to be so valuable to us later on. Two days later we had a head wind. We beat about under sail and made but slow progress. On deck the dogs fared badly with the heavy rolling; we were obliged to put them farther aft. They were thoroughly drenched every time the sea washed over the bulwarks; they kept on lifting their paws from the wet deck, and howled terribly while pulling at their chains. Many of them also suffered greatly from sea-sickness.

One day during my watch in the engine-room the water-glass burst, but fortunately none of the bits of glass struck me in the face. I got off with a douche of the boiling salt water. On the 16th of August we had very bad weather. The dogs suffered greatly. The petroleum launch was very nearly washed overboard.

The large massive iron davits in which it was hanging were bent as if they had been steel wires every time the waves broke over the ship, tearing and dragging at the boat. Time after time they threatened to carry it away, but at last we succeeded in lashing it to the ship's side.

DOG ENCAMPMENT AT KHABAROVA.

Yet we had a lively time on board our "rolling tub" every time we had a stiff breeze. The guns rattled in their stands, the camp-stools flew hither and thither over the saloon floor, the saucepans made a terrible noise in the galley. In the engine-room we had to be careful to avoid being thrown into the machinery.

On the morning of the 18th of August Sverdrup sighted an island. We had not expected to come across any new land on the Kara Sea. The island was named Sverdrup Island, after its discoverer. In the evening we again saw land; evidently it was the mainland near Dickson Harbour.

On Monday, the 21st of August, we anchored near the Kjellman Islands while the boiler was being seen to. We soon discovered that there were reindeer on the islands. There was great excitement on board; nearly all who could handle a gun went ashore, while five remained on the vessel. We landed on the biggest of the islands and set out in pursuit of the deer. The animals were exceedingly shy. We had to creep on all-fours for long distances; the ground was not good for stalking, and the deer scented us long before we got within range, and set off at lightning speed. We had then to begin a wearisome tramp afresh across moors and plains, and again stalk them—with the same result.

Hendriksen and I kept together. We had just sat down on a stone, tired and hungry, when Peder suddenly took the pipe out of his mouth and said,—

"There's a bear," and sure enough there was a polar bear coming towards us from the shore. "What small bullets we have!" exclaimed Peder; he had no faith in the Krag-Jörgensen rifle.

We crept cautiously behind a stone, but the bear saw us and came straight at us. We raised our guns—Peder had a long gun and I a carabine—and we fired at the same time, but both of us missed fire. Peder had probably been too liberal with the vaseline. We fired again, and this time the bear was hit in one of its forelegs. It turned round and made for the shore. It received another shot in one of its hind legs, but it ran on as fast as ever. Peder's gun got out of order, and he shouted to me not to fire any more, but to run after the bear.

OUR FIRST BEAR

I reloaded and set off after it down the stony incline, and succeeded in sending a bullet through its shoulder, which felled it to the ground.

"Have I finished him?" I asked Peder, who had now come up.

"No," he said, "he can stand more," and the bear got on its legs and twisted itself round so that its other side turned towards us, when Peder sent a bullet through its other shoulder. He again walked up to it, and fired a shot at it just behind the ears.

I expressed my opinion that this was rather superfluous.

"No," said Peder, "you don't know how sly these beasts are."

I had to bow to his authority—Peder had shot between forty and fifty bears, while this was the first I had had anything to do with. We skinned it and then set off to find our comrades.

We heard some shots; the sun was standing just above the ridge of the rising ground, and as we walked along we saw something in front between us and the sun, which at intervals was shut off from our view. We then saw the big antlers of a reindeer, which came limping towards us. We threw ourselves down on the ground; it came nearer, but suddenly it saw us and set off at full speed in the direction of the shore. One of its legs was broken and hung dangling by the skin. We ran to cut off its retreat, but before we got within range several shots were fired, and the next moment we saw Nansen strike his knife into the neck of the animal. He told us he had already shot another reindeer, and we told him about the bear. Later on, when we all met by the boats after a hard struggle through the boggy moors, we were glad to get some biscuits and butter to stay our hunger with. It was settled that Sverdrup, Jacobsen, and Scott-Hansen should return in one boat to the *Fram* and move her nearer the shore, while we went in the other boat for the bear and the reindeer. As we approached the spot where the carcass of the bear was lying we saw another one, a fine white specimen, lying asleep a little higher up on the land. It was awakened in rather a rough manner; we approached it quietly and silently, treading in each other's footprints, and when we came within suitable range we closed round him, and a bullet in his forehead and several others in his body sent the bear into a still sounder sleep. It was a fine long-haired beast and was quite wet. It had, no doubt, come straight out of the sea and had been sitting on the shore watching for the young of the whitefish, of which we found the remains near the spot.

The carcasses of the bears lay some distance from the shore, and we had considerable trouble in getting them cut up and carried down to the boat. We were already tired and hungry, and this work did not improve matters. A stiff breeze began blowing, and while we had been busy with the bears the sea had turned the boat over on her side and filled it with water, so that our guns and bread were soaked. After much exertion we got the boat emptied of water and drawn up on land. We, of course, got wet through. When at last we had got all the flesh and skins into the boat by hauling them on board with a line, we began rowing for the ship. It was very tough work. The current and the wind were against us and we seemed to be stuck to the spot. We again saw a bear on the shore while rowing along it, and Nansen seized his gun, took aim, put it down again and once more took aim, but he did not fire. The swell of the sea was too great to allow him to get a good aim, and so we let the bear go. We pulled away at the oars as hard as we could. Nansen, Blessing, Mogstad, Hendriksen, and myself were in this boat. First we rowed along the shore till we got abreast of the ship, when we made straight for her. The boat was heavily laden and the seas were continually breaking over her. The current and wind were as strong against us as ever and we began drifting back. Then we went at it again. We were very much knocked up after all our toil on the

JOHANSEN AND PETTERSON AFTER CLEANING THE BOILERS.

island, but all of us set to with a will and pulled with all our might. At last we were near the *Fram*, and a buoy was lowered for us. Peder was rowing on the bow seat, and was to catch hold of the buoy as soon as he should get a chance.

"Have you got it, Peder?"

"No, not yet."

Nansen urged us on and we made another spurt. At last Peder cried out,—

"I have got it!"

This was a great relief to us; but we were not yet on board—the line might break, so we kept on rowing. At last we got on board with the flesh, skins and all. Oh, what a treat it was to get into dry clothes and to get some warm food and then to creep into our berths!

Later on the weather calmed down a little. Sverdrup, Nordahl, Bentsen, and Amundsen rowed ashore to fetch the two reindeer that had been shot. On returning to the ship, they kept along the shore for a longer distance than we did before they made for the *Fram*. This made it easier for them to get on board, and they managed it splendidly.

On the 22nd of August we made an attempt to get away from these confounded currents near the Kjellman Islands; but even with the steam at its highest pressure we did not succeed in making any headway. We had to anchor again and remain there with the steam up.

Later it began to snow and turned very cold. We had bear's flesh for dinner, and found it excellent. The heart especially was in great demand. A bear's heart is no trifle. Two of them suffice for thirteen men.

On the 24th of August we weighed both anchors, and put on all the steam we could command in order to get away from the currents. This time we succeeded, and we steered our course to the north with sails close-hauled. The next day we passed seven unknown islands on the starboard side. Peder was busy cleaning bear and seal skins. The beef-steaks made from bear's flesh were to our taste as good as a "Chateaubriand" at the "Grand."

The wind, which had been so long against us, now

## A FORTUNATE DISCOVERY

began to go down. On the 27th of August we again sailed past some islands and skerries which are not to be found on Nordenskiöld's chart. We were sailing through unknown waters, and had therefore to take soundings from time to time. The dogs were beginning to like their quarters on board much better, and became more friendly with us.

The 28th of August was a notable day, for an important discovery was made in the engine-room. In the morning, while busy firing with the kerosene oil under the boiler, we discovered in the very nick of time that the oil had eaten away a part of the boiler to such an extent that it threatened to burst. A thick crust in the shape of a pointed bullet had been formed in the plate, which would have burst and sent the terrible hot, scalding steam from the boiler over Petterson and myself, who were then in charge of the engine-room. Fortunately this vulnerable spot was discovered in time, and we were not likely to use oil for firing in the future. We of course had to be careful even when using coals.

That afternoon we had been lying moored to a large ice-floe and had been refilling some of our tanks with fresh water. It was a treat to be able to use our legs and walk on the ice. We all turned out and had a regular washing-day in the fresh-water ponds on the ice. The dogs were also able to satisfy their thirst properly, for we had been rather short of water on board of late.

# CHAPTER IV

*Death among the Dogs—Taimur Island—Cape Butterless—The Northernmost Point of the Old World—A Walrus Hunt—To the North*

THINGS did not always go as we should like. By August 29th we had lost nearly two days in trying to get through an ice-belt. It turned out that we made this attempt in the wrong place. But this is one of the risks one must run in the Arctic regions. We encountered a good deal of ice here. On the one side we had land—whether that of an island or the mainland we did not know—and on the other we saw open channels, which looked as if they would admit of progress. It appeared as if we should have to turn back and make for land and try again; but the fog prevented us moving. One of the dogs unfortunately died. Several of them had been ill. They had not fared well on the cold, wet deck, exposed to all kinds of weather. If they could only agree with one another, we should have put them under the forecastle; but they fought and quarrelled together, and did not seem to know what was best for them—just like a good many human beings. Some of us went out hunting, and returned on board with a few seals.

On the 30th of August we anchored off the Taimur Island in an open channel. Two dogs had now died and been dissected by Blessing, who declared that they must have died from eating bear's fat, which in some way or another had poisoned them.

Nansen, Sverdrup, and I went ashore with two dogs after a she-bear with its young one. We followed up the track for a couple of hours, when we found they had gone into the sea. We remained off the Taimur Island till the 2nd of September. During that time we

SCOTT-HANSEN AND NANSEN HAULING IN SAIL.

cleaned the boilers and looked after the engine, our guns, and the dogs. We made muzzles for all of them with plaited rope, so that they might be let loose and have a better time. It turned out, however, that the muzzles were not of much use.

The nights were now getting colder, and we commenced using reindeer skins for bed-covering. We steamed for the south-western end of the Taimur Island to try to get through the sound between the island and the mainland. On the 3rd of September we anchored in two different places. Nordenskiöld's chart is not so complete as we had believed it to be. We could not quite make out our whereabouts from it. Nansen, Juell, Nordahl, and I set out on a reconnoitring expedition on the 4th and 5th of September. We rowed for seventeen hours, and had no other food than biscuits and a little dried reindeer meat; we had forgotten the butter. The first promontory at which we touched and rested, we called "Cape Butterless." We rowed on, taking soundings as we went; here and there we had to pole the boat, and even pull it over the ice. We shot five seals, all of which sank. We had taken with us our ski, some clothes and tarpaulins for making a tent, and were on the whole well equipped with the exception of food.

We saw numerous traces of reindeer and bears, but we had no time to trouble about them. We found we could proceed some considerable distance through the sound, but then came an ice-belt which separated us from the open sea, which we thought we could discern in the distance under the blue horizon. It is very strange that every time we went away from the ship for some purpose or other we always met with bad weather on our way back, so that, hungry, wet, and sleepy as we were, we had always to exert ourselves to the utmost to get on board. We were always thinking how slowly we got along, and, whenever we looked round for the *Fram*, she seemed to us as far away as ever.

There had been some talk about taking up our quarters for the night on one of the islands in the strait, but it was a fortunate thing we did not do so, for, on returning on board, the wind increased to a hurricane. We were busy among the coals while we were lying here with both our anchors out. We afterwards tried to push our way through in several places, but without success. Our observations here did not agree with Nordenskiöld's chart.

On the 7th of September we did a capital stroke of business. We forced our way through the worst part of the ice, which, to all appearance at least, separated us from open water. With Nansen and Sverdrup in the crow's-nest, and the electric bell apparatus to the engine-room in order, with the anchor hanging at the bow ready to be dropped, and with one man taking soundings, the *Fram* made great progress, which evidently saved us from being shut up in the ice for a year off Taimur Island, and even then we might not have been able to get through.

In the evening we were stopped by the ice, and we remained moored to it till the 9th inst. Nansen went ashore and shot a reindeer. We discovered new islands, as well as fjords and sounds, in every direction, which had not been observed by Nordenskiöld. On Saturday, the 9th of September, we made splendid progress— thirty-five miles in the watch—under full steam and sail, after we got out of the ice. It looked as if Jacobsen would lose his bet with me and some of the others that we should not get past Cape Chelyuskin before the new year. Jacobsen was a great hand at betting. He made bets with all of us, backing a thing with one and laying odds against it with another, so that he was generally all right in the long run.

We had now a pleasant time on board the *Fram*, and plenty of good food into the bargain—fresh reindeer, seal, and bears' meat—so that we did not use much of the ship's stores. Mogstad was shifted from the galley into the engine-room, and Nordahl took over the cooking, at which he seemed to be unusually clever. We generally assembled in the chart-room after meals, to talk and smoke our pipes in cosiness and comfort. One watch consisted of Sverdrup, Bentsen and Blessing on the deck, and Amundsen, with Nordahl or Mogstad, in the engine-room; and the other of Jacobsen, Juell, and Peder Hendriksen on deck, and Petterson and myself in the engine-room. Nansen was in the crow's-nest early and late, and Scott-Hansen took observations.

By Sunday, September 10th, we reached a point which marked the beginning of a new chapter in the history of the expedition. During the previous three weeks our prospects had been anything but promising, owing to the condition of the ice we had encountered; and, many a time, when lying at anchor, we thought that we should have to winter where we were. Cape Chelyuskin was on everybody's lips during these weeks, and we were all yearning to get there. At four o'clock in the morning of the 10th we reached it. There was great festivity on board. At four o'clock, just as the sun rose, the Norwegian flag and our pennant with "*Fram*" on it, at a given signal, were run up on the mastheads. At the same time we saluted with our three remaining shots, the last of which turned out a failure, as the cartridge was wet. A bowl of punch, containing a concoction which we afterwards called "Chelyuskin-punch," with fruit and cigars, was served in the festively lighted saloon, and we emptied our glasses in honour of our safe arrival here. A festive spirit prevailed; even Jacobsen was delighted at having lost his bets.

On the 12th of September, Nansen, Juell and Peder set out to hunt walrus. Several of them were lying crowded together on an ice-floe, and two out of their number were shot. There was a regular commotion among these colossal creatures, as Nansen fired and Peder threw his harpoon the moment the boat touched the floe. From the ship we could see the walruses flinging themselves into the sea, and we could hear the bulls bellowing. They did not succeed in securing more than the two they had shot first. They had not harpoons enough with which to attack more. In the afternoon two others were shot.

LANDING AT REINDEER ISLAND.

From the 15th to the 17th of September we continued our course, mostly under steam and sail, in different directions, according as the state of the ice permitted. On the 18th we shaped our course northwards from the western side of the New Siberian Islands, which we, however, could not see owing to the darkness. On these islands depôts of provisions had been established for our use by Baron Toll, of St. Petersburg, who also had provided the dogs for the expedition.

# CHAPTER V

*Open Water — Unwelcome Guests — Fast in the Ice — Warping — The Northern Lights*

ON the 19th of September we were in 76° north latitude, and steering due north in open water with a fair wind and with full steam. Every one on board was in the best of spirits at such progress in waters through which no one ever sailed before. We eagerly discussed how far we should get before we were laid up in the ice.

A bottle, with a piece of paper on which the longitude, latitude, and the words "All well" were written in Norwegian and English, was thrown into the sea.

On the 20th we reached 77° 44′ north latitude. In the evening we came into conflict with the ice, and had to alter our course; but, at any rate, it was some satisfaction to know that this was in a northerly direction. The fog came on thickly from time to time.

There was a regular mania amongst us on board for letting our beards assume the most fantastic shapes. Scott-Hansen was exactly like Olsen, the master carpenter who built the *Fram*; Nordahl was the picture of Victor Emmanuel, and Bentsen of Napoleon III. The last-named was indignant, however, at the idea of his resemblance.

We saw some birds, both snipes and sea-gulls. On the 21st we sailed north until we were stopped by the ice. The fog again troubled us from time to time.

During the night we proceeded, as usual, at half speed. We threw overboard six bottles, with letters in Norwegian and English.

To-day we made an unpleasant discovery. We found that we had vermin on board, and every man had to undergo a thorough examination. We blamed the Samoyedes from Khabarova for having introduced these unpleasant visitors to us.

Next day we took our clothes, put them in a cask, and sent the steam right into it direct from the boiler through a hose. We almost thought we could hear our enemies singing their death-song. But they got the better of us, after all, as it turned out afterwards. I was busy steaming the bed-clothes, when the cask, not being strong enough to resist the force of the steam, suddenly exploded, and the deck was covered with clothes enveloped in clouds of steam.

About four o'clock in the afternoon we moored the ship to an ice-floe. We were now in 78° 54' north latitude, in the midst of the polar ice, far away from civilization. The weather was splendid and the view around us magnificent. The ice-floes were of different thicknesses; high and low, with open channels between as far as the eye could reach; while, beyond, on the horizon, the sky, the ice, and the water blended together in all manner of colours. The dogs alone interrupted the solemn silence that reigned around us. Perhaps they scented a bear or some other animal, as they gave an occasional bark.

At seven o'clock on the following day all hands were ordered to help in shifting the coals. The work went on merrily. This coal-shifting was a kind of connecting-link between us, for we all went to work at it together. Of course we became as black as niggers, and at night, even after we had washed, it must not be supposed that we were altogether clean. The eyes especially had

a Southern look about them, and we were quite agreed that belladonna does not have anything like such a beautifying effect upon them as coal-shifting.

We were beginning to make up our minds that we were shut in, and that these would be our quarters for the winter, with almost the same surroundings as now. Observations for determining our position were taken as often as the fog or the overcast sky permitted. The slush ice between the floes was frozen, and it seemed almost as if the ship was beginning to be exposed a bit to the pressure of the ice.

The weather was fine and bright, with 17° to 19° of frost. We began cleaning up the place where the dogs were kept, and stowing away in the hold and in the bow some of the deck cargo of planks and beams, including the windmill, which had been lying on the after-deck. We thus got the deck clear, with ample space for taking exercise.

One day we discovered a big bear behind a hummock, not far away from the ship. Nansen and Sverdrup started off there and then, only filling the magazines of their guns with cartridges. All hands went up into the rigging to get a good view of this rare sport; but the bear would not have anything to do with them; it turned right round and bolted off in a north-westerly direction and then disappeared. It was impossible to get within range of it, although three of the dogs were let loose after it.

We could now get to our stores in the main-hold through the dynamo-room and the passage leading up to the half-deck near the entrance to the saloon on the port side, so that we had access to the stores without going on deck. All the coal dust and rubbish had been swept away and the carpenter's bench put up in the hold, so that the deck was now clean and tidy. The cabins had been washed and cleaned out, and one day all hands had a grand washing day in the main-hold. On this occasion we weighed ourselves for the second time on board. It afforded us a good deal of amusement, as the weighing-machine, through some defect or other, gave our weights, as far as most of us were concerned, altogether in excess of the actual increase during a month's time. Captain Sverdrup was now, as before, the lightest man on board, and Juell the heaviest.

Blessing, for the second time, examined our blood. The water required for washing ourselves and for use in the cabins was heated in the following manner. We took the kerosene oil, which we could no longer use under the boiler, and poured it over some bricks, which burnt on being ignited. This method was satisfactory enough, but we found that the jet apparatus for distributing the oil in the form of spray was better.

On the 28th of September we moved all the dogs out upon the ice alongside the ship. They were immensely delighted, as they were let loose one by one, and were allowed to scamper over the ice during their short span of liberty, until they were again tied up. One of them, called "Billettören" (ticket collector), set off at once straight for the Pole. He evidently wanted to get there in time to collect the tickets, as one of us remarked. We tied the dogs to long boards, which we weighted with blocks of ice, so that they should not be able to get away from us. Nansen was busy during the day catching amphipodæ and other small animals under the ice.

The 29th of September was Blessing's birthday, in honour of which the following dinner was served:—

> Soupe à la Julienne, avec macaroni pâtés.
> Potage de poisson.
> Hanche de renne, avec pommes de terre.
> Pouding à la Nordahl.
> Glace de Groenland.
> Bière.

During dinner we had plenty of music, the organ playing its most appropriate pieces. A festive spirit prevailed, and all of us enjoyed ourselves thoroughly. Every one apparently over-ate himself; at least, no one would have any supper!

There was a good deal to attend to in the engine-room, where Amundsen and Petterson were constantly at work. Bentsen and Peder cleaned walrus and seal skins, and stretched them on the ship's side to dry. The dogs seemed to thrive well on the ice. They were very fond of company, and were mad with joy when any of us came to see them.

On September 30th we were still busy clearing and tidying up in preparation for the winter, and had in consequence plenty to do. We also had snow shovelling on a grand scale, and began a laborious but useful task. We had to warp the ship backwards in the slush ice, which was now frozen. Our position was not quite satisfactory, as we ran the risk of being exposed to severe ice-pressure. The great ice-floe on our port side might have fallen in upon our deck at any moment if the squeezing had begun. Moving the ship was not quick work. We fixed two ice-anchors in the ice some distance aft the ship, and by means of the capstan, wire ropes, twofold purchase straps, etc., we managed to heave her inch by inch through the frozen slush ice, which, however, had first to be broken up.

Now and then some of us fell through this deceitful slush. I remember Peder falling plump into it, but he managed to turn himself round on his back. He knew he could not get out of it without help, so he remained quietly with outstretched arms and legs, and shouted out to Sverdrup, who was close at hand, "Come and catch hold of me, captain." Then Sverdrup came and helped Peder up on to a solid ice-floe.

We had now a fine display of the Northern Lights in the evenings. They quivered across the mid-heavens in ever-changing spirals and tongues of fire. At times, too, we saw the grand sight of a shooting star exploding like a rocket, as it was suddenly stopped on its long, curved trajectory.

# CHAPTER VI

*First Day of Rest—Surprised by Bears—The Dogs are let Loose—Ice Pressure—A Hunt in the Dark*

SUNDAY, the 1st of October, was the first Sunday we had as a real day of rest on board. Otherwise the Sundays had been very much like any other day, so we were glad of a day on which we could have a complete rest. In the forenoon we had some sacred music on the organ, and read books from our well-stocked library; in the afternoon we had a nap, and after that we settled down for a quiet evening.

Next day at noon we stopped warping the ship, and her final position for the winter was settled. The *Fram* now lay with her bow to the south; she turned herself southwards at the time when we got fixed in the ice, and afterwards drifted stern forwards.

Scott-Hansen, Blessing and I were engaged in erecting a tent for magnetic observations, sufficiently distant from the ship to prevent the iron on board from having any influence upon the instruments. Just as we were busily engaged in levelling the ice where the tent was to be pitched, I happened to catch sight of a bear about fifty paces off, coming straight towards us. "There's a bear," I shouted. Our first thought was not to defend ourselves, but quietly to signal to the ship, so that the bear should not be frightened away like the first one we saw here. We decided that Blessing should run and fetch the guns from the ship. But the bear seemed to have made up its mind; there was no need for us to be anxious about frightening it away, for it came straight at us. It was evidently in want of a meal. The situation was becoming serious. When Blessing set off to go on board, the bear altered its course, a manœuvre which told us, as plainly as if the beast had opened its mouth and said, "Here, my bold fellow, just keep where you are; you have no business on

Johansen.        Sverdrup.
SHOOTING BEARS.

board; none of your nonsense." We then began gesticulating energetically, and to shout and scream with all our might; but all of no avail. The bear was now close upon us, and Scott-Hansen took an ice-staff and I an axe, the only weapons of defence we had. Blessing came back to us, and we put ourselves in position to receive the bear. Fortunately, it first walked up to the tent and sniffed at it, and then we began beating a retreat; but it came on in pursuit of us. Just at this moment those on board suddenly became alive to our situation, and Nansen and Sverdrup jumped out on the ice with their guns. Nansen raised his gun to his shoulder, and we saw our pursuer fall down. One more shot through the head, and all was over.

It was a fine he-bear. No trace of food could be found in its stomach, so it must have been famished with hunger. The only thing we found in the stomach was a piece of brown paper, which it must have swallowed just before, as we could plainly distinguish the name of a Norwegian firm, "Lütken & Moe," stamped on the paper. This was a lesson to us for the future always to take arms with us whenever we left the ship, even if only for a short distance. The bear was photographed by Nansen as it lay on the ice in the last throes of death.

On the 4th of October we took soundings, and found a fine, bluish clay at the bottom, at a depth of 800 fathoms. On the same day the ice cracked suddenly astern of the ship, and the clear water that appeared looked like a long ribbon stretching from east to west. We noticed that the ice was beginning to pack. A strange feeling came over us when pacing the deck at night during watch; we heard the distant roar and the weird sound made by the heavy ice-floes as they ground against one another by wind and current. There was nothing to be seen except thirty-three dark bodies lying on the floe close alongside the ship. These were our dogs, which now and then gave a sign of life by a bark or a movement which made their chains rattle.

Next morning a bear was seen approaching the *Fram*. Nansen and Hendriksen went off towards it, moving cautiously from hummock to hummock, but it scented them and trotted off. Nansen, however, succeeded in shooting it down with two bullets at quite a long distance. For dinner we had the great pleasure of eating cutlets from the very bear which had evidently intended making a meal of us. The cutlets tasted excellent. The observations showed that we were now in 78° 47·5' north latitude. The rudder had been hoisted up out of its well and put on the deck. Another unpleasant discovery had been made: the vermin had not yet been completely exterminated on board.

The windmill was put up on the port side, close to the half-deck, and the "Grand" was in consequence moved forward, with its bow resting on the forecastle. The dogs were let loose. They made a terrible row, and at once began quarrelling and fighting; it took several of us with rope-ends in our hands to quiet them and get them in order; it seemed as if they had suddenly become wild, and imagined themselves back on the Siberian steppes again. When two begin to fight, the entire pack rushes at one of the combatants, and, strange to say, it is always the weaker one that they all go for. All the dogs were going about in a more or less wounded condition, but they seemed greatly to enjoy their frequent fights all the same. These dogs were very curious animals; they were a constant topic of conversation, and the object of various kinds of observations. We had given them all characteristic names. Thus we called one " Job." This dog was remarkably quiet and timid; he had long, upright, donkey ears of a yellowish colour, and was of a low, longish build. He kept himself to himself, went all alone on long excursions, renounced everything, and never once growled or snarled at any of us. Then we had " Billettören," with his inquisitive " ticket-collector's " face. He generally stood near the companion leading to the engine-room, and barked at us as we put our heads up through the hatchway. Then we had " Barabbas," and " Pan," and " Narrifas," a small and active animal with black hair, bright black eyes, and shining white teeth, which he always showed; "Ulinka," dark-spotted and smooth-haired, with a pointed head, and very affectionate. This cannot be said about "Sultan," a brown and white, strongly-built creature, with brown eyes, and the reputation of being a great fighter. "Caiaphas" had a thick, whitish, woollen coat, and a hoarse bark; he seemed to suffer from a chronic cold. And, above all, I must not forget the most important of the pack—the one representative of the fair sex—"Kvik," brown-spotted and smooth-haired, with a black nose and strongly-built frame.

Altogether there were three different races represented among our thirty-three dogs. It generally took some time before all of us could make out how many there were, as long as they were kept on deck, and this frequently gave rise to a little wagering, more than one bet being made regarding the number.

We had now finally disposed of the vermin that had been troubling us. The last five of us who were still infested with them had to take off every stitch of clothing, and deliver up all the old clothes in the cabins, and put on bran-new ones, while the old things were thrown out on to the ice. The clothes specially made for the expedition were now handed out to us. They were made of grey Norwegian tweed; knee-breeches with leggings, and Greenland anoraks for the upper body, with fur-bordered hoods, and Laplanders' boots made of sealskin for our feet. Scott-Hansen and I, in addition, received a wolfskin suit each, for use while taking observations. We were now using sleeping-bags in both the four-men cabins. They were simply grand to sleep in.

The rigging-up of the windmill turned out to be a long job, as so many preparations and rearrangements had to be made on deck. On October 8th the ice began to press in earnest. We were drifting in a south-westerly direction. The soundings showed a depth of water of 150 fathoms.

On the previous night all hands had to go on deck, as there was a great movement in the ice. It pressed with great force against us and cracked in several places, so that we were obliged to fasten several ice-anchors to the ice to prevent the floe with the dogs and the one with the observation tent from drifting away from us. On my night watch, between four and five, the pressure was terrible. The *Fram* trembled in her timbers, but she bore the strain well. The pressure against the bow was so great that a thick wire rope, which was fixed to one of the ice-anchors, snapped as if it had been a sewing-thread. I had just stepped on to the forecastle, and, seeing the great strain on the rope, I jumped quickly down on to the deck, and had no sooner got hold of the rope in my hand to let it go, than it snapped with a shower of sparks. Fortunately this did not happen at the moment when I was just above the rope.

The 10th of October was Nansen's birthday. No preparations for celebrating it had been made, as Nansen was not well. He had been feverish for several days. As yet we had not taken down the running-rigging, stored the sails, nor fixed the awning over the ship; nor had we begun to restow the provisions, sew boat and other sails, nor made any of the necessary preparations for suddenly leaving the ship. There was, in short, a good deal of work to be done besides the daily observations. After eleven o'clock at night we had each an hour's watch in turn, but Nansen, Sverdrup, Scott-Hansen, and the cook for the time being were exempt from these watches. Juell was, by rights, storekeeper and cook, but Mogstad and Nordahl had hitherto attended to the kitchen department in turn. Just now it was my turn to be cook, and I found it as much as one could do to cook and serve up food for thirteen men. We used petroleum lamps when cooking, but they had an obstinate way of their own of getting out of order. One day I was going to boil some corned beef for dinner, and the meat had been hung in a bag under the ice to soak. But it had been taken out of the water too soon and put on the deck, where it of course froze into a solid mass. As it happened, the lamps were just then giving me a lot of trouble. Nansen had to come to my assistance with the "Primus," but it was six o'clock in the evening before dinner came to table. There was, of course, no necessity for getting any supper ready that evening, and I was not afterwards called upon to cook.

On the 11th of October we experienced a good deal of ice pressure. We had to turn out and heave or slacken on the four ropes with which we were moored to the different ice-floes.

The same day poor "Job" departed this life. His comrades made an end of this unobtrusive and remarkably shy animal, which never did any harm to man or beast. All the other dogs attacked him and tore him to pieces while we were having our dinner.

Nansen continued his researches regarding the seawater at different depths, and caught a great number of crustaceans and other marine animals. We prepared a thermometer house, and placed it on top of the hummocks on the "dog floe." Blessing had been occupied for some days in unpacking and arranging in order all our books. He arranged the library in the room by the companion on the starboard side, and we had now about six hundred volumes in all.

The ice was troublesome again on October 13th. All of a sudden it began pressing with such a force that we thought the *Fram* would be ground to pieces; then the next moment we had clear water round the ship. At five o'clock the pressure was tremendous. The biggest floe in our neighbourhood, the "dog floe," split in two, and the floes pressed together from all sides. All hands had to set to work. An ice-anchor was lost by being buried under a mass of broken blocks of pack-ice. Shortly after being thus blockaded the ice slackened again, and we now discovered that five or six floes were drifting off with the dogs, all howling and barking. A wild chase ensued to get them on board, and with the aid of our light larch-wood pram we finally succeeded in recovering them.

Scott-Hansen and I had been to the observation tent and taken a magnetic observation, and on our way back to the ship the ice was packing and cracking in all directions round about us, even under our very feet as we jumped from floe to floe.

When evening came we settled down to cards. All at once we heard the dogs beginning to bark furiously. One of us—I think it was Peder—ran on deck to see what was the matter. He came down and said he thought he could distinguish a bear behind a small hummock not far from the ship. We all rushed on deck in the dark, lightly dressed as we were, notwithstanding the 36° of frost. Peder, Scott-Hansen, and myself were the first to get hold of our guns, which hung in readiness. We ranged ourselves along the railing, eagerly looking out over the ice and among the scattered, barking pack of dogs. And, sure enough, away among the hummocks, one, if not two massive forms were seen moving parallel with the ship. And so we looked along the barrels of our guns and fired away, taking aim as best we could, and loading as rapidly as possible.

A muffled roar was heard, and a form seen sinking

to the ground close to one of the hummocks. The ice pressed and creaked; ice-floes were tilted up and set on end. The dogs roved about from floe to floe, barking all the time in one particular direction. From the railing of the *Fram* flash followed upon flash. The shots resounded through the stillness of the night, while the men ran to and fro, most of them only half dressed. We refilled the magazines of our guns,

ICE HUMMOCKS NEAR THE *FRAM*, AS SEEN BY MOONLIGHT.

and then set out over the ice, one after the other, in the darkness. With our finger on the trigger, feeling our way with our feet, gazing all around us into the night, we stole along, and at last saw a shapeless form on the ice. It was a bear. We fired a shot at it to assure ourselves that it was dead. Yes, it was as dead as a herring.

Hush! What is that? We heard a pitiable groan

further out on the ice. So there must have been two of them, after all. We got hold of a rope and a lantern, which, however, went out, and we made a running noose round the beast's head and dragged it on board. It was a young one, so it must have been the mother which was moaning out on the ice. The cub had only been hit by two or three bullets, but that was not bad shooting, seeing that it was so dark. Later in the evening we were busy mooring the ship.

Next day, Sunday, the 15th of October, the dogs were taken on board and chained up in their old places. Another of them, little "Belki," now died. Two disappeared; whether they had been lost during the ice pressure, or caught by the bear, we knew not. They were "Fox" and "Narrifas." On examination we found that not only had there been a second bear near the ship the previous night, of which we had felt sure, but we also discovered traces of a third. Nansen, Sverdrup, Blessing, Jacobsen, Bentsen and Mogstad—perhaps more of them—set out on the ice, while Scott-Hansen and I cast longing eyes after them as we stood over by the observation tent, which we were about to take down and bring on board. The sportsmen discovered a young bear with a broken back dragging itself over the ice by the help of its fore-body, while the hind part of it appeared to be disabled. It was put out of its misery by a bullet and dragged on board. Nothing was seen of the mother. This result of a bear hunt in the dark—two tender young bear cubs, one a year and the other two years old—could not be called bad.

## CHAPTER VII

*More Bears—The Power of Baking Powder—"Johansen's Friend"—Electric Light—Shooting Competition*

SCOTT-HANSEN and I were one day on the ice, determining the deflection with the magnetic apparatus, when the ice began pressing, and compelled us to pack up in post haste and hurry-scurry on board. The daily meteorological observations consisted in investigating the direction of the wind and its strength, the clouds and their drift, in reading the different thermometers, barometers, and the barograph (a self-registering aneroid barometer), the thermographs, and the hygrometers. This was done every fourth hour, day and night. Later, it was done every other hour.

One morning, while I was busy with these observations, I heard the dogs, which we had on board since the ice had been packing so much, beginning to howl and whine. I especially noticed "Caiaphas," which stood with its paws on the deck-rail, staring intently at something down upon the ice, and barking all the time with its hoarse bark. I looked cautiously over the rail and saw the back of a fine white bear close to the ship's side. I stole across to the saloon door for a loaded gun. The bear, however, advanced along the side of the ship with a suppressed growl, and would very likely have come on board to us if it had not got my bullet in its shoulder. It gave a roar, jumped a few steps, and fell down. I put two more shots into it. The others were down in the saloon at their breakfast, but came rushing on deck as soon as they heard the shots.

An hour later Scott-Hansen and I were busy with some observations on the floe, not far from the ship, when we suddenly discovered a large bear trudging towards us; but as soon as it noticed the blood of the bear which we had just skinned on the ice, it bent its steps in that direction. Scott-Hansen seized the revolver, our constant companion when on the ice; but just then we caught sight of Peder on the after-deck of the *Fram* with his Krag-Jörgensen gun. He took aim, pulled the trigger, cocked the gun again, aimed and fired, but the gun would not go off. Peder began cursing the gun. "The confounded thing won't fire!" he growled. He had, as usual, been too free with the vaseline. At last the gun went off, and the bear, which in the meantime had got close to the ship, set up a terrible roar, raised itself on its hind legs, and bent its head to tear the place where it was wounded, beating the air with its paws. It then wheeled round and set off among the hummocks. Scott-Hansen ran after it with his revolver, and sent two bullets into its head as it lay on the ice. We afterwards discovered that Peder's shot had gone right through its heart. That was not a bad catch so early in the morning. It seemed likely that we should keep ourselves going with fresh meat for some time.

Nansen was busy sledge-driving with the dogs. They go excellently when all pull in one direction, but they are not always inclined to do this. On the way back to the ship, however, they pulled well together, and went at first-rate speed.

Sverdrup made up his mind to make some kind of a trap for catching bears. He experimented on a steel trap, but there was also some talk about a bear-pit.

"So long as we don't catch dogs instead of bears," was Nansen's remark. The dogs were always breaking loose, and if one got away on to the ice, the others at once began barking. They seemed to envy each other the pleasure of getting free.

The temperature was now $-12°$ to $-13°$. In the saloon it was between $42°$ and $53°$ above zero. We began to be troubled with dampness in the cabins. We had to make thin wooden frames to put between the sleeping-bags and the walls in order to preserve them. Jacobsen invented a very complicated arrangement, with cotton wicks and tin boxes, to absorb the damp in the cabins.

One day Juell was going to make a cake, which, by the bye, was not an uncommon occurrence, and for this he had used a kind of baking powder with the raising properties of which he was not quite familiar. Before long we noticed a somewhat suspicious smell coming from the galley. Suddenly Bentsen appeared at the saloon door, crying out, "The cake is coming after me, boys!" It appeared that Juell had painted "FRAM" in big letters on the top of the cake, and Bentsen meant to imply that these letters were crawling out through the galley door, the one after the other. "The 'F' and 'R' and the 'A' are outside already," he continue "and now there is only the 'M' left, and that is so big that it covers the whole cake."

We were not using any heating apparatus in the saloon; we only kept a lamp burning there. Blessing had been engaged in examining the proportion of carbonic acid in the air in the saloon and in the open. On the 23rd of October the *Fram* again lay in open water; the ice had slackened and a big lane had been formed in the ice to the north and the south of the ship. The next day the ice closed in upon us again and began to pack. We had a net for catching marine animals hanging in the water, which was only saved in the nick of time; we found a big catch in it.

We had a black and white dog on board which had taken a decided objection to me; as soon as he saw me or heard that I was on deck he would bark and growl continuously. Even when I went up into the crow's-nest to read the thermometers which we had up there, and he saw the light from the lantern which I carried on my breast while climbing up the rigging, the dog knew it was I, even if he was far away on the ice, and would then begin to bark and growl. The dog, I suppose, must have been frightened the first time Scott-Hansen and I put on our wolf-skin clothes. The dog had no other name than that of "Johansen's friend."

On the 25th of October, the windmill, which drove the dynamo for our electric light, was tried for the first time. The result was more successful than we expected after the trials we had made while lying at the wharf of the Akers Engineering Works. We sat down to our dinner in the best of spirits, the saloon being brilliantly illuminated by the electric light. Mr. Oscar Dickson, who had presented us with the electric light installation, was gratefully remembered, and his health was drunk in Norwegian Lager beer. Our supply of beer lasted up to the first Christmas in the ice, after which we restricted ourselves to a mixture of lime-juice, sugar, and water.

The electric light was a source of great usefulness and enjoyment to us. When the wind was blowing 4–5 metres in the second, it was sufficiently strong to drive the windmill, and we always called that kind of wind "mill-breeze."

On the 12th of October there were great festivities on board and on the ice. The first birthday of the *Fram* was celebrated in a worthy manner. We inaugurated the day's proceedings with a splendid breakfast, French rolls and apple cakes being the great attraction. Scott-Hansen, Blessing and I set about at once arranging a shooting competition in honour of the day. We quite felt the greatness of the occasion as we assembled on the ground with our guns. Two flags were hoisted on the spot where the competitors took up their position, and the *Fram*, the hero of the day, had also flags flying. The range was 100 yards long, and each competitor had five shots. It was the last day on which we saw the sun before it left us altogether. It set blood red as it disappeared before our eyes, not to return again until the next year. The moon, however, was in the sky day and night, shining bright and clear.

The result of the competition was as follows:—

| | |
|---|---|
| First prize | Jacobsen. |
| Second prize | Johansen. |
| Third prize | Scott-Hansen. |
| Fourth prize | Sverdrup. |
| Fifth prize | Blessing. |
| Sixth prize | Hendriksen. |
| Seventh prize | Bentsen. |
| Eighth prize | Petterson. |
| Ninth prize | Nansen. |
| Tenth prize | Nordahl. |
| Eleventh prize | Juell. |
| Twelfth prize | Mogstad. |

The thirteenth prize was awarded to Amundsen, although he did not take part in the competition.

The committee had collected a few nick-nacks for prizes, each of which was accompanied by suitable mottoes in verse. The presentation of the prizes was to take place in the evening with great ceremony. Scott-Hansen had prepared as the first prize a handsome star, made of birchwood, decorated with a piece of lace which he had procured from goodness knows where. This was awarded to Jacobsen, the champion marksman. The second prize, a night-cap, was presented to me. The other prizes consisted of a pipe made out of a reindeer horn, a needlecase, cigars, a roll of tobacco, a memorandum book, etc., etc.

We spent the rest of the evening pleasantly and merrily round a bowl of punch, to which we had given the name of "Fram-punch." It was made of lime-juice, sugar, and water, and was flavoured with strawberry or cloudberry jam.

On the 27th of October we again took the rudder out of its well, where it had frozen fast in the ice. While engaged in this work a sharp, bright, bluish light fell suddenly over the ship and the ice around us. It came from a fireball of unusual size and splendour. It left behind it a long double trail of burning particles which was visible for quite a long while.

Blessing still continued his monthly examination of our blood. Instead of decreasing, the number of blood corpuscles in most cases increased.

Nansen had for the first time been dredging, and brought up from the bottom of the ocean a wonderful collection of plants and animals. It appears that there is plenty of life under the polar ice, both animal and vegetable.

The 31st of October was the birthday of Sverdrup, our commander, which, as a matter of course, was kept up with great festivity. We fared grandly on the very best things to be found on the ship. The elements were friendly enough to contribute towards the celebration. There blew such a fine "mill-breeze" that we could use all the electric lamps in the saloon. The arc-lamp sent its powerful rays through the skylight and illuminated the half-deck, where the dogs were lying, just as if it were broad daylight. The light shone far out over the ice, and must have surprised any animals that were out there. We had a revolver competition in honour of the day, and on this occasion Scott-Hansen turned out to be the champion.

Mogstad and Blessing challenged each other to a revolver match, and a number of bets were made on the event. The match took place amid great excitement. In the end Blessing won with twenty-five points, while Mogstad scored twenty-one. Loud cheers for the victor resounded over the ice.

## CHAPTER VIII

*Foot-races on the Ice—More about the Dogs—The Northern Lights—Adulterated Beer—Ice Pressure—Peder Attacked by a Bear*

WE had now 54° of frost. Notwithstanding this low temperature, we had still no heating apparatus in the saloon. We now received our supply of underclothing for the winter. With the exception of the stockings, made by Norwegian peasants, all the rest of the hosiery was of English manufacture.

Sverdrup invented an excellent foot-gear, which consisted of wooden clogs with long canvas leggings. Many of us followed his example and made ourselves similar boots. They were very roomy in the foot, so we could put on plenty of socks. To Scott-Hansen and myself, who had often to remain motionless for hours on the ice during the magnetic observations, they were simply invaluable.

For Sunday, the 5th of November, we had arranged some foot-races on the ice. A long lane which had frozen between the floes formed a splendid course, which was measured and got ready for the occasion. Juell had prepared thirteen prizes, which all turned out to be cakes. The first prize was a very big one and the thirteenth quite a tiny one. But when the day arrived, the course had cracked right across. The gap, however, was not very wide, and we could easily have jumped over it and continued our course on the other side. When, however, the time came, we were too lazy and out of trim for running, and the races did not come off. We were not, in the meantime, to be cheated out of the prizes. It was decided that they should be apportioned by lot, a method which we all agreed was far more easy and comfortable than having all the trouble and bother of running for them.

The next day there were several openings in the ice owing to the strong south-westerly wind that had been blowing for some time. This was the wind we liked, for it took us further to the north, nearer to the goal we were longing for. Here we were only in sixty fathoms of water. On the following day the temperature rose suddenly to 21° and the barometer fell steadily down to 734 mm., when the temperature again fell.

The dogs again killed one of their comrades. "Ulabrand" was the victim. He was attacked in the stomach, and his blood had been sucked from him in the same way as poor "Job's" was. There were two more of the dogs which the rest had got their eyes on. One was a brother of "Job," and the other a small white dog. But since these savage beasts seemed to be unable to make a right use of their liberty, they had to suffer confinement, and we therefore chained them up again on board.

We were now in 77° 43′ north latitude and 138° east longitude. We had thus been drifting to the southeast, but we could not, of course, expect to drift due north from the very outset.

We had been considering how best we could make use of the kerosene oil, which we could not use for firing under the boiler, but up to the present we had not been able to come to any decision. The lamps which we used for cooking required a great quantity of the large, round woven wicks, and we were afraid that our supply of them would run short. Sverdrup, who understands everything, began making a weaving loom.

It is not an easy matter to find snow which is entirely free from salt, even in the crow's-nest, for the "earth-drift"—as we called the snow which the wind whirled up from the ice—penetrated right up there. The ice was cracking round the *Fram*, and the pressure becoming violent. They were indeed magnificent trials of strength which we saw before our eyes, when the floes collided with one another and were ground to pieces, forming ridges and hummocks all around us.

We had begun making harness of canvas for the dogs, so that it might be ready for use whenever it was wanted. These dogs were really very curious animals. It now seemed as if the whole pack had got their eyes on "Sultan," and as if they had agreed amongst themselves upon his fate, which obviously meant death. No sooner did they see their opportunity than the whole pack, with "Pan" as the leader, rushed at the doomed one and attempted to strangle him. It was in this way that they killed "Ulabrand" and "Job." And the doomed dog was perfectly aware of what was in store for him. He looked depressed, crest-fallen and frightened, and sneaked about by himself. We dare not let him loose on the ice during the day with the others, but always kept him fastened up on board.

On November 15th we had a "mill-breeze," and the dynamo was going, so that one might have taken our ship for a factory, or something of the sort, particularly below in the main-hold, where we had our carpenter's shop and the noise and whizzing of the machinery and the belting could be heard.

On deck, however, the cutting wind made us feel the cold twice as much as we otherwise would, penetrating, as it did, to our very bones and marrow, while the eye only faintly discerned in the darkness the interminable ice-fields, where our little community represented the only visible life.

At times the Northern Lights gave the sky the appearance of the whole heavens being on fire. From the zenith the light spread itself out in fiery flames over the vault of the heavens; the arch with its tongues of fire stretched downwards and was met by draperies and bands of light, while fanlike rays suddenly ignited and gradually merged into soft waving streamers, which assumed all the colours of the rainbow, while close to the horizon the luminous haze of the Northern Lights formed a long, hazy belt of mystic iridescence. We were becoming so accustomed to displays of the Northern Lights that we scarcely took any notice of them, unless they were exceptionally magnificent.

The darkness and the cold had the effect of making all our work slow and tedious. Whenever we had any work in hand, were it ever so slight, we had always to carry lights with us. This, together with the heavy clothes which we were obliged to wear, encumbered us in all our occupations, so that we found our work gave us quite enough to do.

Scott-Hansen showed an exceptional perseverance and patience in his difficult work in connection with the magnetic observations. Hour after hour he would remain on the ice with his instruments, in the severe cold and darkness, observing the deflection and oscillation of the magnetic needle and reading the fine gradations with a magnifying glass, while holding his breath, lest the cold should cover everything with frost. It was a wonder his hands and feet did not get frost-bitten oftener than they did.

The first winter, when I assisted him in the magnetic observations, he was obliged to take them on the bare ice, as it was of no use erecting any tent owing to the pressure of the ice. We afterwards built a snow-hut, where we were very comfortable. We used, therefore, the first winter, to set out on the ice in the darkness with our boxes and tripod stands; and when we had been standing still for some time, we would take a run, walk on our hands, turn some somersaults, or dance to some national tune. Our hands fared the worst, for we were now and then obliged to uncover them during the observations. It was a great treat when we got on board again and settled down in our cosy saloon with a cup of warm tea before us.

On the 17th of November we were in 78° 27′ north latitude and 139° east longitude. We had thus been making good progress towards the north.

Bentsen came one day and asked Amundsen if he had heard that a brother-in-law of Blessing was living on the New Siberian Islands, where he carried on the business of a trader, and was a kind of governor over some thousands of Poles, who had been exiled thither. We began a rather amusing discussion as to whether we ought not to pay a visit to Blessing's brother-in-law, as he was not so very far off after all.

One Sunday evening, just as Scott-Hansen, Blessing, Sverdrup, and I were in the middle of a pleasant game of *mariage*, the two first suggested that we should have some beer. They had both for some time been saving up their share—or at least part—of their dinner beer. Some practical joker or other—most probably Bentsen—had evidently got the idea that some fun might be obtained from this mania for saving up the beer; without letting any one know of it, he mixed some coffee and water with the beer in one of the bottles. As it happened, this very bottle of "bock-beer" was brought in, and Sverdrup and I were invited to partake of the precious beverage; but no one cared to drink first—we all seemed to have our suspicions about that beer. I shall never forget the expression of Scott-Hansen's face when he took a draught, nor that of Blessing when he was going to taste it, in order to decide what kind of stuff it was. A roar of laughter drowned the imprecations hurled by the victims at the culprit's head. They tried hard to discover the guilty one, but all in vain; this only tended to increase the fun. We tried to make as much as we could of this incident, and the discovery of the coffee adulterator became the burning question of the day on board; but he was never found out.

On the 21st of November we took soundings, and reached the bottom at a depth of not quite fifty fathoms. Nansen had been busy photographing by electric and magnesium light.

After each meal we generally got hold of our pipes and took refuge in the cook's galley, which we made our smoking-room, as we were not at first allowed to smoke in the saloon. In the galley we would stand packed like herrings in a barrel, smoking away till we could hardly see one another, and listening to stories and yarns of all sorts, at which Bentsen and Sverdrup were the best hands. Now and then the cook would grumble and wish us far away, and no wonder, for there was not too much room for washing up.

The dogs, with no roof over their heads, had not been having a very good time. We now made kennels for them round the skylight, with shavings for them to lie on. In the mornings they were let loose to get some exercise, and one of us, for a week at a time, had to look after them. They did not seem to like leaving their quarters, although these were anything but warm.

On the 23rd of November there was a ring round

the moon, with two mock-moons. The thermometer stood at 22° below zero. For some time we had suffered from damp in the cabins, and we had the greatest difficulty in preventing our sleeping-bags from being damaged. In both the four-berth cabins we made an awning of canvas above the berths, and greased it well with tallow, so that the drops rolled off and fell into a receiver.

DR. NANSEN AMONG THE PACK-ICE NEAR THE *FRAM*.

On the 25th of November we were in 78° 38' north latitude, and were drifting along quite satisfactorily. In order to control our four chronometers, we now and then observed the time when Jupiter was being passed by his satellites. We had an excellent astronomical telescope, and in clear weather we got brilliant observations.

On November 29th the dogs again killed one of their comrades. This time "Fox" was the victim.

When we cut our hair we used a clipper; some of us had it cropped quite close to the head. There was, consequently, not much to protect our heads from the cold, but then we always wore our cat-skin caps. Scott-Hansen, when cropping us, left, unknown to us, a small tuft of hair on the nape of our necks, very much like a Chinaman's pigtail, which caused great merriment among the others whose hair had not been cut.

While dozing in the saloon after dinner, on Friday, December 8th, we suddenly heard a heavy crash on the deck, accompanied by several smaller falls and a rattling noise, as if the whole of the rigging had fallen upon the deck. All hands rushed on deck in an instant. It was the ice, which was in a perfect uproar, making a rumbling noise like an infuriated man who cannot control his temper. This morning masses of ice pressed up against both sides of the stern in great piles. Suddenly, and without our having been warned by any previous sound, these piles of ice must have fallen down over the stern as the floes receded from the ship.

It was a tremendous crack, but the *Fram* withstood it. We all agreed that no other ship could have stood the pressure we had experienced up to the present time. The ice broke up into pieces, which, as a rule, were forced in under the ship, which, in consequence, was gradually lifted up. The pressure went on for some time during the afternoon. At six o'clock it began again, this time accompanied by a thundering noise and uproar. We were having our supper, but some of us went on deck to have a look at the turmoil around us, while those who remained behind in the saloon had to shout at the top of their voices in order to be heard. Nansen, who forgot nothing in connection with the equipment of the expedition, had been thinking of taking a phonograph with him, but it came to nothing after all. It would, however, have been most interesting to be able to bring home with us the voice of this generally silent desert of ice, groaning in anger, as it seemed, because mankind had ventured to force their way into it to lay bare its hidden secrets. The *Fram* was screwed 4° over to the port side.

Blessing and Nordahl had been unlucky at cards of late, and had lost their rations of French rolls and cakes for the whole of the next month. Poor fellows, they now had to be content with the hard rye biscuits.

On the 10th of December appeared the first number of our paper, the *Framsjaa*.[1] It began well, and discussed all sorts of subjects; Blessing was the responsible editor.

December 13th was a day full of events in our usually quiet life in the ice. During the previous night all the dogs suddenly began to bark and make a terrible row. We ran on deck and found that they were all out of their kennels, and those near to the railing had jumped up on it, while all were barking in the same direction. They were, however, all tied up. We could not, of course, see anything in the darkness, but Mogstad and I thought we could hear something like the screech of foxes out on the ice among the hummocks. The dogs did not become any quieter during the night; they seemed to be afraid to settle down and go to sleep. Each watch had the same report to make about their uneasiness, especially of those which had their kennels at the foot of the half-deck on the starboard side close to the gangway, which stood open for passing to and from the ice. Three of the dogs, which were fastened close to the

[1] *Fram's Outlook.*

F

gangway, disappeared in the course of the evening. We thought it was because these three had torn themselves loose, and got out on the ice, that the others were whining and making a noise, which they generally did on such occasions.

Next day Hendriksen and Mogstad went to fetch ice for the galley some distance away from the ship. They had not taken any weapons with them. When they had gone some way on the ice they caught a glimpse of a bear coming in their direction, fighting with the dogs, which were close round it. The bear was making straight for them, and they had to make all haste on board to avoid getting the bear's claws into them. Mogstad, who knew his way about better in the darkness than Hendriksen, having been minding the dogs earlier in the day between the hummocks on this part of the ice, succeeded in getting on board, but it had fared almost fatally with Peder, as he was anything but light-footed with his big, heavy foot-gear. When he had run some distance, and believed that the bear was not following him, he turned round and cast the light round about him with the small lantern he was carrying; but before he was aware of it the bear was right upon him, and struck him in the side. Peder, believing his last hour had come, uttered a fearful roar, then, quick as lightning, he struck the beast over the head with the lantern, which then went spinning over the ice. The bear let go its hold and sat up on its hind legs, staring in great surprise at Peder, who at once took to his heels. The bear, however, was not going to let off an enemy so easily—one who had treated him so uncivilly—and set off after Peder, when a delivering angel, in the shape of one of our dogs, appeared upon the scene and attracted the bear's attention, so that Peder this time escaped the brute's clutches. The dogs, which had been barking furiously the whole time, now surrounded the nimble and agile bear, which set off straight as an arrow for the ship, from which shots were now being fired in the darkness. Mogstad was on board, and had got hold of Scott-Hansen's carbine, which hung near the saloon door. At this moment Peder, quite out of breath, got on board. The first shot missed its mark, and so did the second, and then the gun got out of order. Peder came clattering down the companion in his heavy boots, crying out, "A bear has bitten me in the side! Cartridges! cartridges! Shoot him! shoot him!" Scott-Hansen, Jacobsen and Nansen seized their guns and turned out; but, as bad luck would have it, the guns were not quite ready for use, the barrels being stopped up at both ends with wadding. It was no easy matter to put the guns in order in the dark. There they were, standing with their guns, while the bear had now got close up to the side of the ship and had just struck down a dog and was standing over it. In the meantime Peder was rummaging about in his drawer and calling out for cartridges. Blessing and I now came on deck; I had my gun in perfect order, and Jacobsen, who had been running about looking for a walrus-spear with which to stick the bear, cried out, "Shoot! shoot! he is just down there! He is killing the dogs!"

I caught a glimpse of something down on the ice and fired three shots; we could hear the blood trickling from the bear on to the ice. "Give him another!" cried Jacobsen, which I did. As the beast lay on the ice in the agonies of death, Nansen, who now had his gun in order, sent one more bullet into it. At my first shot one of the dogs jumped up from under the bear, happy and quite unwounded.

We now saw that the chains of three of the dogs were broken; the bear had simply gone in through the gangway, seized the dogs, torn them from their chains, and carried them off over the ice. On searching among the hummocks we found the bodies of two of the dogs; they were "Johansen's friend" and the brother of "Suggen," two of our best dogs. I could now approach "my friend" without being snarled at; poor creature, there he lay with his back all torn to pieces, a flat, misshapen mass. I felt great satisfaction at having avenged his death by killing his murderer. The other dog had been bitten right across the snout, and it was no doubt this one which had been screeching like a fox. We could see that the bear had been lying right across him while eating away at the other.

It was lucky for Peder that things happened as they did. Fortunately, we were now able to see the incident, with all its accompanying disturbance and noise, in a comical light. The bear was not even fully grown, but it was a smart one for all that. But if we lost some dogs on this December 13th, we also got some in return, for "Kvik" gave birth to thirteen puppies—one for each of us on board. The much-talked-of number thirteen on several occasions proved quite a lucky number for the expedition. We killed five of the puppies, as "Kvik" could not very well manage all of them in this cold climate.

# CHAPTER IX

*Deep Soundings—The Bear and the Trap—Christmas and New Year—The Drift—Our State of Health-- Walrus*

I WAS now a pupil of Scott-Hansen. With his usual kindness and patience he instructed me in the method of taking observations. We were now in 79° 13′ north latitude. According to this we had drifted 4′ to the north in about a week.

One day Peder came into the saloon and said, "There's a bear about." Guns and cartridges were brought out, and all hands rushed on deck. The dogs were barking and running about in the moonlight as if possessed. Some of us set off running in the direction in which the bear had been seen. We did not, however, see any bear, but found the tracks of a monster, which must have been in a great hurry to get away from the ship. Sverdrup thought it was now high time the bear-trap was fixed up, and he set about fixing it. Soon afterwards the trap was suspended between two supports some distance away from the ship.

On the 21st of December, our shortest day, we took soundings the whole of the day without reaching the bottom, although we had run out 1,000 fathoms. The temperature of the water at a depth of 800 fathoms was 23° F. Ten of us had been busy all the forenoon and afternoon hauling up the line with its heavy lead, weighing about a hundredweight. We kept trudging along, one after the other, with the line over our shoulders, for some distance over the ice, and then back again to the hole. This afforded us excellent exercise and diversion; and with the light from the forge, where Petterson was busy repairing the windmill, the scene on the ice was quite a picturesque one.

The dogs were now doing well, and there seemed to be a better understanding between them since they became aware that they were threatened with death and destruction by their common enemy, the bear. "Billettören" was at his old tricks again; he kept stealing dried codfish, which he hid away among the hummocks, whither he set off as soon as he was let loose in the morning, and did not appear again except at meal-times. "Caiaphas's" tail was adorned with ornaments in the shape of lumps of ice, which rattled like a rattlesnake whenever he moved his tail. "Kvik" ran away from her pups to take an airing on the ice, and "Baby" was, as usual, ready to give us his paw whenever we came near him; "Cannibal" was somewhat ferocious, but not dangerous; "Pan" was still king of the pack as far as strength was concerned, but "Suggen" was really in command; "Barabbas" was "Kvik's" favourite, and in consequence was greatly hated by the others; "Bjelki" always kept a sharp look-out for bears, and stared at us with his great, black, melancholy eyes.

At four o'clock on the morning of December 22nd a bear was near the ship. Jacobsen saw it, forward on the port side. He fired a shot at it, but did not succeed in hitting it at such a long range in the moonlight. Hendriksen, Mogstad, Bentsen, and Sverdrup then came on deck. In the meantime, the bear approached the trap, which was on the starboard side of the ship. It had evidently crossed in front of the ship to have a look at the strange object. It raised itself three times on its hind legs and cautiously examined the whole arrangement. It then carefully put a paw against the supports on each side of the trap, sniffed at the bait, which consisted of blubber, and looked all round. It then lowered itself carefully and walked along by the steel wire with which the apparatus was fastened to a small hummock, sniffing round this as if it wanted to see whether it was properly made fast, after which it walked away with-

A SKI COMPETITION.

out troubling itself any further about the whole arrangement. "That fellow has as much sense as a man," said Sverdrup. "I'll swear, now, that a Samoyede would not have been able to make anything out of it, but would have walked straight into the trap."

The bear, on coming nearer the ship, was shot; a bullet through the shoulder settled it. Jacobsen and Peder could never agree as to whose bullet it was. The bear was not very large, but it was pretty fat. We discovered, on cutting it up, that it had devoured a considerable portion of a copy of the *Illustrated London News*, which it had found close to the ship.

Our first Christmas in the Arctic regions was upon us, and the saloon of the *Fram* resounded with the old greeting of "A Merry Christmas!" We kept Christmas all by ourselves, free and independent of everybody, in our own ice-bound kingdom. We did not need to trouble ourselves about authority and laws; we had none other than those we ourselves made; and our little community thrived admirably. Yet how much should we have liked to be among the dear ones at home, if only for a little while! Thoughts every now and then overcame us like a warm current, thawing all the ice which separated us from the south, and then everything up there in the darkness and the cold became quite light and warm.

We were seated round the table on Christmas Eve, in our thick woollen jerseys or anoraks, when suddenly an elegantly dressed person, with collar and cuffs and a white tie, stood in our midst. It was Scott-Hansen, who had dressed in his cabin for the occasion. He looked just as if he had come straight from Norway with greetings as he shook hands with us all. From the captain's cabin came another well-dressed figure. This was our commander, who, in his usual quiet way, silently took his seat. All this seemed to us like a breath of civilization.

After supper Nansen fetched two boxes from his cabin. They contained presents to us all from Scott-Hansen's mother and *fiancée*. With child-like pleasure we received our gifts of knives, pipes, cigarettes, etc. I got a target with darts, and I think it would have pleased the fair donors if they could have seen how, on many an evening and far into the night, we amused ourselves with this game, winning cigarettes and gingerbread from each other as the result of our skill.

Cakes, which did great honour to Juell, almonds and raisins and other fruit, as well as some toddy, were then placed on the table. The organ was out of order, and Mogstad had not yet got out his fiddle, so I had to play on my accordion. And then we sang, and Nansen gave us some recitations. Now and then we took a trip on deck, and it was then that the absolute solitariness of our position impressed itself upon us, with the magnificent moonlight shining over the endless ice-fields around us which separated us from civilization. It was very cold, the temperature being 36° below zero. We were in 79° 11′ north latitude. Our paper, *Framsjaa*, appeared this week —a specially well-filled number. We had now an artist on the staff of the paper, and he contributed some clever sketches, entitled " The Nansen Boys in Time of Peace," and " The Nansen Boys in Time of War." In the former, when no danger was at hand, we were represented as armed with guns, revolvers, and long knives; in time of war, when the bears were about, we had nothing but a lantern.

Between Christmas and New Year things went on as usual. Some of us complained of being unable to sleep at night; sometimes we lay awake the whole of the night. I, for my part, could not complain. Blessing had begun taking notes of the sleeping on board for statistical purposes.

The Old Year was rapidly coming to an end. As yet we had not proceeded very far to the north since we became fixed in the ice. The wind had most to do with our drifting. If it was northerly we drifted to the south, and if southerly we drifted to the north. On Christmas Day we had a fire in the saloon for the first time. It was very pleasant, but we were not very well off with regard to fuel.

The last day of the year arrived dark and cloudy,

but the weather cleared up in the course of the day, and when the Old Year bade us farewell the whole of the heavens were ablaze with Northern Lights. We were then in 79° 6' north latitude, and the thermometer stood at 33° below zero.

We spent the evening pleasantly and merrily. The *Framsjaa* contained, among other news, "telegrams" from Norway about most remarkable political changes. "Hutetu," our artist, contributed a drawing in pastel, representing a female figure sitting on the horn of the moon, surrounded by flaming Northern Lights running in spirals and bands, and looking in surprise at the *Fram* as she lay in the ice below. Nansen made a speech just as the Old Year was passing, thanking us all for our pleasant comradeship throughout the Old Year, and hoping this would continue in the New.

We welcomed the New Year with the hope that it might be a good year for us, and enable us to reach our goal. It brought cold, with the thermometer at 36° below zero; but then it also brought light with it. The heavens were radiant with Northern Lights. It also brought us another great light, one that we could discern from day to day on the horizon in the south. We felt, however, that perhaps it might be darkness in grim earnest that the New Year had in store for us. The days, as they passed by, the one after the other, grew longer and longer.

When the sun arrived we decided to have a grand sun festival—a kind of service, a sort of sun-worship, if you like. Let me here mention that there was no kind of divine service held on board; each one was left to worship in his own way.

With regard to our life on board the *Fram*, I can only say that on the whole we got on well together, and that our relations with one another were all that could be desired. It was, of course, impossible to avoid frictions altogether. The continual intercourse, day and night in such limited space, with its monotony, in the very nature of things would tend to ruffle one's temper on the slightest provocation. The Arctic night, no doubt, had also to a certain extent a depressing influence upon our spirits. I think, however, that the whole thirteen of us will agree that we got on well together.

During the month of January we had almost continuous southerly winds, and we drifted, therefore, at a good pace towards the north. Now that it was clearly proved that it was the wind upon which we had to depend, we all, naturally, only wished for southerly winds, so that we might push on further and further to the north. Never were such beaming faces seen as when a regular gale from the south-east was blowing. Then the question of reaching the Pole itself was often discussed, the time in which we might possibly get there, whether we were likely to reach it in the ship or by sledges, whether we might after all be compelled to leave the *Fram*, and so forth. Maps were brought out, and the history of former expeditions was read and discussed. We lived through all their experiences, but at the same time we knew that we were far better off than any other Arctic expedition before us. Many a life had been lost in the service of Arctic exploration, and dearly bought were the experiences upon which Nansen built, when he prepared his plan and fitted out the expedition which was destined to excel all others in its achievements. Here we were, on our splendid ship, with all the comforts one could desire, with plenty of food and with no fear of hunger or cold. The horrors of the Arctic night were unknown to us; we sat safely in our gallant craft, and let the ice outside thunder and crash as it liked. Of illness we knew nothing, and scurvy, that terrible and most dreaded enemy of the Arctic explorer, we did not fear, for our provisions had been well and carefully chosen.

On the 6th of January we were in 78° 57' north latitude, and two days later in 79° 6'; during the following days we went on drifting steadily to the north. The thermometer was at 40° below zero; the quicksilver was frozen, and we were obliged to use thermometers with spirits of wine and other liquids.

As early as the 14th of January we were discussing the idea of making a sledge expedition to the Pole, when we had got further north, and thence to Franz Josef Land, while the *Fram* was to try to get out of the ice and steam thither and meet the sledge expedition there. The sledge expedition was only to consist of three men, while all the dogs were to be used.

Scott-Hansen had begun taking observations with the pendulum apparatus; this had to be done at night, when everything was perfectly quiet. The thickness of the floes on the side of the ship was four and a half feet, while the floes before the bow were five and a half feet through.

On the 22nd of January a large open lane was seen not very far off in a north-easterly direction. We then enjoyed the rare sight of seeing the reflection of the moon on the surface of the water. Next day the lane was covered with a thin sheet of ice. Later in the morning we heard one of the dogs making a terrible row in that direction; we thought, of course, that a bear must be about. Nansen and Sverdrup had gone over to the place, and Nordahl and I also set out in the same direction to measure the temperature of the water and to take a sample to test its saltness. As

I lay on my face on the ice, reading the thermometer by the light of the lantern, I heard a puffing noise and the splashing of water and ice. We got the guns ready and jumped upon a small hummock to receive the animal, shouting to the men on board that we thought there was a bear about. We could hear Nansen shouting back that it was a walrus and that

A SEA OF ICE.

we must not fire; they had gone on board for harpoons and lines with which to catch it.

When we got on board we heard that Nansen and Sverdrup had come across a walrus lying on the ice, when they came to the place where "Caiaphas" stood barking. It threw itself into the water and vanished. They were now trying to find it again, but they were not successful.

It gave rise to a good deal of speculation, to meet

with a walrus here in the midst of the desert of drifting ice, with hundreds of fathoms to the bottom of the ocean, where it seeks its food. There must, we thought, surely be land in the neighbourhood, or we must be above some banks. We had taken soundings with a line nearly 130 fathoms long, without finding any bottom. For some time that walrus remained a mystery.

When we were out on the ice the *Fram* looked quite picturesque as she lay there somewhat coquettishly on one side, while the ice-floes lovingly embraced her powerful hull, the masts pointing majestically towards the sky, and the rigging thick with hoar-frost. The windmill as it whirled round and round showed that there was life in the midst of the solitude.

## CHAPTER X

*Changes in the Ice—Trying the Dogs with the Sledges—The Return of the Sun—A Ski-tour in 60° below Zero—An Eclipse of the Sun—Unsuccessful Bear-hunting—Spring*

WE had now begun taking long walks on the ice, and had a kind of notion that we might find land to the north of us. One after the other came down from the rigging, believing that he had caught a glimpse of land.

On the evening of the 27th of January a violent pressure began in the ice. We got through it all right, however. In the lane, about 200 yards to the north, there was a terrible hurly-burly. But although it was some distance off, and the ship lay as securely fixed as if in a vice, we now and then felt violent shocks, as if there were a wave-like motion in the ice. And these waves of ice, which were about six feet thick, and in many places packed together to treble and even greater thickness, were not to be despised.

Scott-Hansen and I had to set out to save the anemometer and the thermometer on the floe close to the ship, as the ice was beginning to crack on the port side about thirty yards off. The following day we set out to look at the terrible havoc around us. It was an imposing sight to see the results of the forces which had been at work. The ice was crushed to pieces and piled up in blocks and smaller fragments to a height of nineteen feet. In one place we saw an ice-floe in the shape of a monolith raised on end, and reaching twelve feet in the air, while it was only two or three feet in breadth. The *Fram* now lay as if in a valley, surrounded by ridges of ice on all sides, but mostly astern. Between the ridges, which generally ran in a western-easterly direction, the enormously thick ice had cracked and been ground to pieces, so that our surroundings were now quite new.

Towards the end of January it was so light that we could read a newspaper in the middle of the day, but still no land was to be seen. On the 1st of February we assumed that we had passed, or were passing, the 80°. On account of the overclouded state of the weather we had not been able to take any observation. Nevertheless, as we had had a splendid wind, we decided upon celebrating the occasion in a small way. The more *fêtes* and celebrations we had the better, and we always tried to avoid amalgamating them.

The next day we found we were in 80° 9′ north latitude, and 132° east longitude, showing a drift of 19′ in three days.

During the whole month of February we made but slow progress. On the 9th we again passed the 80°, having drifted southwards. And after that we drifted forwards and backwards, so that in the beginning of March we found ourselves still in 79° 53′ north latitude, and 134° 57′ east longitude.

There was now great activity on board; we were busy making sledges and mending our ski. We were driving with the dogs and learning how to guide them with whips similar to those used by the Eskimos, consisting of a short handle with a very long lash. Occasionally, also, we were to be seen on the ice alongside the ship busily engaged in practice at hitting the empty tins which Juell had thrown there.

When out driving, however, we did not succeed in guiding the dogs in the Eskimo manner. We were obliged to drive them in the way to which they had been used, that is, by letting a man go on in front and show them the road. When the ice is flat a team of four dogs can easily draw two men. We also tried experiments with different sledges to ascertain which were the best for hard and for loose ground.

PETTERSON TAKING A "CONSTITUTIONAL" ON THE ICE.

Nansen and Sverdrup had the experience gained on their Greenland expedition to help them in these experiments.

We tried different kinds of runners and metal fittings: round, concave, and flat runners, and fittings of aluminium, German silver, and steel. It was, of course, important to have all these thoroughly tested, so as to ascertain which was the best.

G

"Billettören," poor fellow, now died quietly and peacefully. He had been poorly some time, and died, so to speak, in his bed. The climate was, no doubt, too severe for him; so he had to leave this life and his favourite occupation of gathering together dried codfish away among the hummocks. The editor of the *Framsjaa* offered a prize for the best epitaph on "Job" and "Billettören." I believe it was Juell who won the prize.

The saloon had been transformed into a workshop for all kinds of work. On the deck lay sledges which had to be lashed, and ski which wanted new fastenings. Some of us were repairing *komager* (Lapp boots made of reindeer skin), while others looked to their canvas boots, which they preferred. From Sverdrup's cabin came the homely sound of a sewing-machine; he was making sails for the boats.

We also took tours on ski round about our quarters. The temperature was generally about 45° below zero, but it took a good deal to make one feel cold when on ski.

On the 16th of February we saw a mirage of the sun above the horizon in the shape of a red flaming torch. This was the occasion of a preliminary sun festival. The proper celebration was held on the 20th of February, although we could not see the sun on account of the cloudy sky; we could only see the reflection of its light in the clouds above. We had another shooting competition in honour of the day, but without prizes. Peder and Nansen were the best shots on this occasion.

Our first Arctic night was thus at an end; but we did not find that any of us had suffered in any way during this dreaded period. The sun did not meet those pale and emaciated faces and bowed figures of which we heard so much in connection with other

A TEAM GROUP AFTER THE FIRST ARCTIC NIGHT.
(Photographed March 8th, 1894.)

[*Page* 82.

*With Nansen to the North.*]

expeditions. It was our good ship and our excellent provisioning which we had to thank for this.

We measured the thickness of the ice in several places. In a lane which was formed about a month earlier, where the snow was thinnest, the ice was thickest; viz., twenty-two inches, while where the snow lay thicker it was only seventeen inches, by no means a slight difference.

On the 1st of March we attempted to take some soundings. In our first attempt, however, we lost the lead through the breaking of the wire, and in our second we ran out a line of about 1,700 fathoms, but did not reach the bottom.

No one had thought of such a depth in these regions. For this reason we were not too well supplied with materials for soundings; but we started a rope-walk on the ice, and began making sounding-lines from wire ropes in a temperature of 40° below zero.

One day Nansen caught in his net a great number of small infusoria, which looked like a kind of living fireworks. They shone with a wonderfully pretty greenish-blue colour as he shook the net.

The severe cold did not have any injurious effect upon us worth speaking of, but we, of course, had to be careful.

Peder had his cheek frost-bitten, while Bentsen had one side of his nose frozen every day. He thought that part of it would become quite black when he got back to warmer climes. Scott-Hansen often had his fingers frost-bitten when taking observations, and on one occasion, when Nansen was photographing me, my nose all of a sudden turned white without my being aware of it. Nansen had to tell me to make haste and rub it with snow.

One day Nansen, Sverdrup, Scott-Hansen and I set

out on a ski tour, the temperature being 60° below zero. We wore fur coats, but only our ordinary thick tweed trousers. When we had proceeded some distance we discovered that we had nearly lost all feeling in our knees, and had then to begin rubbing and beating them to get life into them again. We now altered our course so that we got the wind, which was travelling about three metres in the

A SKI EXCURSION.

second, obliquely, instead of directly against us. The ski are easily broken in severe cold, as the wood becomes very brittle. Many a pair were destroyed in consequence. As for Jacobsen, none of the ski were strong enough to carry him. Eventually some were specially made for him with steel runners underneath, but they also went to pieces.

When we were out on these excursions we generally used our Iceland woollen jerseys and wind-clothes. The latter are made of a light material through which the wind cannot penetrate, the trousers being made wide enough to pull on over the usual ones, and the jacket in the shape of an Eskimo anorak, with a hood to draw over the head which can be pulled tightly with a cord. We found these clothes most useful as a protection against the biting wind.

On the 12th of March the temperature was 60° below zero. This was the lowest temperature observed by us.

One day we heard the dogs making a terrible row and barking loudly. We all thought there were bears about. "Ulinka" and "Pan" were let loose, and they set off westward towards a lane which had been formed in that direction. Nansen and Sverdrup followed the dogs, and soon discovered some holes made in the ice in the lane by a walrus. More of us went to join in the search for the walrus, but all in vain. It is most difficult to understand how these animals can manage to exist here in the midst of the thickest and closest drift-ice: but the fact remains that they are found here.

We were having westerly and south-westerly winds, and, in consequence, were unfortunately drifting southwards. Our life on board went on as usual: we had now more opportunity for taking exercise since daylight had returned. Our library was in great request; on more than one occasion it had been a great comfort and pleasure to us. Books about earlier Arctic expeditions were those read at first. A number of volumes of English illustrated papers were great favourites; we enjoyed the pictures almost as children do.

The dogs were let loose in the mornings, as usual, to take exercise on the ice; they barked and carried on terribly to get loose, but no sooner had they got on the ice than they wanted to get on board again. But they were not allowed on board until dinner-time, when most of them crept back into their kennels. One of them, little "Bjelki," who had a remarkably thick coat, always remained outside, and went to sleep in a temperature of $-60°$! Another one, "Haren," a long-legged, white, smooth-haired dog with pointed ears and a long snout, would never come on board with the others; he never felt cold, and liked best to be on the ice. "Sjölike," a small, snappish brute with a tangled white coat, and a great fighter, although he had scarcely any teeth left, was taken down into the saloon to be dried. "Kvik," who had the privilege of being there, became exceedingly jealous at this. When any of the dogs were brought down into the saloon, they became so quiet and docile as to seem quite embarrassed at all the grandeur and finery to be seen there.

We had to shoot one of "Kvik's" pups, which suddenly went mad and ran round and round the deck, frothing at the mouth.

Daylight was now shining right down into the saloon to us. We had taken away the kennels round the skylight and put in double windows. The electric light was well enough, but it was not to be compared with sunlight.

At the end of March we were in 80° 4' north latitude, and the temperature stood at $-26°$. The sun was now quite high in the heavens, and we were using it for our observations. In spite of the cold, the sun gave out so much heat that the snow in the bow of the *Fram* began to melt. The dogs basked in the sunshine, and showed their joy by trying to tear each other to pieces. The puppies took after their elders, and every morning they fought on the deck to their hearts' content.

JOHANSEN ON A HUMMOCK WATCHING FOR THE BEARS.

[Page 87.

*With Nansen in the North.*]

On the 6th of April we expected an eclipse of the sun. Scott-Hansen had made a calculation as to the time it would occur, and how long it would last. He, Nansen, and I began in good time to watch the sun. We used the large telescope and the theodolite, two of us observing, one at each instrument, while the third kept the time. Scott-Hansen and I were observing as the time drew near, and we both almost simultaneously cried out, "Now!" when the moon entered upon the disc of the sun, which occurred a few seconds later than Scott-Hansen had calculated.

The next morning, while I was taking the meteorological observations, my attention was drawn, by "Ulinka's" barking, to two bears close to the large hummock astern of the ship. It was difficult to distinguish them in the bright sunshine, as they were as white as the snow. I seized a carbine which hung ready loaded with a few shots, and Mogstad, who in the meantime had come on deck, seized another. The bears, which stood scenting the air, and had probably been disturbed by the noise of the dogs, faced right round and made off. We jumped down on the ice and ran after them. I had low wooden shoes on my feet, and was constantly losing them in the snowdrifts. It was a she-bear with her one-year-old cub that had been near the ship. I was to be responsible for the mother, and Mogstad for the cub. When we reached the large hummock we could see them some distance ahead, but at rather a long range. We fired, and could see that both the bears were hit. The mother was hit by three bullets, and then fell over, and the cub was also seen to fall. But neither of us had any more cartridges besides those that had been in the guns, and, unfortunately, these did not contain expanding bullets. The cub raised itself and made a spring forward. The mother twisted herself round, got on to her legs, and trudged off as if in a dazed condition. Then she lay down for a while, and then again set off after her cub. I ran on board to fetch more cartridges, and to give the alarm that two bears had been fired at close to the ship. All hands helped to get guns and cartridges ready. Nansen set off on ski without having had anything to eat. We did not see him again until the evening.

Quite an expedition was now fitted out and started for the place where the bears had been wounded, but we saw neither them nor Nansen. I climbed a hummock to get a better view, while the others went on in advance with sledges to fetch the bears, of which we felt sure. Suddenly I caught sight of two other bears, not far away, but they discovered me at the same time, and took to their heels. It was only the work of a moment to get the gun off my shoulder and to load it, and off we ran, across ridges and past hummocks and lanes, while we now and then caught a glimpse of the bears in front of us. Peder, who was the only one besides myself who had a gun, followed up the chase for a while, and Nordahl and Petterson also joined. I was lightly clad, and pushed on as fast as I could. In about an hour and a half I was the only one in a pursuit which, after all, led to nothing. I could see by the tracks that the bears had reduced their speed, and I hoped to have gained upon them; but at last I saw it was impossible to overtake bears on ski, and, when shortly afterwards a fog came on, I had to retrace my steps to the ship, which I reached in time for dinner. In the afternoon many of us set out in search of the bears, but all in vain.

Nansen came back in the evening after a long and difficult pursuit of the wounded bears; he had followed up the blood-stained tracks as far as he

We remembered that at home the spring was approaching, and the birds were coming from the south as its first messengers, and all nature was brightening up and enjoying the new life around. At home the sun and the snow were fighting the old battle with greater results than with us.

Where we were, however, everything was just as before, excepting that it was light both night and day, while before it was dark. But we could see no fields requiring to be laid bare, no plants or trees anxious to shoot forth; no flowers, and could hear no birds singing. We could see nothing of all those things we now thought were so wonderfully pretty when we were at home.

When May arrived the weather became milder; we had plenty of favourable wind to gladden our hearts, and on Whit Sunday, the 13th, we had reached a latitude of 80° 53′. The same day we saw a sea-gull come floating over the big hummock. It was a message of spring. In the course of the summer we shot several birds: ivory gulls, Arctic petrels, snow bunting, and no less than eight young specimens of the very rare Arctic rose gull, or Ross's gull. Peder would not allow us to shoot the black guillemots. "They are lucky birds," he used to say.

Our paper, the *Framsjaa*, appeared pretty regularly, but one Sunday no number was published. In the next number the editor informed his readers, in reply to many anxious inquiries, that the new rotary printing machine had been delayed by ice in the Elbe, but that now it had arrived safely, and the paper would thereafter be greatly enlarged and appear regularly. A column for "questions and answers" would be a new attraction, and the editor would undertake to reply fully to all kinds of questions, no matter what they might be. The last number contained a remarkable poetic effusion, with the title, "What is eternity?" This contribution, the editor remarked, had arrived after the edition was printed, but he was so impressed with the poem that he would not keep it from his readers for another week, so he decided, quite regardless of expense, to print a new edition containing the poem. "With our new rotary machine nothing is impossible for us," said the bare-faced editor.

## CHAPTER XI

*Summer Excursion on the Ice—Midsummer Day—" Suggen" and "Caiaphas"—The Drift*

THE 17th of May, 1894, the anniversary of the Norwegian Day of Independence, opened with bad weather, like the previous day. But we took no notice of the weather, for we had been in a festive mood since the early morning, and were bent on celebrating the day in a worthy manner. Such a curious procession the world has probably never seen as that which on this day, high up on the interminable ice-fields in the far north, wended its way around a ship lying fast between masses of ice. The weather was such as no festival in honour of the Norwegian Day of Independence had ever been celebrated in before. The *Fram* was, of course, decorated as befitted the occasion.

First of all came Nansen with his small Norwegian flag on a bear-spear, and then Sverdrup with the pennant of the *Fram* waving in the breeze. Next came a sledge drawn by two of our best dogs, while the other dogs ran about, apparently surprised at the strange sight. The sledge was driven by Mogstad, while I sat beside him with my accordion, representing the band. The music was not brilliant, but it must be remembered that with the thermometer at 10°, and a biting wind, one's fingers were somewhat affected by the cold. After the sledge came Jacobsen and Peder, the former with his gun, and the latter with his long harpoon and walrus-line round his shoulders; then Amundsen and Nordahl with a red banner, in the midst of which stood a Norwegian viking breaking a spear in two, with the inscription, "Forward! forward, Norwegians! What we do, we do for Norway!" Then came Blessing with his banner; it was one of his own shirts, on which was painted in large red letters, "N. A." (Normal Arbeidsdag, or Normal Working Day). The shirt was fastened to the end of a harpoon-spear with a cross-piece for the sleeves, and in defence of his banner he carried rifle, revolver and knife. After him came Scott-Hansen with the meteorologist's banner, consisting of a large tin plate, on which stood, on a red background, the letters "Al. Str." (Almindelig Stemmeret, or Universal Suffrage). It was a striking banner enough, but it gave us a lot of trouble; it was blown to pieces during the procession, and had to be repaired, and later on, when Nansen was speaking, it would persist in keeping up a rattling noise, and had, at last, to be turned edgewise to the wind. Last of all came Juell, our cook, with the kettle belonging to our cooking range on his back, and a big fork in his hand.

In the early morning we had decorated ourselves with bows of the national colours. We had some trouble about the blue colour, and had, at last, to use paper, but for the red and white we found some suitable cloth. Even "Suggen," the patriarch among the dogs, went about with a long ribbon bow at his neck. Bentsen and Petterson did not join us, as they were devoting themselves to the preparation of the dinner.

At twelve o'clock the procession started in the order mentioned above. A strange, solemn sight, no doubt, it must have been to see us, with our banners and devices, gliding on our ski around the *Fram*, which lay there, safe and sound, pressed a little over on one side by the ice. I played the Norwegian national song, "Yes, we love this country," etc., and we all thought it sounded most impressive. We marched twice round the ship, and thence to the big hummock astern, where Nansen proposed a cheer for the *Fram*, which had hitherto borne us so well on our expedition, and which he hoped would do the same in the future. The ringing cheers resounded far out over the ice. We then returned to the ship, where we made a halt by her side, while Nansen ascended the bridge and delivered a speech in honour of the day. He hoped that all at home were well; there were, perhaps, some whose minds were filled with anxious thoughts on our account, but he only wished they could know how well we were faring, and they would be quite easy in their minds. Up to the present we had reason to be satisfied, and if some unforeseen circumstance did not occur, we might succeed in bringing honour to our country, and make it respected in the eyes of the world, should we really succeed in reaching our goal. The speech was received with cheers for our country, which were given with the full force of our lungs.

Then followed the salute: four shots from our cannons thundered forth over the silent ice-fields. Some of the dogs took to their heels, frightened out of their wits. "Baby" and "Rattlesnake" did not appear for some time afterwards.

A splendid dinner was then served in the saloon, which was festively decorated with flags. The conversation turned upon our return home, a subject upon which, in our happy moments, we were generally apt to fall back on, and which always carried us away. After dinner we had cigars and coffee. In the evening refreshments, consisting of figs, raisins, almonds, and ginger-bread, were served round.

On May 18th, "the day after," there were no visible

after-effects among any of us. The wind continued with drifting snow. It was E. to S., and travelled about ten metres in the second. The ship had been twisting herself round, and was now lying in the direction of S. ½ E. instead of S. ½ W. The sky was overcast, and we could take no observations. The temperature was 14° below zero.

A MERIDIAN ALTITUDE OF THE SUN IN THE SUMMER OF 1894.

Two days afterwards we took an observation, according to which we were in 81° 12·4' north latitude, and in 125° 45' east longitude.

Amundsen made an apparatus with which to measure the current at different depths, and Petterson, who is fond of cooking, relieved Juell as cook.

On the first of June we took a sounding with a line 4,400 metres in length, made out of a wire rope. We only got back 3,200 metres; the rest of the line, with ten iron grids and a bottom-sampler, are lying at the bottom of the ocean.

In the beginning of June the ground was in the best possible condition for ski-running. On our tours Sverdrup and I saw several "breathing-holes" made by walrus or seal in various places in the lanes. One evening we played a game of "bold"[1] on the ice

A SUMMER EVENING, JULY, 1894.

close to the ship; we played with heart and soul till the snow flew about our ears and the steam rose in clouds from our bodies.

We hoisted our sails one day in order to get them dried. The sails swelled out in the wind, but of course the *Fram* did not move.

The summer brought with it misty rains and a mild temperature up to 40°. The snow was melting, and pools of water were being formed here and there on

[1] A game something like the English game of "rounders."

the ice. Numerous indications on the sky in all directions told of open water in various places. In this mild weather, light as it was both night and day, we promenaded the deck, which was kept nice and trim, smoking our pipes and talking to each other about the ice, the drift, and our chances of reaching our goal. When the wind blew from the south, our spirits rose. For the present our object was to get further to the north than any ship had previously done, such as the *Alert*, the English ship, which reached 82° 27′ north latitude, and the *Polaris*, the American ship, which got as far as 82° 26′ north latitude. We were also on the look-out for land, especially Peder, who was constantly spying from the crow's-nest. Every time he appeared at the door of the saloon he was greeted with the ironical query, "Well, have you seen anything?" or "Have you heard anything?" which Peder received with imperturbable calmness.

On the 16th of June we reached 81° 51′ north latitude. The temperature was maximum 39°, and minimum 19°. Scott-Hansen, Nordahl and Peder had been away on an expedition, the longest that had hitherto been undertaken across the drift-ice. From the crow's-nest Peder had seen an unusually large hummock with black stripes down its sides. They took its bearings and set off for it one Sunday morning on ski, taking plenty of provisions with them, and more than half the dogs. They did not succeed in finding the same black hummock which Peder descried, but they came across another one about twenty-five feet high, from which they brought back with them some clayey soil. They also found a log of driftwood, a piece of which they also brought with them. On their way back they found in an open lane a curious animal or plant, they did not know which. It turned out to be an alga. When they got back they were much fagged and knocked up with toiling across hummocks and lanes on the heavy slushy ground. Scott-Hansen and Peder became slightly snow-blind after this expedition, and Blessing had to cure them with cocaine.

The pool around the ship was gradually getting bigger, so much so that we could practise in our kayaks on it. Scott-Hansen was especially keen at this sport;

THE *FRAM* IN THE ICE, MIDSUMMER, 1894.

he would let himself capsize with his kayak, and then try to right himself with it again. Nordahl held a line, fastened around Scott-Hansen's body, and when the latter was on the point of drowning, he was pulled ashore, and had then to hurry to his cabin and change his clothes. He seemed greatly to like these experiments in capsizing.

From the pools on the higher ice, small rivers ran down the slope to the lower ice-strata, with just the same sound as the rippling brooks among the mountains at home. On board we found that the mould-mushroom thrived wherever there was any dampness. Blessing cultivated the bacteria which he had obtained from the dead puppies. But as yet he had found no bacteria in the air.

On Midsummer Day we were in 81° 43′ north latitude. The weather was bad, with cold northerly wind and sleet. There were no signs of birch-leaves, or of flowers; only ice, ice everywhere. While we were sitting at dinner a bear paid a visit to the big hummock astern, where Mogstad and Jacobsen were building an ice-cellar for our stock of bear, walrus and seal flesh, which we were keeping as food for the dogs. When they returned thither after dinner they discovered the tracks of the bear. Nansen was away the whole afternoon in search of it, but had no success. It was now most difficult to get over the hummocks and across the lanes; in fact, in many places one would want water-ski to get across.

We celebrated Midsummer Day in the usual way, with a really good dinner. We had not many ways in which we could keep up our celebrations. Our life was somewhat monotonous; one day was exactly like any other. There was the same kind of work at the same time, and the same recreations at the same hours. The latter consisted of cards and reading, but we were beginning to get tired of cards. We were, however, very comfortable; of that there could be no doubt, and so we had to rest satisfied.

On June 30th the weather was dull, with an overcast sky and mild rain, which told greatly on the ice. The pools on our floe were now getting bigger and bigger, and the observation-tent and the cage were almost inaccessible, and could only be reached by jumping from one place to another. The next day there was a break in the clouds, and we were able to take an observation. The latitude was 81° 32′, so we had been drifting south again. During June, therefore, we had made no progress northwards at all, though it was a month of which we had really great expectations.

We filled our water-tank with water from the ice-floe. This water was somewhat salty, but for all that we used it for a considerable time. The first time we got new, fresh water, we all thought the tea was poor and weak; it was the salty flavour we missed, and we did not think much of the fresh water. We were not so much afraid of water which was a little saltish as, for instance, the crew of the *Jeannette*. Every piece of ice which was brought on board that vessel for cooking or drinking purposes was first carefully examined; they believed that the smallest quantity of salt would produce scurvy among them.

According to the observations we made, the temperature in the strata nearest the surface of the water varied greatly:—

| | |
|---|---|
| On the surface | 32·76° |
| 1 metre below surface | 32·63° |
| 2 metres below surface | 32·51° |
| 2·5 ,, ,, | 32·00° |
| 2·6 ,, ,, | 31·90° |
| 2·7 ,, ,, | 31·95° |
| 2·8 ,, ,, | 29·25° |
| 2·9 ,, ,, | 29·10° |
| 3 ,, ,, | 29·15° |

At the last depth we found a thin layer of ice, which was easily broken, and pieces of which rose to the surface.

When the ice was measured on the 10th of July, we found that on the old solid floes it had increased about eight inches in one week. It was most remarkable that the ice should increase in thickness while it continually went on melting at the surface. The reason may be that the fresh water, formed by the melting of the snow, ran down through the ice, and there came into contact with the colder salt water, and, gradually assuming the temperature of the latter, froze.

The appearance of the surroundings in the neighbourhood of the ship was not now very attractive. The

SAILING ON THE FRESH-WATER POOL NEAR THE *FRAM*.

*Fram* lay so high above the ice that we had to use ladders to get down to it and back on board again. Down on the ice were heaps of broken glass, the remains of all the beer bottles we had emptied, the last of which was finished many a day ago. Everything which we had thrown overboard during the course of the year was now laid bare by the melting of the snow. The kennels, which we had erected on the ice, and which consisted of two long wooden boxes divided into separate rooms for the worst fighters, looked dirty and rickety as the snow went on melting, while here and there a merry brook made its way under the kennels, forming pools of varying sizes.

The appearance of the ice in the direction of the horizon was no longer white against white; the blackened ice and the pools had now changed it all and given it a cheerless appearance. The snow still left on the ice had the appearance of coarse moist sugar.

On the starboard side we had a fine fresh-water lake, on which we sailed with the longboats. Scott-Hansen, Mogstad and Bentsen were the three who were most interested in this sport. Sverdrup rigged the boats with a square sail of the same kind which they use in the north of Norway. When there was only a slight breeze they got on all right, but if there was a fresh wind, it generally happened that the spectators on board got a good laugh; the water was shallow, and every now and then they went aground, the boat filled with water, and they had often to lower the sail.

One day, all hands started for the fresh-water lake to test the bearing capacity of the boats. All the dogs seemed to understand that there was something unusual going on, and followed us inquisitively; even "Kvik," who was with her pups; left her kennel and a bone to join the others. "Barabbas" at once took her place at the bone, and was the only one that remained behind. As soon as we had got into the boat, which easily carried the whole thirteen of us, and had begun to push her along, the dogs began to show signs of the greatest fright. The poor animals evidently thought we intended going away and leaving them behind by themselves on the ice. They kept whining and running backwards and forwards on the floes. "Suggen," the veteran, set off and ran round to the opposite side of the lake, followed by several of the others. Little "Bjelki," after some hesitation, rushed into the ice-cold water and swam towards us, his thick coat looking very much like a bundle of wool. As soon as our trial trip was over we returned to our starting-place, and then the dogs became quiet once more. "Suggen," who perceived that he had made a mistake, took things quite coolly. He did not return, but took a long tour on the other side of the lake, as if he wanted to show us that he had not been at all anxious about us. "Suggen" was evidently a personage of importance among the dogs. He took no part in any of the fights, and all the other dogs made concessions to him. He was a kind of chieftain, and was not tied up like the others; he went about as he liked, and had his own kennel. He never descended to breaking into the ice-cellar, which the others did; many of them often came out of that cellar stuffed like a sausage after a successful raid. When "Suggen" became tired of his own kennel, he simply took possession of one of the others, generally "Pan's." The latter was the most unmanageable of them all. When "Suggen" used to come and stir him up, he had to go out and lie down on the roof; if he did not go, "Suggen" used to lie down quite coolly on top of "Pan," who, strange to say, quietly put up with it. "Suggen" used to make a sort of long speech whenever he wanted meat. He always kept himself clean and tidy. One dog who did not keep himself clean was "Caiaphas"; he was the dirtiest of them all. His thick coat was always full of dirt. ("Caiaphas" and "Suggen" subsequently proved themselves our faithful friends, and kept up longest on the sledge expedition. They were true to the end, and suffered many hardships before they gave up their lives in the service of science.)

So far (July 18th) the summer had been a disappointment to us. We expected to drift a good deal more northwards at this time of the year, but we had been almost stationary. Many of us were quietly hoping that before the summer came we should be free from ice, and able to steam northwards through the open lanes. Although the ice around the ship was apparently decreasing, she was still in the same slanting position in her solid bed, with masses of ice crammed in both her wells astern. It was the wind, and that alone, which would carry us to the north, and therefore we might wait a long time, as there was no current. When we compared the observations from day to day with the direction and strength of the wind, we saw that it was by the wind alone that our movements were influenced.

On July 20th a slight breeze from the north-east began blowing; and we hoped we were going to have a spell from that quarter now.

In the summer months there was great activity on deck. Foremost, at the smithy, stood Lars and his assistant, hammering out iron for the sledge-runners. Under the awning over the fore-deck Sverdrup was busy building six double kayaks, and Jacobsen was occupied in lashing parts of the sledges together. Strong materials were necessary, in case we had to leave our good ship. Nansen was in the workroom, studying algæ with the microscope far into the night. Blessing was similarly occupied, but often fished for algæ in the fresh-water pools. When he had anything remarkable under the microscope, Scott-Hansen and I went to look at and admire his find.

But Blessing could also do something else besides examine algæ and blood. He was both joiner and sail-maker, and Sverdrup could always find a job for him in his shop whenever he applied for work.

DR. BLESSING COLLECTING ALGÆ.

*With Nansen in the North.*]    [*Page* 104.

# CHAPTER XII

*Snow-blindness—More Dogs—Mistaking a Dog for a Bear—A Real Bear—A Retrospect—Nansen Asks me if I will Accompany Him to the Pole*

DURING the last days of July we had constant westerly winds, and drifted slowly to the south. Now and then we were troubled a little with snow-blindness. Peder, who had sailed in the polar regions since he was a boy, had never been troubled with it, and would not believe there was any such thing. But even he himself had at last to resort to Blessing and get some cocaine, and used snow-spectacles thenceforth. We had also brought with us veils for protection against snow-blindness. They were pretty red, blue, and black silk veils, which, however, were not used very often. I remember Sverdrup walking about with a blue veil covering his eyes and nose, which looked rather ludicrous just above his bright red beard. He, too, was somewhat careless about his eyes, and had to consult Blessing eventually and ask him "to look in his eyes, as he thought he had something in them."

One evening, as I was going on board after a stroll on the ice, I chanced to catch a glimpse of the hind part of a retreating bear some distance off. I seized the watch-gun, which always stands loaded near the companion leading to the cabin. The others thought it was merely fun on my part; but soon Blessing saw the bear as well, and all hands were speedily on deck. Some ran up the rigging and began shouting to one another, so that the bear was frightened and made off. Nansen and Sverdrup set off in pursuit, but, of course, it was impossible to overtake it, the ground being in such a terribly bad condition.

On the 31st of July, "Kvik" brought into the world eleven puppies, one of which, being deformed, was at once killed. Of the first litter of thirteen there were now only four left, "Sussine," "Barbara," "Gulen" (the yellow one), and "Freia." "Sussine" is alive to this day, and thrives well in her home in Norway. She has been the mother of a large progeny, many of which, however, have died.

In the beginning of August we had the loveliest summer weather it is possible to conceive. Scott-Hansen talked about having a dip, but perhaps it was as well that he did not carry out his intention, for the water was only 32·70° at the surface. We were on deck the whole of the day, while in the evening we smoked our pipes and played cards.

Scott-Hansen and Nordahl went away on an excursion and found two pieces of driftwood in the ice, probably pine-logs from the Siberian forests. Peder, who was always on the look-out for anything curious, found a tuft of grey moss among some sand on a floe—another message from some land or other.

The examination of the temperature and the saltness of the water at different depths began on the 2nd of August. It is conducted in the following manner:—Four men heave the line up on a winch with two handles. The line passes out through a metre-wheel, so that we can read how much has been paid out. We reached the bottom at a depth of about 2,000 fathoms.

About this time we one day discovered a virtuous point in "Cannibal," one of our dogs. He had no doubt been accustomed to look after things. For several days

TAKING SOUNDINGS

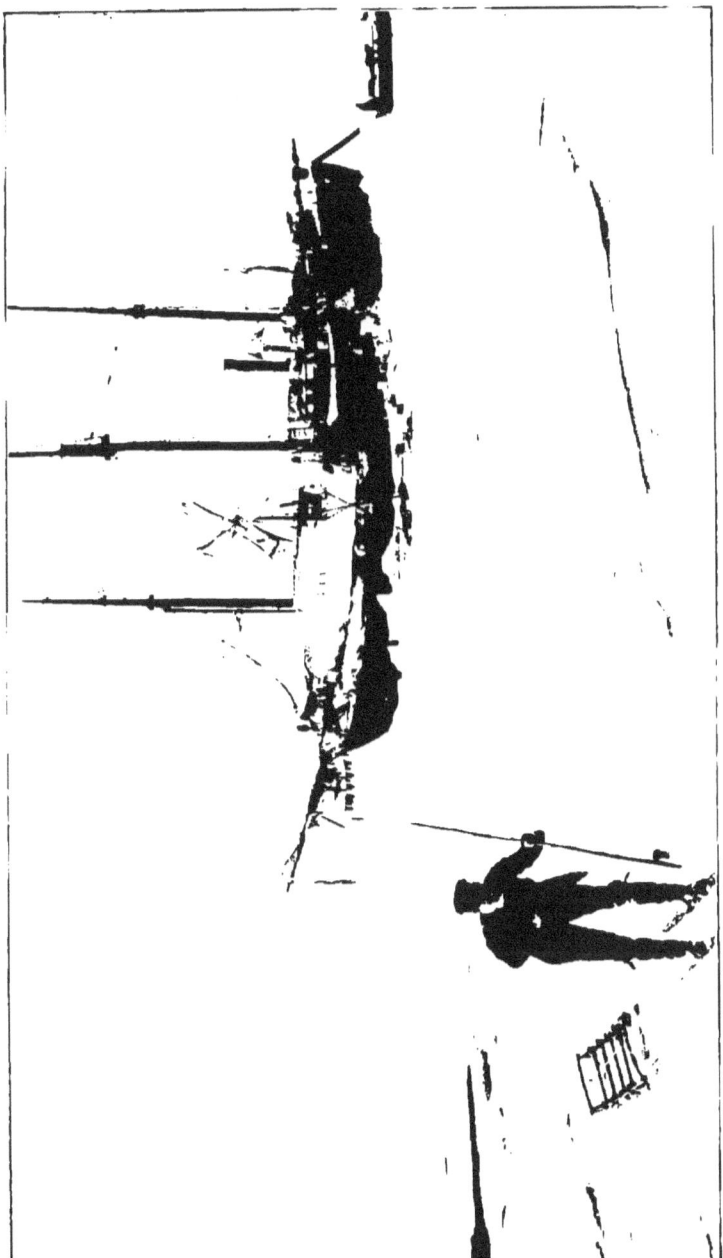

now he had been lying continuously on a bag of biscuits which we kept on the ice for feeding the dogs. He never stirred away from the bag, and showed his teeth to every dog that approached it. Yet he never attempted to steal anything from the bag himself.

A wet fog set in during the morning of August 10th. In the forenoon the weather cleared up, and Scott-Hansen and I decided to start on a short expedition to the north to measure the ice-pressures with the photogrammeter. There were enormous accumulations of ice to the north of us, and when one sees such colossal masses of it piled up from twenty to thirty feet in height, three or four times as long as the *Fram*, and a good deal broader, and how even the biggest ice-blocks are ground to pieces and lifted high up on to the top, then one is apt to lose all faith in the stability of any kind of ship if it were exposed to a pressure such as this. We had splendid warm weather during our expedition, so that we were able to take off our anoraks and walk in our shirt-sleeves, just as we do at home in the summer.

We put up our apparatus and began our work, feeling quite lonely in the midst of this silent desert of ice. We could just catch a glimpse of the ship in the distance, the only object which indicated that man had penetrated so far ; we gazed at it with pleasure and admiration, and felt that we were fortunate to be so comfortable as we were on board her. This excursion gave us a foretaste of what it would be to work our way across the ice if ever we should have to leave the ship. We should not be able to make great progress, if we had to proceed over ice like this in search of some land or other, and it would be in any case an arduous and fatiguing undertaking.

On August 16th we had fine rain. The previous night, after twelve, when it was my watch, I was nicely taken in. There was a thick fog which made all objects loom unnaturally large in the distance. I fancied I saw a bear over by the big hummock, scratching and digging his way into the meat-cellar, so that the ice flew about his ears. I could only see part of his back and his paws; but feeling that it could not be anything else but a bear, I fetched the watch-gun, rested it on the railing, and took aim carefully, as the distance was about two hundred yards. I took my time and waited, in order to be able to see something more of the animal. At last more of its body came into view and I pulled the trigger. Then all was silent for a moment. Nansen came at once on deck and asked what was the matter. I told him I had fired a shot over to the big hummock, as I thought there was something over there. The next moment we saw the supposed bear advancing leisurely across the ice towards us; but as it came nearer to us we discovered it was one of our dogs, to which, curiously enough, we had given the name of "Icebear." The fog had magnified it into a big bear; at the same time it was partly due to the fog that I, fortunately enough, missed it, for "Icebear" was one of our very best dogs. I heard frequently from my comrades of this exploit afterwards!

We had several times seen seals in the lanes about here; Sverdrup shot one, one day, but it sank before any one could manage to get it on to the ice. We had not expected to be drifting back during the summer. We had been depending so much upon it. It was the winter in which we now put our faith. We believed, of course, we should reach our goal; but we also believed we should have to fortify ourselves with a good deal of patience.

Towards the end of August it began to grow cold again, and the pools were soon covered with ice. After a fall of snow on the new ice the ground was in

JOHANSEN SHOOTING AT THE DOG, "ICE BEAR."
*With Nansen in the North.*] [*Page* 108.

excellent condition for ski-running, which was soon in full swing. One morning, in the small hours, when I came on deck to relieve Blessing on his watch, we discovered, while standing by the railing, something moving about on an ice-floe about five hundred yards away. It was a bear, which was lying on its back rolling itself luxuriously in the newly-fallen snow. A strong north-westerly wind was blowing towards it, at the rate of nine metres in the second, and the windmill was going at full speed. But it did not seem to mind this in the least, for we plainly saw it raise itself, first with its fore-legs, and leisurely begin to move towards the ship, moving its head from side to side as bears usually do when they are after their prey. With its extraordinary sense of smell it had, of course, scented the dogs.

The watch-gun was full of vaseline, so I went quietly into the saloon for a couple of guns, whereupon we went cautiously forward and laid ourselves in ambuscade on the forecastle. The bear came steadily nearer; the fellow was not in the least afraid, although the windmill was making a great noise. We lay quietly with our fingers on the trigger. When it had reached the other side of the lane in front, about 100 yards off, it crossed this on the thin ice and jumped up on to the other side. Now was our time. As the bear was making a tack eastwards we both fired at the same time, and the monster fell backwards over the edge of the floe. We found that it had been hit by both shots. One had cut the artery just where it issues from the heart, so the bear had, of course, been killed on the spot. The dogs, which were tied up on the ice and had thus escaped danger, had not noticed the bear till they heard the shots and saw us on the ice with our guns, when they became quite frantic with excitement. We hauled the bear up from the thin ice, but not before Blessing had fallen through, and dragged it up to the side of the ship, where we left it with its jaws wide-open, so that the next watch, which happened to be Nordahl, might have a surprise.

The dogs sat the whole day barking in the direction from which the bear had come; I suppose they remembered the bear of last winter which came on board, stretched its paws into the kennels, tore a couple of the dogs away from their chains, and carried them off to make a meal of them. Such things are not easily forgotten even by a dog.

On the 28th of August our observations showed we were in 80° 53′ north latitude, having thus drifted back past the 81° again; but on the 4th of September we were again in 81° 14′ north latitude, and 123° 36′ east longitude, although the wind had been easterly and even north-easterly. During the next few days we again drifted south.

"Cannibal," who was one of the most ferocious of our dogs, was attacked by the others and severely maltreated. As many as could get at him attacked him in the belly—they seemed to know this is a vulnerable point—with their greedy teeth, but he survived under the care of Blessing, who sewed up the wounds.

The daily routine of life on board went on somewhat in this fashion:—

The cook (Juell and Petterson took the post in turns, a fortnight each) got up at six o'clock, when the last watch went to bed. The coffee or chocolate was on the table at eight o'clock, when all hands were called. But there was not much breakfasting till a little later on; the two doctors, Nansen and Blessing, were generally the last. Mogstad, who was an early riser, reminded us of the old saying, "In the morning hours the finest gold is found"; but Blessing thought this was a mistake, and that it should run, "Morning slumbers are sweet and sound." After breakfast every one began his particular work. The dogs were fed and let loose. Later on it was decided that every man should take exercise on ski for two hours daily. This was carried out in all sorts of weather, and we found it agreed splendidly with us. Nansen was busily employed in making a kayak to

JOHANSEN AND AMUNDSEN RECONNOITRING IN THE NEIGHBOURHOOD OF THE *FRAM*.

hold one person. Blessing and Sverdrup had for a long time been making some canvas coverings. We had dinner at one o'clock and supper at six. In the evening we either played cards or searched the treasures of our library. Amundsen would never touch cards—"They are the devil's playthings," he used to say. Jacobsen went early to bed and seldom joined us at cards. But some of the others went in frequently for gambling, and they were in the habit of paying their losses with I.O.U.'s, which ran up to such big amounts that it was difficult to keep account of them, and then we wiped them out altogether and began again. There was generally a good deal of betting and bartering of bread going on. Sometimes we had heated discussions on the state of affairs in Tromsö or Horton.

We now began to build splendid solid snow houses for the dogs. It was again beginning to be cold, and darkness was increasing day by day. The winter was approaching.

On September 22nd it was just a year since we became fixed in the ice. We could now look back upon the year's drift. Scott-Hansen made a chart of it, and so we could see what our progress had been. Notwithstanding the many zigzags which we had made, we saw that the drift had gone on in one particular direction, viz., N. 36° W., and about 120 miles in length from east to west, and about 140 miles towards the north. The progress had been slow, but in the right direction. We fully believed that during the coming year we should drift more rapidly northwards than we had hitherto done, and that we should not be driven back to the same extent as during the last twelve months. At the rate we drifted during this time we should want about seven years before we could get out of the ice. We did not think we should be able to drift right across the Pole, or in its neighbourhood, but we might most likely traverse the Polar Sea in 86° north latitude.

There had been some talk about two of us leaving the ship and setting off for the Pole with all the dogs; not, however, with the intention of returning to the ship, which, of course, it would be impossible to find again, but with the view of making for Spitzbergen.

Our captain asked me this afternoon if I would go with him on such an expedition, and to this I, of course, declared myself willing. We amused ourselves with calculating distances, weight of provisions, the number of miles per day, etc., etc., just to see how the plan would work out. But this was not the first time this matter had been discussed.

Nansen invented an apparatus for firing with kerosene oil in the galley, which turned out a great success. From a reservoir of oil on the wall a pipe leads into the fireplace, where the oil falls in drops into an iron bowl in which some asbestos or cinders are placed, the flow of the oil being regulated by a valve-cock. A ventilating pipe conducts a current of air from the deck straight into the grate. Now we did not need to be so careful about our best paraffin oil, and could use it more liberally for our lamps.

Petterson was at first unfortunate in the use of this new apparatus: one day the whole arrangement exploded when he was standing near it, and we thought that both he and some clothes, which were hanging in the galley to dry, had been sent aloft. When he came to report what had occurred he looked quite furious and hot. He would, no doubt, have exploded himself if he had not let off the steam, accompanied by blessings and curses about "that devil of a black oil."

September 29th was Blessing's birthday. We kept high festival on mackerel and meat-pudding, with cauliflowers, rice with cloudberries, and malt extract for dinner. When we occasionally got malt extract it was not served out in spoonfuls as suggested in the directions on the labels, but in bottlefuls, and it did us a lot of good.

Next day, when Sverdrup and I were out on a splendid ski tour, we again discussed our favourite topic, the expedition to the Pole and thence to Spitzbergen. He did not know if Nansen would let him go; he said he thought Nansen wanted to go himself.

We had been experimenting in drawing loaded sledges on ski and on foot. About 250 lbs. were placed on the sledge, but we had no proper harness for drawing, and, in the then condition of the ground, it seemed as if "trug"—something like the Canadian snow-shoes—would be better than ski. We tried three dogs to the same sledge, and they managed the load exceedingly well.

October 10th was Nansen's birthday. The flag was set flying from the mizzen-masthead and the saloon was decorated. The thermometer marked 22° below zero, and in the forenoon we took a long ski-tour. Petterson did his best to provide a specially choice dinner, and Blessing treated us to Lysholm's Aquavitæ (a favourite Norwegian gin). After dinner we had coffee and cigars, the latter being Nansen's gift. In the evening followed the usual *fêting*. During the succeeding days we had fair wind from east and south-east, and on the 21st of October we passed the eighty-second degree.

In the course of the day we discovered tracks of a bear and two cubs; they had evidently not scented the ship, but the tracks of the ski had apparently interested them greatly. We took soundings again, and found the bottom at a depth of 1,800 fathoms. In the evening there was such merry-making on board as had not been witnessed for some time. We played on the organ and danced like mad, although the dance-music was not of the best.

On the 31st of October we again had a festival on board, this time in celebration of Sverdrup's fortieth birthday. "No one is quite sure about the date," he said, "for I have two different birth certificates."

A MONSTER BEAR.

*With Nansen in the North.*) [*Page* 115.

On November 4th we had a change in our otherwise monotonous life. Peder discovered a she-bear with two cubs west of the ship. The whole crew became animated. Sverdrup, Mogstad, Peder, and I set out at once after it. It was not light enough for shooting. We had all the dogs with us, and in about a quarter of an hour we saw the three bears quietly pursuing their course to the south, much more quietly now than by daylight. The dogs were very courageous, as they had us at their heels. We quickly overtook the bears, but we had to get quite close to them, as there was not light enough to take aim properly, and even then we had just to look along the barrel and fire at random.

The bears stopped and turned round when they found that the dogs were getting at close quarters. The latter at once struck off at a right angle, as if by word of command, and began worrying the bears sideways. The mother now helped us in obtaining a good aim at her in the dark, as she, followed by the cubs, made straight for us, now and then making a rush at the dogs, and striking out at them with her paws. We dropped on our knees and fired at the mother. Peder's gun, as usual, would not go off, and Mogstad's also missed fire twice; but just as Sverdrup and I fired, his gun also went off. The first volley practically settled the bear, so that she could not, in any case, get away. One of the cubs was killed outright by a bullet, and the other was set upon by the dogs, which, having thrown it down on its back, were biting and tearing at it. Some of the others wanted to try on the same game with the old bear when they noticed she was disabled, but she raised herself on her legs, and struck out viciously with her paws. Peder was going to settle her for good, and fired, but the gun missed fire again. "You give her a shot, mine won't fire!" he cried, and one of us sent a bullet through her head. The dogs were tearing away so madly at one of the cubs that Mogstad had the greatest difficulty in sending a bullet into it, after which they tore and pulled away furiously at the carcases, "Ulinka" and "Suggen" being the worst. All this passed in less than no time; twelve shots were fired in all, and in a very few minutes the three bears lay there dead. At this moment Nansen arrived upon the scene. He had seen us in the distance, and could not make out at what we were driving, as we lay there firing in all directions. The bears' flesh was a welcome addition to our larder, as it was a long time since we had tasted any fresh meat. On our return on board all the guns were cleaned of the vaseline, so that there should be no missing fire again when we had bears about. Peder had gone about with his gun in this state on long excursions with the dogs, thinking that as long as he had a gun he was safe and all right. If he had met a beast like the one which " struck him in his side," I fancy he would have been badly handicapped.

We now had magnificent displays of the Northern Lights every evening. They flashed in all the colours of the rainbow, and, notwithstanding the bright moonlight, the aurora was exceedingly brilliant. With an incredible speed it travelled silently across half the vault of the heavens in incessantly changing flames, bands, streamers, spirals, and arches. It seemed as if we had passed north of the belt of the Northern Lights, as there was less of the aurora in the northern sky. Blessing decided to take the observations of the Northern Lights in the daytime, while at night the watch on duty had to make notes and sketches of the aurora in a journal.

On November 17th we had again a south-westerly wind, 5-6 metres in the second. The temperature was − 20° We were now mostly engaged in mending our clothes in our leisure moments. Old trousers and woollen shirts were cut up and made into swathing-bands for the feet, or used for mending socks. We had all become accomplished clothes-patchers. The work was not exactly what you may call superfine, but it was strong and durable, and that is the main thing.

One of the puppies of the last litter had a nasty accident to-day; it was caught by, and carried round with, the axle of the windmill, till Bentsen, who was on deck, stopped the mill and released the unfortunate creature. It was completely dazed, but it soon got better, after having been taken down into the saloon, which was like a new world to it. It was somewhat stiff in the limbs, but not injured in any way, which is a wonder after such an experience. The dog is alive to this day, and its name is "Axel."

It was on November 19th that Nansen asked me if I was willing to go with him on an expedition to the North Pole. He explained his plan to me in the presence of Sverdrup. His idea was to leave the ship at the end of February or in the beginning of March next. We were to take all the twenty-eight dogs with us —four sledges, with seven dogs to each. The course would be direct north to the Pole; thence, under favourable circumstances, to Spitzbergen, or, if unfavourable, to Franz Josef Land. According to his calculation we should be at Cape Fligely [1] ($82° 5'$ north latitude) in the beginning of June—that is, if progress could be made at the rate of eight miles a day on an average, when there still would be left provisions for eighteen days, after all the dogs, with the exception of five, had been killed in order to feed the others. We should only take provisions for the dogs for fifty days. Two kayaks, to carry one man each, would be used. From Franz Josef

[1] The most northerly point of the group of islands known as Franz Josef Land.

Land we should make for Spitzbergen or Novaya Zemlya, in the hope of falling in with the whalers. As soon as we reached the coast of one of these islands we should have to depend upon hunting for our subsistence. This is, in rough outline, the plan which Nansen explained to me most carefully in the course of nearly three hours.

A FROZEN SEA.

He laid stress upon the dangerous nature of this expedition. We should both be running the same risk; if we were attacked by scurvy, we should be hopelessly lost. He had decided upon asking me, he said, because he thought I was specially fit for such an expedition, but he begged me to consider my answer well.

As of late I had been thinking a good deal about such a journey, especially after my conversations with Sverdrup, I had been imagining to myself that I was likely to be asked to take part in the expedition, particularly as this also seemed to be the general opinion among my comrades on board. I was, therefore, able to answer that I did not require any time for consideration, as I had already been thinking it over, and that I was willing to go with Nansen. I looked upon it, of course, as a distinction that the choice had fallen upon me.

I made up my mind that I would, at any rate, do my best to obtain a successful result; and I thought that if we failed, it would be no disgrace to die in such an attempt.

# CHAPTER XIII

*Nansen's Lecture—Fitting out the Sledge Expedition—Christmas and New Year Once More—Our Worst Pressures*

ON the evening of November 20th, when we were north of the eighty-second degree, Nansen called us all together in the saloon, where he had hung up a polar map, for the purpose of giving a lecture. He began with the origin and theory of the expedition, and dwelt upon the knowledge possessed of the conditions of the ice in the Polar Sea, and upon the discoveries we had made with regard to ice drift. In all probability the *Fram* would be able to keep to the route originally laid down, perhaps a little more to the south. But it had always been the object of mankind to get as far north as possible, even to reach the Pole; and the question now was whether we ought not to make an attempt in that direction. There would scarcely be such a good opportunity for some time to come as we should have in the coming spring, when a sledge expedition for the Pole would have a starting-point much further to the north than that from which any former expedition had set forth.

He had decided that two men should set out on such an expedition—himself and I. He then recounted his plan and calculations regarding the expedition. It was possible, of course, that something might happen to the *Fram* during her drift. The ice pressure might become too severe, she might be forced on to the land, or she might be burnt, which would be the worst of all. He then went on to explain that it would be quite possible for the crew to save themselves and reach land, for there was little or no chance of the *Fram* drifting so far to the north as to render any difficulty in getting to land. Next summer the *Fram* would most probably lie in open waters. The lecture was most interesting, and all of us listened intently to it.

A busy time now began on board the *Fram* in fitting out the sledge expedition. No little work was put into its equipment; it had cost our chief a good deal of brain-work to think out all its details. There are numerous things required for such an expedition; nothing must be forgotten. A Russian expedition to Novaya Zemlya, for instance, could not attain anything because snow-spectacles were forgotten. Success depends upon getting everything as serviceable and as light as possible. The question of weight is especially an important one; three or four pounds saved in packing means provisions for a couple of days more.

My duties as assistant in taking the meteorological observations on board now ceased, and Nordahl assisted Scott-Hansen instead. Nansen finished a one-man kayak, and Mogstad began to make another. These are necessary craft on such an expedition, in order to get across lanes and open water which we were likely to meet with near land, whether it might be Franz Josef Land or Spitzbergen. The frame of the kayak is made of bamboo cane, and is afterwards covered with sail-cloth. Nansen and I were busy making these coverings. The kayaks are broader, but not so long as those of the Eskimos, in order that they should be more durable and easier to manœuvre on the sledges while going across the ice. In the middle of the upper covering of the kayak there is a hole encircled by a wooden ring, over which we could turn down the lower part of our kayak fur coats. After having pulled the hood tightly round our faces, and tied the sleeves round our wrists, we could sit perfectly dry in the kayak, no matter how much the sea might wash over us. In order to get easily at the provisions and other things stowed away in the kayak, we put trap-doors fore and aft in the deck.

Scott-Hansen and I each wore two watches, and compared them daily with the large chronometers, in order to check their rate exactly, so that we might take the two best watches with us on our expedition. Sverdrup made our two sleeping-bags of the skin of reindeer calves, in order to make them as light as possible. Juell was our saddler. He measured the dogs, and made new, strong harness of canvas for them. For those which were the worst at biting the harness in pieces, he put wire inside the canvas, upon which they had an opportunity of trying their teeth. Mogstad was very handy at almost everything, and he also made the sledges which we took with us.

The sledge expedition was now, of course, the topic of the day. We had discussions for and against it—about the condition of the ice, about open water, the endurance of the dogs, the provisions, the cold, etc., etc. All of us, of course, wished it every success and good fortune. We were going to take letters with us to their dear ones at home. The post we should thus carry would be rather a unique one. The letters, as a matter of course, were not heavy ones. The writers, in fact, had to count their words and keep down their number.

The days passed rapidly. We were about to enter upon our second Arctic night, which would bring with it the same cheerless darkness that we experienced last winter. I did not feel the cold so much this year as last, nor did my companions. As a contrast to this,

I may mention that the members of the Tegethoff Expedition found that they stood the cold best the first year.

The dogs kept up their "howling-concerts," just as they did last year during the time they were tied up on deck. Those of us who had our berths on the port side were next-door to the kennels, and were furious over these concerts, as we could not get any sleep during the night. Those on the starboard side could scarcely hear them.

Our cooking arrangements for the coming expedition were of the greatest importance, and we carried on experiments in cooking in the tent, erected close to the ship. The tent we were going to use was of silk, and of the same size as a military tent for four men. It was made in one piece, and had a small opening in one of the corners for a door. We fixed it up with a ski-staff, and used plugs for the straps.

Sverdrup had been suffering from a stomach catarrh, which he contracted by carelessly exposing himself to the cold. He was obliged to diet himself, and had not been at all well for a week. During a part of the time he had taken no food, and had no sleep. But he recovered from his illness.

Nansen and I went out on a ski-tour in the moonlight to try how the wolfskin clothes suited us. The ground was in a bad state except on the new ice in the lanes. The temperature stood at $-43°$. We both perspired freely, and agreed that the wolfskin clothes were too warm to wear when out on ski in this temperature. It was, of course, some time since we had any exercise, as, during the dark period, there was no opportunity of taking much of it.

During December we had a good deal of south-easterly wind, and on the 13th we were able to hold a festival in honour of the *Fram*, as being the ship which had travelled farthest north of all, the observations showing that we were in 82° 30′ north latitude.

From this time all of us followed the observations with the greatest attention. As soon as Scott-Hansen had got hold of the stars, he had always to determine our position. It was especially after south-easterly winds that we were intent about the result of his calculations, and many a wager was lost in betting upon how far we had gone.

In the hole in the ice, where we took samples of the water and the temperature of the sea, we also had hanging on a long line a bag net made of thin silk for catching small animals, and according to the direction taken by this line, we could guess the drift. If it showed to the south, we knew that the ice was drifting to the north. Peder was even able to say almost to a minute how much we had drifted, according to the more or less slanting position of the line. Never were we in better spirits than when the line "lay dry" under the ice in a southerly direction, and when the windmill was going round with reefed sails before a regular "south-easter." We then knew that we were making headway to the north and getting nearer to the open water on the other side of the Pole, and we two who were soon to start were glad, because it made the way to the Pole shorter for us.

From time to time we tried the dogs with fully laden sledges, using different teams, bad and good together. The trials went off satisfactorily. On even ice they went splendidly; when hindrances came in the way they pulled up. There was a great deal of fighting going on between the dogs. "Baby" and "Pan" fastened their teeth into each other as soon as they got a chance, and we had the greatest difficulty in separating them.

Scott-Hansen was now carrying on his magnetic observations in the snow-hut which he and I had built. He said he was exceedingly comfortable in there; it was nice and warm, the temperature being only 6° to 8° below zero, and the interior was brightly illuminated by a petroleum lamp under the clean, white vaulted roof. There stood Scott-Hansen, half a day at a time, "scratching at the pin" and gazing at the movements of the magnetic needle. The self-same individual possessed remarkable patience and perseverance, and his good humour never flagged.

Johansen. Scott-Hansen.

RACING TO THE SHIP ON THE WAY BACK FROM A SLEDGE DRIVE.

On Christmas Eve the wind was blowing hard from the south-east, and the barometer fell right down to 726·65 mm. While the storm raged over our heads across the ice-fields in the dark Arctic night, a feeling of real comfort and security came over one at the thought of being so well housed as we were on board the *Fram*. Christmas Eve came upon us like any other day, lying here as we did far away from the noisy world and all the Christmas fun. It was a quiet Christmas which we thirteen celebrated. We had a kind of cleaning up of the saloon and the cabins. The weather being cloudy and overcast both night and day, we could not take any observations. In the meantime, however, we could safely say that we were a good way north of the eighty-third degree. Perhaps it was as a sort of Christmas present that we had the satisfaction of reaching 83° 24′ north latitude, the most northerly point of the world that any human being had ever reached.

Nansen and Blessing were up in the work-room the whole of the day, busy with some mysterious brew. When the bottles came upon the table in the evening it turned out to be nothing less than champagne—" polar champagne 83°"—undoubtedly the most unique in the world. It was made from spirits of wine, cloudberry jam, water and baking-powder, and there was as much as two half-bottles for each of us.

It seemed, however, as if the true festive spirit was wanting, for this Christmas was not a very lively one. We spoke little, and there often occurred pauses in our conversation, which plainly showed that our thoughts were far away.

And there was nothing wonderful in that. There was nothing strange that we thirteen, on an eve like this, should let our thoughts dwell where we ourselves should like to be. No, no one can find fault with us for being so quiet on board, although we were so comfortably off. In regard to food we were perhaps better off than a good many this Christmas Eve; we were well and warmly housed there in the ice-desert, but we were prisoners. We lay, far away from the world, fast in a frozen sea, where all life was extinct, and in the exploration of which so many lives had been sacrificed. With such surroundings one might well, after a long absence from home, think of those left behind.

This Christmas Day we were also treated to " polar curaçoa," which was really good, and in the evening we danced to Mogstad's fiddle. We read the same Christmas numbers, and looked at the same illustrated books as we had brought out from the library the last Christmas.

The ice began cracking on Christmas Eve not far from the thermometer house, and we had to set to work and save the instruments. The crack occurred in the ice on the old channel, which had now been frozen for nearly six months.

The day after, or "Second Christmas Day," as it is called in Norway, was Juell's birthday. Blessing had two bottles of brandy left, and treated us to a genuine glass of toddy.

"Halma" was our favourite game during Christmas. Amundsen, as usual, supplied us with music, and there was one old-fashioned, monotonous valse which had such a special attraction for him that he went on playing it until we had to relieve him and turn the handle for him.

The dogs on the ice outside, surrounded by the continual darkness, did not come in for any of the Christmas cheer, although they, too, had their mission up there, and perhaps not the least important. We felt that the taking of the lives of these animals, after they would have done their best to help us on towards our goal, would be the most painful task on our forthcoming expedition.

Next day we took soundings with a line 1,700 fathoms long, without reaching the bottom. In the afternoon the *Fram* received a very violent shock, which reminded us that the ice was in motion. The following day the pressure was again violent and continuous in the lane ahead of us, and the *Fram* shook herself several times in her firm bed. A large upheaval of ice-floes took place not far from the bow.

We closed the Old Year by welcoming the New, with a hope that it might bring good luck with it! Light it would bring with it we knew in any case. But we wondered whether it would shed more light upon these unknown parts of the globe. We were now in 83° 20·7′ north latitude, and 105° 2′ east longitude. The temperature was −42°.

In the evening we sat round a bowl of "polar toddy" waiting for the New Year. Nansen spoke about the Old Year, which had passed by more rapidly than he and we others had expected; and that, he believed, was due to the good relations existing between us. There had been frictions now and then,—each of us had had his own dark hours,—but that was unavoidable; there had, at any rate, been a good understanding between us. As the clock struck twelve we drank to each other in Lysholm's Aquavitæ, to which Blessing treated us. Sverdrup then took his glass and, in his quiet manner, wished the whole expedition every success in the New Year, and success especially as far as the sledge expedition was concerned. Nansen spoke to those who were to remain behind on board the *Fram*. There was, he said, an Irish saying something to this effect—"Be happy; and if you can't be happy, take it easy; and if you can't be easy, be as easy as you can." He would ask those who were to remain behind to take this to heart. If they would act according to the old saying, the New Year would, no doubt, pass quickly for them also, and that would probably be their last year in the ice.

We kept up the New Year far into the morning, till we became sleepy, and then went to our bunks, ready to get up as soon as our turn came for the watch.

Our cabins had in course of time received the following names: Sverdrup's was called "Old Age Retreat"; Blessing's, "Relief"; Jacobsen's, Bentsen's, Mogstad's, Nordahl's, and Hendriksen's cabin on the port side, "Eternal Rest"; and Amundsen's, Juell's, Petterson's

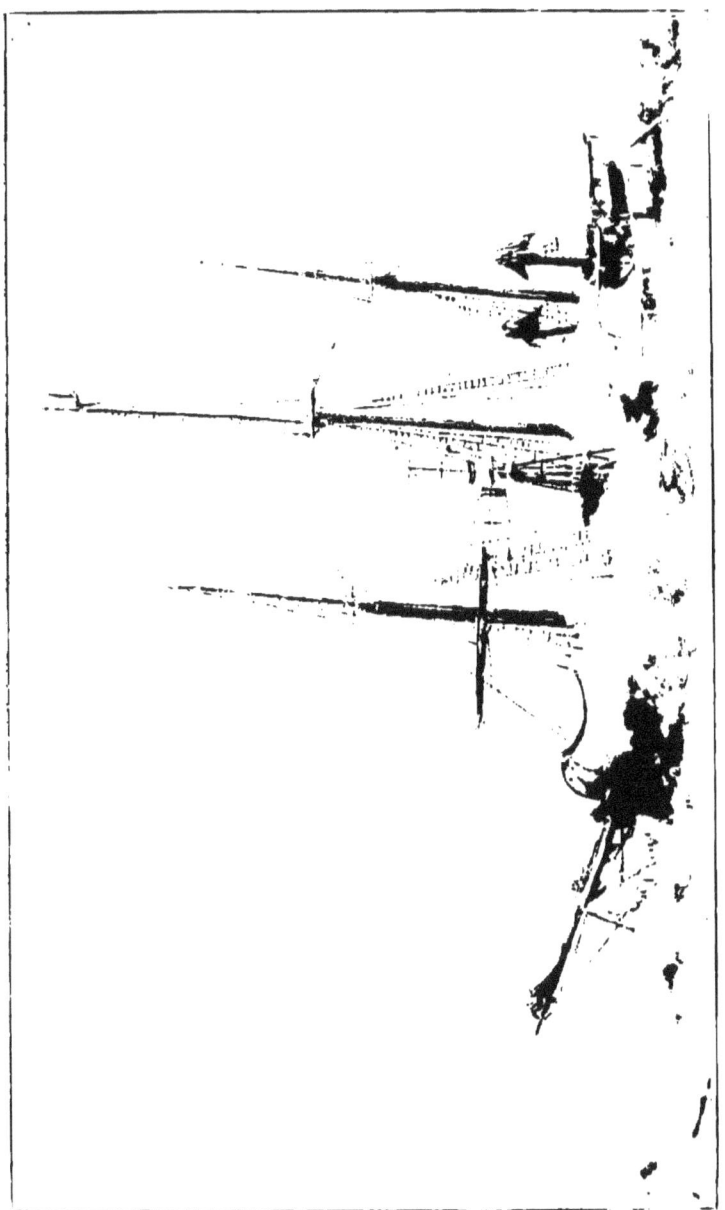

MOONLIGHT EFFECT OF THE GREAT ICE-PRESSURE, NEW YEAR'S DAY, 1895.

and mine on the starboard side, "The Mysterious Room." Hansen's cabin was called "Hôtel Garni," and Nansen's, "Phœnix." //

On January 2nd, 1895, nearly all hands had begun their letters for home. The thing was to get as much as possible into a minimum of space. Fine pens and thin, strong paper were therefore in great demand; all were practising a fine, microscopical hand. Scott-Hansen's letter was a masterpiece in this respect. The writing was so small that it could only be read with a magnifying glass. The ice had again been in motion of late, and on New Year's night the ship received a severe shock; we had not had such a violent one since the last winter.

Though on the following night everything was quiet, early on the morning of Thursday, January 3rd, at half-past four, the pressure began again and continued till about nine o'clock. On the port side the ice packed and pressed closer and closer upon the ship, which from time to time trembled from the pressure which transferred itself to the ice under the ship. Scott-Hansen and I took a walk round about it to have a look at the havoc. There was a high ridge on the port side, with a fissure on the side near to the ship, about eighteen paces distant from it.

On the other side of the ridge behind the tent and the observation hut was a lane, extending in an oblique direction towards the stern of the ship. In two places the ice in the lane was unbroken, and they bore the pressure of the floe against the vessel. The pressure had been going on from time to time in the forenoon and the ice cracked in several places over in the neighbourhood of the new lane. After dinner came a fresh pressure. The ridges on the port side came tumbling down, reaching up to the big fissure near the ship. The Samoyede sledge with the sounding appa-

K

ratus and another loaded sledge, which were on the ice, had to be placed in safety.

While we were at supper we felt another shock. We found that our floe had cracked again in several places, both amidships and in front of the bow. This solid floe, of which we were so proud and on which we felt so safe, was thus breaking up into pieces and being pressed together. We had got everything in readiness in case we should have to leave the *Fram* suddenly. The sledges were placed ready on deck, provisions were brought up and put in a safe place, the cases containing dog-biscuits were out on the ice, and the kayaks were made clear. As yet the main body of our floe—the thickest part of it, in which the *Fram* lay embedded—had not been attacked. We all agreed that, to move these great masses of ice in the way which we were now witnessing, terrific forces must be at work.

"It represents millions of horse-power," said Amundsen, and had not the *Fram* been so built that she was lifted up so as to let the pressure under her bottom go on as much as it liked, she would not have been able to withstand the enormous squeezing. But the vessel was so constructed that she could withstand any pressure whatever, and she could hardly have got into a more dangerous position than that in which she was on this occasion, when she lay as if in a vice, resisting the pressure from the pack-ice as it advanced against her side.

We were sitting in the saloon, playing "Halma," in the evening, when another terrible pressure began, and Peder came rushing in, crying out that the dogs were drowning. All hands ran on deck, but Peder had already managed to open the doors for the terrified creatures, which were whining and howling in their kennels, where the water was steadily rising.

We next set to work transferring the provisions on to the ice close to the big hummock, about 200 yards off. Three sledges were in constant use. With these we kept trudging backwards and forwards in the darkness. We then fetched provisions for men and dogs from the main and the fore-hold: pemmican, bread, chocolate, and different kinds of meat. The dogs ran about in a state of expectation and terror, looking in vain for their old abode. It was some time before they at last went to rest in various places on the ice under some protecting ice-crag.

Clothing had been served out to us all, and separate bags prepared for each man, so that we should only have to throw the marked bags on to the ice, in case we were surprised by any severe ice-pressure.

On Friday night the watch was placed, as usual, at eleven o'clock. The ice was uneasy, and was packing hard on the port side. The part between the ship and the lane was exposed to a severe pressure, and masses of snow fell in here and there over the ship. New fissures were being formed crossways in the ice, the edges of which were being doubled upwards by the continuous pressure of the ice.

I was on watch from one till two, and during this time the same incessant pressure continued. Sometimes it roared and moaned in loud and exceedingly deep tones, like a thing of life. In the dark night it made one's flesh creep. It lasted the whole night, until five o'clock in the morning, when all hands were called. The pack-ice was by this time close upon us, and had crept up almost to the gangway. We had then to transport the remaining boxes of provisions to our depôt by the big hummock, and we had the same trudging backwards and forwards with the sledges in the dark as that of a day or two before.

We had a regular rummaging in the hold to find

the boxes containing provisions, and we were hard at work until dinner-time getting them on deck. Cartridges were taken from our stores, ten being apportioned to each of us to carry in his bag, and a box containing shot and ball cartridges was sent over to the depôt. At night we had supper later than usual on Saturdays. We hoped we should be able to get some good rest for the night, but it was to be otherwise. About eight o'clock the pressure began again, and this time with a vengeance. The mass of ice on the port side came rushing in over the awning on the fore-deck and piled itself up aft on the deck to a level with the bridge. It was now high time to save ourselves, as Nansen called out, "All hands on deck." He had hurried on deck and set loose the dogs, which the awning had protected from the masses of ice that had fallen upon it, and it was really a wonder that the awning withstood the strain.

I was in the galley at the time, waiting my turn for a wash after Sverdrup had done, and had just managed to dip my hands into the water. I was barefooted, and only lightly dressed. It was not at all pleasant to sit there dressing while one after the other of my comrades vanished on deck, and the pressure went on with deafening noise, the *Fram* groaning in every timber. I did not get on deck till nearly all was over and the others came down again to fetch up their bags, clothes, and sleeping-bags. Everything was in readiness, but at the last moment we found that there were still a good many things which we ought to take with us. Fortunately, the temperature was only about 8° below zero.

If the *Fram* were to be lost, we were so far in safety on the ice, with provisions for a year, clothes, sleeping-bags, tents, sails, sledges, and dogs; but we should, of course, be in the midst of the polar ice, about a thousand miles away from the nearest known land. We did not feel despondent, but we thought ourselves remarkably lucky when the pressure suddenly stopped. It seemed as if it had spent its fury, and was satisfied now that it had driven us out upon the ice. We found afterwards that the *Fram* had been lifted up about a foot and shifted somewhat backwards, also righting herself a little towards the port side. She was now listing over $6\frac{1}{2}°$; on Friday night, January 4th, it was $7°$.

When everything had been placed in safety, we returned to the ship and assembled in Sverdrup's cabin for a small merry party. Sverdrup treated us to gingerbread from his store of accumulated winnings, and we drank to each other in malt extract, hoping that this would not be the last time we should drink a glass together on board the *Fram*.

It was decided that we should remain on board for the night. The watch was taken in turn, while we settled down in the empty bunks, ready to jump out at a moment's warning. Soon after the pressure began the door on the port side had been shut up, as it was dangerous to pass the ice on that side. On account of the present state of things we slept even less than the night before. We dozed for a while, then went on watch, and then back to doze again. But, during the night, and up to Sunday dinner-time, when I was sitting making these notes on a piece of paper, as our journals were now over at the depôt, the ice was at rest.

# CHAPTER XIV

*Beating the World's Record—The Depôt on the Big Hummock—The Second Arctic Night—More about the Equipment of the Sledge Expedition*

ON Sunday afternoon, January 6th, 1895, all hands were hard at work clearing the ice away from the side of the ship. It was not such an easy job as we imagined, for a mass of ice and snow slush had forced its way in and filled the deck between the windmill and the half-deck.

The same day we beat the world's record. The observations showed that we were in 83° 34·2′ north latitude, and 102° 2′ east longitude. The occasion was duly celebrated in the evening, but we were all tired and sleepy. We drank "polar toddy," ate cakes and fruit, and went to bed in the empty bunks with our clothes on. There had been some pressure going on in the course of the day, but the *Fram* did not suffer from it in any way. During January and February we were busy digging and carting away the ice. I believe the crew kept at this after Nansen and I left the ship in March.

From time to time Petterson prophesied that we should have fair winds. If his prophecy did not come true, which happened now and then, he did not get off without a good deal of chaffing. Once he expressed himself something like this: "I am not a sailor, but I feel sure that, very shortly, we shall get a devil of a hiding from the south." As the "devil of a hiding" did not come, Petterson was asked for it at every meal-time. When a south-westerly wind sprang up a long time afterwards, blowing at the rate of ten metres to the second, and accompanied by snow, Petterson was again in his glory.

On January 11th some of us went to the depôt and put our provisions, clothes, etc., over there in order. Boxes of bread, dog-biscuits, ammunition, guns, flour, barley, chocolate, ski, sledges, kayaks, sails, tents, and implements of various kinds were lying topsy-turvy all over the ice, but now they were arranged in various heaps, with an assortment in each, so that we should not lose all we had of one kind in case of an accident to the floe in any place.

The next day, January 12th, we found that we had not altogether escaped the influence of the polar night upon us. Our tempers naturally were not always what they should be. Though one may be among the best and kindest of people, it really requires, under such circumstances as ours, a great deal of tact to keep on good terms with everybody. For we were always the same thirteen persons together, both night and day, under exactly the same conditions, and learned to know each other thoroughly, with all our various little weaknesses and tender points. One's spirits were apt to become depressed now and then, and one easily became cantankerous and irritable, taking offence at utterances of the most trivial description. It was a capital thing, however, that we could have recourse to the library when we were out of sorts.

We had some difficulty with regard to the distribution of heat in the saloon, as the ship was lying over on the starboard side. The heat was greatest on this side of the saloon, but it happened that those of us who liked heat best had their berths on the port side, and these fellows kept up a big fire in order to get their side warm, while we on the starboard side found it so hot that we had to lie outside our sleeping-bags. Scott-Hansen often sat bared to the waist in his cabin when working out his observations.

When Nansen and I were gone, Sverdrup moved across to Nansen's cabin on the warm side, and Jacobsen removed from "Eternal Rest," where there were five men, to the "Old Age Retreat," and lived there by himself for the rest of the voyage.

"Pan" and "Baby" were still trying to put an end to one another. Bentsen and Nordahl were one day trying for a long time to separate them; the former had to give it up, however, as he was continually losing hold of his trousers, having taken off his belt in order to thrash the dogs.

On the 15th of January we were in 83° 27·3′ north latitude, and 103° 41′ east longitude. We had been drifting south again on account of the north-westerly wind.

One of the dangers of which we were most apprehensive on the sledge expedition was that of breaking a leg or an arm. In order that we might be prepared for any such accident, it was necessary that we should understand how to splint and bandage broken limbs. Blessing gave a lecture on the subject one evening, with practical demonstrations of the treatment to be used. Nansen sat on the top of the table in the saloon, representing a person with a broken leg. The rest of us stood round and watched the operations. When Nansen was ready I was placed under treatment, and was supposed to have a broken collar-bone. Blessing's instructions were clear and interesting, but we both hoped that the time might never come when we should require each other's aid.

Jacobsen, assisted by some of the others, built a fine smithy of ice-blocks over by the ridges on the port side. Fire was now constantly in the forge, and Petterson let his hammer dance merrily on the anvil, feeling not a little proud at being the world's most northerly smith, working away in a temperature of 40° below zero, in a smithy where he was quite safe from fire, and where he need not trouble about insurance.

He made an axe for the sledge expedition, the blade of which was no bigger than a matchbox. He could not understand what we wanted with anything so "devilish small." He also made a small bear-spear for Nansen. This was, however, never used upon any bear, but as a soldering-iron when we had to make our kayaks watertight in the seams with stearine. We made the spear hot by warming it over our train-oil lamps. We had a regular soldering-iron with us, which we also used for the same purpose.

But the smithy was also used for many other purposes. For instance, the many pairs of ski which we took with us had to be carefully impregnated with a mixture of tar, tallow, and stearine, so as to stand better the wear and tear over all kinds of ground. The runners for the sledges were steamed over a cauldron on the forge in order that they might be more easily bent. Afterwards they were impregnated with the same composition as that applied to the ski before the German-silver plates were fixed under the runners. Mogstad had prepared thin guard-runners of maple to be fixed outside the German-silver plates.

We found it was far easier to draw sledges with wooden runners impregnated with the above composition of tar, etc., than with metal plates under the runners; and besides, these double runners strengthened the sledges considerably. Petterson also manufactured small nails in his smithy. Mogstad used silver for soldering the German-silver plates. This was the only occasion upon which the question of money was raised on board the ship. Scott-Hansen had a five-kroner note, but that was of no use. It was real silver that was wanted, and Mogstad managed finally to raise some half-kroners, which he used for solder. We had a miniature fire on one of these occasions; the lamp exploded, and our table bore the marks of this conflagration.

Amundsen had a difficult job repairing the windmill; it was getting old and the pinions were much worn. It was not pleasant work to lie boring holes in the hard iron in the severe cold up there on top of "Franz Josef," as Amundsen called the mill. He wanted, however, to try to get it into working order, and to get the electric batteries thawed up, so that we might all be photographed by electric light in the saloon before Nansen and I left the ship.

Our departure, for the present, had been fixed for the 20th of February—that is to say, if it should not be too dark at that time. Blessing, after having gone through his apprenticeship with Nansen, had taken over the photographic work, and he was now much patronised. I had been busy copying all our meteorological and deep-water observations on thin, strong paper with ink which will resist water. We had taken every precaution to preserve and bring these home safely. We again took deep-sea soundings, and all hands were thus fully occupied, so that all were contributing in some way or other towards the success of the expedition.

On a sledge expedition such as ours it was, of course, of the greatest importance that the provisions should be chosen with the greatest care; above all, they must be wholesome and nutritious, so as to avoid scurvy, and they must be prepared and preserved in a light and concentrated form.

It was also important that they should be so prepared that they could be eaten without any cooking or preparation. The principal food on sledge expeditions is generally pemmican, which experience has proved to be the best. Pemmican is, as every one knows, fresh meat dried in the wind. On Nansen's expedition across Greenland the explorers suffered from want of fat, the pemmican being too dry. Nansen had taken precautions that this should not happen again. Our pemmican was made from the very best kind of beef cut from the solid, fleshy parts, dried quickly, and pulverised, to which the same quantity of fine beef suet was afterwards added. It was almost entirely free from water. We had also some liver *pâté* prepared in the same way. Then we had some pemmican which had been prepared with vegetable oil instead of suet, but this was not a success. We took a good supply of this staple food, as the dogs had also to be fed upon it. The pemmican came from the makers in the form of small cheeses in tins, but as we did not care for loading ourselves unnecessarily with any heavy packing, we took the contents out of the tins and made boat-grips of them in the following manner. It was necessary to use grips under the kayaks, so that they could rest safely and steadily when passing over the uneven ice. Instead of making these grips of wood, Sverdrup sewed some canvas-bags of a shape to fit the bottom of the kayaks, and after having warmed the pemmican, we filled these bags with it, just as one does a mattress. As soon as they came into the open air they became hard and solid.

Professor Waage's fish-meal proved to be an excellent food during the sledge expedition. Mixed and boiled with flour and butter it made a splendid dish; one actually became warm all over the body after a meal of it. We took also some dried potatoes with us; mixed with pemmican it was the most delicious lobscouse in the world. Nansen preferred the "fish-gratin," as we called it, while I fancied the lobscouse—at any rate, at first.

When Nansen and his companions crossed Greenland they were always feeling hungry. In order that we should feel properly satisfied and comfortable now and then, we took some steamed oaten groats and maize with us for making porridge. We had also some "vril-food," a kind of sweet meal, which we soon learnt to appreciate; in fact, sugar and flour were most highly prized. And we did not forget chocolate, of which we had both the ordinary kind and another sort made with powdered meat, the latter being hardly distinguishable in taste from the former.

Of "serin," or whey powder, we had a good supply with us. This is really nothing else than pulverised whey, which we mixed with boiling water. We used to drink it at night, before we put our frozen bodies to rest in the sleeping-bag. It did us a wonderful amount of good, and we often longed for this drink on our laborious journeys in the cold.

The bread we took, of course, contained as little moisture as possible; we had two kinds—wheaten bread and aleuronate bread.[1] Peder saw to the butter, and kneaded all the water out of it, but it became very hard for all that—in fact, so hard that

---

[1] Bread made of wheaten flour mixed with aleuronate (vegetable albumen).

on one occasion on our journey I broke a knife in trying to cut off a piece.

Sverdrup made three small sails for the sledges, as we should have to make as much use as possible of the wind, both on the ice and on the water. He also made some special oar-blades to be fixed on to our ski-staffs and to be used as oars. The blades consisted of frames made of cane covered with canvas. A small sledge with a white shooting-sail, such as is used by the Eskimos when they hunt the seal, was also made ready for us.

Guns and ammunition were, of course, matters of paramount importance. After much deliberation and many trials, we decided to use the same guns which Nansen had with him on his Greenland expedition. These were two double-barrelled guns, each having a barrel for ball of 360 calibre, and one for shot of 20 bore. Our ammunition consisted of 180 rifle-cartridges and 150 shot-cartridges.

We took several knives with us. Nansen had a large, fine, Lapp knife, of the same kind as the Lapps use in the summer, with a large, flat, broad blade of iron and steel. This knife could also be used as a hatchet. One of the excellent "tolle-knives," from Toten, with handle covered with birch-bark, turned out a most useful implement. We also had several small knives. Sverdrup made me a present of one combining gimlet, saw, file, screw-driver, etc. This was in such request that when we returned there was only one blade left in it.

Of foot-gear we had each two pairs of Lapp shoes and one pair of "komager." The former are made of the skin of the hind legs of reindeer oxen, not of the skin of the head, which, although it may be warm, is not so durable. The "komager" are made of tanned sealskin, well impregnated with tar and train oil.

We used "senne" grass (*carex œsicaria*) inside the shoes and socks of wolfskin and hair, and foot-bandages of thick "vadmel" (Norwegian homespun tweed). Stockings we did not use. We took a pair each with us, however, but these we cut in two so that we could use the legs and the feet separately.

Our cooking apparatus was so arranged that we could cook our food and melt as much ice as possible for drinking purposes, with the least possible expenditure of fuel. It consisted of several vessels, the innermost being the cooking vessel proper, made of German silver. This was inside a ring-shaped vessel, which was filled with ice. Above the two a flat vessel was placed, also for melting ice. The whole was surrounded by a thin, light mantle or cap of aluminium, and outside this we again placed a hood of wolfskin, so that none of the heat should be lost. For heating, we used petroleum in the "Primus" lamp; this apparatus proving itself the most economical of all in regard to fuel.

We had been living high of late on the flesh of the last three bears we shot. Juell had a masterly way of cooking excellent beefsteaks with parsley-butter from bear's meat. We all agreed that we lived like fighting-cocks, especially when we remembered how other expeditions had fared.

On the 23rd of January we took two soundings, and reached the bottom at a depth of 1,800 and 1,850 fathoms respectively.

On January 25th I was in the hold with Nansen, getting our ski ready. The weather was clear; the streak of light on the horizon in the south at noon, which heralds the approach of day, was gradually growing bigger. We had now fought through the worst part of the Arctic night. The temperature was down to 58° below zero. We had hardly any wind, but Petterson was prophesying again. Our carpenter's shop was in the hold; it was, no doubt, the coldest in the world, the temperature there being 36° of frost.

On February 1st Sverdrup and I were busy bending laths of ash by steam for the sledges. When we

DR. NANSEN AND JOHANSEN LEAVING THE *FRAM* ON THEIR SLEDGE EXPEDITION ACROSS THE POLAR ICE.

were over in the smithy on the ice it did not often strike us that the sea-bottom was only 1,800 fathoms below. It was not at all warm inside the smithy as a rule, but then we were getting used to the cold. The saloon, our only warm room, was now in the greatest confusion. It was an improvised workshop for fitting, soldering, lashing, and all kinds of work which we could not do in the cold.

On the walls and under the roofs were hanging wooden materials, ski, sledge-runners, plates of German silver, and ash laths, together with pictures, a barometer, a barograph, watches, clothes, fur coats, guns, and provision bags. There was hardly room to move about.

Nansen announced that the letters we were going to take with us from our comrades on board ought not to be heavier than an ordinary letter ($\frac{1}{2}$-oz.). It might happen, he said, that we should have to throw away everything in order to save ourselves. The letters we would, of course, stick to as long as possible, and they ought therefore to be light. Our comrades, however, had not reckoned upon being allowed to send even as much as that, but as they all were writing in a small hand, they got a lot into $\frac{1}{2}$-oz. of thin paper.

Nansen and I tried the two sleeping-bags which Sverdrup made for us, to ascertain if they were warm enough. They only weighed $6\frac{1}{2}$ and $4\frac{1}{2}$ lbs. respectively. We lay out on the ice for a couple of nights, but we felt rather cold; the bags were evidently too thin. Sverdrup had then to set to work to make a double bag from the thick skins of grown-up reindeer, so we did not save anything in weight here.

Out of an anemometer, which had been standing on a hummock going round day and night, and which we were continually repairing, Mogstad made an odometer, which was affixed to the hindmost of the sledges.

By the 10th of February it had become so light in the middle of the day that we were able to read. The dogs were having a fine time just now. All over the ice, near the ship, biscuits were lying about, but they did not seem to care much for them. They got as much food as they wanted, in order to get them into good condition for the hard work on our expedition. The carcases of the four dogs, which had been hanging all the winter under the jib-boom, and on which they had their eyes, were devoured in a jiffy. They also got pemmican and blubber. With the exception of "Livjægeren" they were all in good condition. Times had changed since the days when our late friend, "Cannibal," lay on the top of the biscuit bag, guarding it against the others.

On February 21st we were in 81° 40′ north latitude. We had another weather prophet on board besides Petterson, namely Peder. He only prophesied when we were going to have northerly winds, and used the nautical almanack to assist him. It was, he said, when Jupiter was in a certain position that we might expect these winds. As Peder had once or twice been successful in his prophecies he soon found a great believer in Amundsen. When occasionally the north wind failed to put in an appearance, and we found ourselves drifting in the very opposite direction to that in which we should have been according to his prediction, he did not look upon himself as beaten, but maintained that the north wind was sure to be blowing some little distance out on the ice, say about a couple of miles or so from the ship.

We got over the worst by February 22nd. The ski were now all ready, with fastenings and a double layer of birch bark; the provisions were carefully stowed away on the sledges, all four of which were now at last standing ready packed by the ship's side. We made a list of the provisions, and found that there was about 200 lbs. of overweight when the instruments and ammunition were included. Our equipment had to be gone through again and rearranged. As the time drew near for our departure, a number of small things were added which had not been thought of before, such as small harpoons for fixing on our ski-staffs, pumps for the kayaks, dogs' shoes of sealskin, and two wire ropes, provided with short, double leashes for stretching between the sledges and fastening the dogs to when we encamped for the first few nights. We imagined that they would prefer their old quarters to remaining with us on the ice, but with the aid of these leashes we had no need to be afraid of their getting back to the ship.

## CHAPTER XV

*The Departure—We Make Two Starts—I Act as Snow-plough—Sun Festival and Celebration on Passing the Eighty-fourth Degree*

FEBRUARY 23rd and 24th were to have been days of rest before our departure, but instead they turned out to be two of the busiest days we ever had. We were in a regular bustle, and everything was being hurried on before we could get ready to start. In spite of all the commotion, however, our comrades had found time, in the course of the night, to decorate the saloon with flags, and three new electric lamps, embellished with coloured paper, over the sofa.

The dinner on Sunday, February 24th, was a solemn affair. Scott-Hansen produced some claret, which he had been carefully keeping all the time. Blessing made a speech, in which he congratulated Nansen on the result the expedition had obtained up to the present time, and wished us both a successful journey, hoping we should find everything well at home.

Nansen, on behalf of us both, replied that we would be sure to think with pleasure of our life on board the *Fram*, and that as surely as we reached home safely we would remember our comrades in the ice. He hoped that no one on board would ever regret having joined the expedition, and asked us to drink to our next meeting—a happy meeting of all of us home in Norway. After dinner we had coffee with curaçoa and a short rest, and then we had to set to work again with sewing, loading cartridges, and packing away fishing tackle, sewing materials, and kayak pumps. Some of our clothing had also to be looked to, and bands and straps had to be sewn on our wind-clothes. There was something to do up to the last moment.

I sat up writing far away into the night. I had my letters for home to finish, and finally I was thinking of having a good wash. We all kept awake, and Bentsen was sitting in our cabin telling yarns. We had a festive gathering in the evening, with polar toddy, raisins, almonds, and other fruit. Captain Sverdrup spoke a few hearty words, wishing us all success on our journey. Afterwards Nansen went back to his work, which consisted of dictating to Blessing a lot of instructions relating to his observations of the small marine animals.

On Tuesday, the 26th of February, we were at last ready to say farewell. But the weather was anything but inviting for a start. The morning was grey; there was a slight snowfall, and the wind was east to south. The last good-bye was said to those who were to remain on board, while Sverdrup, Scott-Hansen, Blessing, Mogstad, and Hendriksen were to accompany us some distance on the way. They took a tent and the necessary equipment with them, in order to spend the night with us in our first encampment. Nansen glided off in front on his ski, leading the way, and next came the first sledge, with "Kvik" as the first dog in the team. But the journey did not last long. We had not proceeded very far from the ship, and the sound of the guns had only just died away, when one of the heavily-laden sledges broke down in being dragged across a ridge; a projecting piece of ice had smashed three of the cross-bars, and there we were left standing. There was nothing else to do but to return whence we came. We should not have believed that we should see each other again so soon; we had only just said good-bye.

It was fortunate, however, that we had not gone very far away with our things. It appeared that the sledges were not strong enough for the heavy load we had put upon them. We should have to strengthen them. Nansen decided that we should add two new sledges to the four we had, making in all six, and the load on each would thus be considerably less. The same activity began again on board; Sverdrup and I were once more in the smithy, busy tarring the two new sledges. All were now fitted with a long, broad board, which was lashed underneath the cross-bars with steel wire, so that any projecting pieces of ice should not again damage them. The sledges were once more overhauled. We had finished all the repairs and outfitting on Wednesday night, and the next day we were to start again.

We set out on the morning of Thursday, February 28th, with our six sledges, accompanied by Sverdrup, Blessing, Mogstad, Scott-Hansen, and Hendriksen, who had fitted out a sledge with a tent and other necessities for one or two days' journey. Our other comrades also accompanied us for some distance, Jacobsen and Bentsen being the last to leave us. Although we now had a man to each sledge to assist it over ridges and other obstacles, we travelled very slowly. It took us all our time to assist in pushing on, and helping the sledges over, when the dogs pulled up, and this not only when there were obstacles, but even when we were on flat ice. It was clear that the loads were too heavy, and after having journeyed some distance we pulled up and took off two boat-grips with pemmican, which lightened the sledges to some extent. At this point Bentsen and Jacobsen returned to the ship, the latter expressing his opinion that we were sure to have to come back to the *Fram* once more. The provisions we left behind were placed on a hummock, and a ski, which had been broken on the way, was set up as a mark, so that our comrades could find the place later on and bring the provisions back to the ship.

We then proceeded on our journey with the reduced loads, but we did not make much progress, and soon decided upon pitching our tents and encamping for the night. The dogs were fastened in couples, side by side, and fed. We thus obtained an idea of how long a time it would take us to encamp when we two were left to ourselves. We soon found that we must be prepared to take a considerable time, especially at the beginning. We spent a pleasant evening in the great tent which our comrades had brought with them. We felt quite warm and comfortable as we sat there in our wolfskin clothes. The five treated us to an excellent supper, consisting of chocolate, bread, butter, bacon, and cake, the latter bringing with it some of the smell of the kerosene oil on board the *Fram*. Afterwards our hosts brought out some pure spirits of wine and brewed toddy for us, which we drank out of our tin cups with great relish. Our pipes were soon alight, and speeches were made by Nansen and Blessing. After having had a pleasant time we went to rest in our sleeping-bags. But we did not get much sleep, owing to the dogs, which fought and howled during the whole night.

Next day the weather was dark, the wind east to south. After several hours of work, occupied in cooking and getting the sledges and dogs ready, we broke up, and the whole party set out again. In the afternoon came the hour for leave-taking. The weather was cold and depressing, and so were our spirits; the Arctic night had not yet come to an end. All were moved as we shook hands for the last time and sent greetings to all at home.

And then Nansen and I were left alone on the desert icefields with the dogs and sledges. We did not get very far during the rest of the day, as we found progress very difficult. Nansen was in front, leading the way. When the sledges came to a stop through some impediment or other—and we could hardly proceed many paces at a time without this happening—we had to get them started again. We were continually running backwards and forwards in order to be able to make any progress at all.

Next day things went on in much the same way. We soon discovered that the loads were yet too heavy, both for the dogs and ourselves, although they were becoming somewhat lighter the farther we proceeded northwards. The ice, moreover, was in a very rough condition and difficult to get over. We therefore made a halt, and Nansen declared that the loads would have to be still more reduced. "If the others had not gone back to the ship," he said, "the best thing would have been to return with them at once." He then went some distance to the north to reconnoitre, while I fed the dogs and got our encampment in order. When he came back we lighted our cooking apparatus, had our supper, and then crept into our sleeping-bag.

When the morning came, Nansen selected a strong team of dogs and set off on one of the sledges for the ship to get assistance in bringing back the sledges.

Thus I was left entirely alone in the solitude. This was on Sunday, the 3rd of March. The weather was fresh and cold, and I could hardly believe that it was really the sun I saw away on the horizon, but there could be no mistake. There it stood, fiery-red, on its first appearance, but no ray of heat reached us. To us it meant light, and light to us meant new life. Far away I saw the masts of the *Fram* through the clear air. I took her bearings in case this might be wanted.

Instead of lying inactive in the tent waiting for the others to return, I thought I would begin moving in the direction of the ship with the whole caravan. I began the return journey in the following manner. I started with three of the sledges, using all the dogs,

CROSSING A RIDGE.

and leaving the other two sledges behind. Then, when I had proceeded some distance on the way, I took the dogs from the sledges to go back and fetch the remaining two, and tied the traces round my waist. I tried first to stand on my ski and let the dogs drag me along; but I soon had to give this up, as the ice was rough and uneven, and the progress became too violent and jerky. The dogs set off at lightning speed as soon as they became aware of the lightened load, but the speed was too much for me. Down I went, sprawling in the snow, and the next moment I was being dragged along with the ski on my feet as if I were a snow-plough. This was the first and last occasion on which I acted in this capacity during the expedition. At last this undignified method of progress was stopped by a ridge, over which the dogs scrambled, while I was landed right up against it. The wild creatures tore themselves loose, dragging my knife-belt away with them on their mad career. I was afraid they had left me for good; but, strange to say, they pulled up as soon as they felt themselves free, and stood staring at me just as if they wanted to see how I was getting on.

I enticed them back to me, and giving up the ski, I fastened the dogs again to my waist, and set off trotting behind them in my Lapp boots till the snow flew about my ears. Now and then, of course, I had a fall, but I was soon on my feet again. I thought it was splendid exercise to be flying about like this alone on the icefields much farther north than any living beings had been before.

In this way I reached the sledges, which were brought up to the others one by one. The chief difficulty was to get them over the rather high edge of a frozen lane near the camp, but, owing to my "free and easy" method of travelling, we managed to get on quickly enough; so much so, that when the evening came we had travelled back a greater distance than we had advanced the day before.

I found a nice place for encamping, gave the dogs some pemmican, and began getting my supper ready. I pictured to myself how nice some warm food would taste, lighted the "Primus," and crept into the sleeping-bag, where I could make notes in my journal of the events of the last few days in peace and comfort. While

I was attending to the cooking apparatus "Suggen" began to bark, and presently I heard some one answer away on the ice. I turned out, and could now hear voices not far off. Soon afterwards I caught a glimpse now and then, between the hummocks, of dogs drawing a sledge, on which sat two men. In a few minutes they came driving at full speed into the camp, while the dogs made a terrible row. It was Scott-Hansen and Nordahl, who had returned with Nansen's sledge and team to keep me company during the night. To me this was a pleasant surprise. Scott-Hansen told me he had just worked out his last observation, which showed that we were in 84° 4' north latitude, and that they had been celebrating the return of the sun on board that day, and so we decided we also would have a celebration of our own.

After partaking of a plain supper, we settled down to our pipes. Sverdrup had sent his best pipe with them, as he knew I had none; neither Nansen nor I had taken any pipes or tobacco with us on the sledge expedition. We then made some toddy of some spirits of wine which they had brought with them, and we spent quite a pleasant time in the tent where we three sat, far away from home, singing many of our national songs.

It was late at night before we went to rest in our sleeping-bags, Scott-Hansen and I in the double one, and Nordahl in a single one he had brought with him.

Next morning Nansen, Sverdrup, and Peder arrived from the ship on ski. We broke up the encampment and returned for the second time to the *Fram*. In the neighbourhood of the ship we were stopped by a long lane of open water which had been formed in the ice. It was impossible to get the sledges across it at any point, and as we did not care to get out the kayaks, we put the sledges on a safe part of the ice and left them there until the lane should be sufficiently frozen for us to bring them across to the ship. We and the dogs managed to scramble across on some small ice-floes.

It was pleasant to be again sitting in the warm, cosy cabin of the *Fram*, doing justice to the well-stocked table.

When we started for the first time with the four sledges, each load weighed about 550 lbs.—we could not tell to a few pounds, for every little thing was not weighed. The total weight of the provisions was not quite 2,000 lbs. On starting the second time the same weight was distributed over the six sledges, but shortly afterwards two boat-grips and one bag with pemmican were left behind, reducing the weight by about 300 lbs. There were thus about 300 lbs. on each of our six sledges. On the two sledges with the kayaks, however, we had rather heavier loads, besides the weight of the sledges themselves. The biggest of these, with guard-runners and ski, weighed 70 lbs.

It was clear that we could not manage so many sledges, or so great a load upon each sledge. After renewed deliberations and calculations, Nansen decided that we should take only three sledges with 440 lbs. on each. This would give us sufficient food for 100 days and the dogs sufficient for 30 days. The three sledges were strengthened in every possible way—ash ribs were lashed over all the cross-bars, and between these and the uprights iron supports were likewise lashed. The wolfskin clothes had not turned out suitable for our journey. By using them at night in the sleeping-bag they, as well as the bag, became damp, the latter having the hairy side out; and when we put on the wolfskin clothes in the evening before going into the bag they were so stiff that we could hardly pull the hood over our heads. The last night we were out on the ice the temperature was −43°, and in the thermometer house near the ship it had only been −38° the same night.

We made our blankets into a sort of night-shirt, so that we could button them round us when we crept into the bag. We also used this garment to throw over our shoulders when making a halt on the journey. Sverdrup made the sleeping-bag somewhat larger, as it proved to be too small when we turned the hairy side in.

We lay out on the ice one night and tried this new arrangement, with the blankets and the hairy side of the bag turned in. We had on two thick woollen shirts, drawers, leggings, socks, Lapp shoes, and woollen knee-breeches with leggings. Outside the upper part of our bodies we wore a smaller woollen jersey, another of camel-hair, while Nansen had one of Iceland wool, and I an anorak of vadmel (Norwegian tweed), with woollen hoods covering our heads. This arrangement gave entire satisfaction, and we felt much drier in the bag than before.

The third equipment was now ready, and the time had arrived for us to exchange our third and last farewell with our comrades and the *Fram*. I had been down in the hold with Jacobsen, lashing iron fittings to the sledges, and while there he told me that he would not say good-bye any more to us, since we kept on coming back every time. We were sure, he declared, to come back the third time as well.

Well, we did come on board again, but that was not until we met again in the harbour of Tromsö, after many a long day had passed.

## CHAPTER XVI

*Off at Last—The Fight Across the Ice to 86° 14'— Farthest North*

ON the 14th of March, 1895, the guns again thundered forth across the desert icefields, and the flag was hoisted on the *Fram*. This time our journey began in earnest. Several of our comrades came some distance on the way with us. Sverdrup and Mogstad left us in the course of the day, but Scott-Hansen, Hendriksen, and Petterson remained with us until the following day. Nansen went in front, as before, and led the way; next came the sledge with his kayak and the following dogs in his team: "Kvik," "Baro," "Lilleræven," "Sjölike," "Narrifas," "Freia," "Barbara," "Potiphar," and "Rattlesnake." Then came the middle sledge, and lastly mine with my kayak. The teams of these two sledges consisted of the following dogs: "Suggen," "Baby," "Haren," "Gulen," "Flint," "Caiaphas," "Blok," "Bjelki," and "Sultan"; and finally, "Barabbas," "Kvindfolket," "Perpetuum," "Katta," "Livjægeren," "Storræven," "Russen," "Icebear," "Pan," and "Ulinka." On the flat ice everything went capitally, but the ice-ridges caused us a great deal of trouble and loss of time. I broke one of my ski soon after we started, but I obtained a new one from Mogstad, who had to return to the ship on a ski and a half. When we made a halt to camp for the evening, the odometer on the hindmost sledge showed that we had covered six miles, and we ourselves were both hungry and thirsty. We had been merry-making the night before on board the *Fram*, and maybe that was the reason we felt somewhat more thirsty than usual. We did not feel quite at our ease till we were comfortably seated inside the tent with plenty of food and drink before us. Petterson gave vent to his feelings by exclaiming, "Now I feel as happy as a prince!"

Next day we parted with our three comrades; they had spent the night in a snow-hut which they had built with the aid of their ski and staffs. They had not been very warm, and had been astir early in the morning. They now helped to break up the encampment and to look after the dogs, whereupon we thanked them for accompanying us on the way, gave them a farewell hand-grip, and then shaped our course to the north, feeling not a little emotion at parting.

Through some trouble which I had with one of the teams, as well as through my long leave-taking with Scott-Hansen, I got left behind and had to hurry on after the sledges. I found time, however, to look back after our three comrades, who were standing gazing, no doubt with strange thoughts in their minds, after us, who were setting out for the unknown regions in the north.

On Monday, March 18th, the fifth day of our journey, the odometer showed that we had done over twenty-four miles. Sometimes we went over the flat, even ice at a great pace, but at times we came across ridges and lanes over which we had to climb. The lanes were the worst, as we had to look for safe places by which to cross, and this took time. The *Fram* had long since vanished on the horizon; there were only our two selves and the dogs in that lonely region. The ice improved as we travelled farther north, and the sledges became lighter day by day. We had a good deal of trouble with one sledge, which had to look after itself pretty well. It often capsized, and whenever I had to right it the other one came to a stop, and then I had to get it started again. We suffered greatly from the cold, the temperature being about 40° below zero. During the daytime we had to toil along till we perspired, and it was then warm enough, but it was during the night that it was worst, especially as our clothes and sleeping-bag were damp. We spread our blankets over the kayaks, in the hope of being able to dry them in the sun as we went along. But it was a vain hope to look for the sun. It was still far away, and its rays were not likely to dry anything for some time yet.

In the evenings we longed to get into our sleeping-bag, and in the mornings we were all intent upon getting away; but this took some time, especially as we were now obliged to take each dog out of the leash and harness it.

We fed the dogs in the evening, after the day's work, as they then had something to which to look forward after their exertions during the day.

I had been obliged to tie up one of our dogs, "Livjægeren," to one of the two sledges I was minding, as he had become a total wreck, and only gave us trouble when in the team. One day he was very near being strangled; he could not keep up with us, and was being dragged along the ground by the rope, which I had to cut in order to save him. One of my fingers became frost-bitten, and Nansen had to rub it with snow to revive it.

On March 19th we had a misfortune with our

middle sledge, which came into contact with a sharp piece of ice, and one of the bags with fish-flour had a hole cut in it. This caused some delay, as the whole sledge had to be re-packed and lashed The odometer was broken, and my kayak got a hole in its side through capsizing. Nansen lost the sheath of his bear-spear, and left his pocket-compass behind on a hummock, but I fortunately discovered it in time.

We made a short halt in the middle of the day, and had some beef-chocolate and bread-and-butter, but we soon began to feel the cold, and then we had to be off again. In spite of our mishaps, however, we had done eight miles. I found that the morning was the best time for making progress, for then one could get the steam up, so to speak, and keep the body warm.

The days which now followed—before the sun had risen very high in the heavens, and the cold had abated—must be reckoned as the worst we had experienced during the whole expedition. Throughout the day we had a continual struggle to get forward at all, and in the night we suffered exceedingly from the cold and from want of sleep. The exudations from our bodies during the march collected in our *vadmel* clothes, so that during the first days they became stiff and frozen. As the time went on, the icy surface on the clothes gradually increased, and during the continuous and severe cold, which froze the quicksilver, they became a veritable glacial suit of armour. For a time, I used to change my outer clothing when we crept into our sleeping-bag, and used alternately my anorak and my camel-hair jacket; but this plan I soon had to give up, as it was too painful to have to turn one's frozen garments inside out with one's benumbed fingers. We had just to leave them as they were, and they cut into our wrists and loins until we were quite sore. The dogs gradually became intractable, and would not pull. They would come to a stop all of a sudden, and jump over each other's traces until these looked as if they had been plaited. Over and over again the traces had to be disentangled — rather a nasty job with frozen, bleeding fingers. Some of the dogs were in the habit, as soon as a halt was made, of gnawing through the traces. For some of the worst of them the harness had been interlaced with steel wire, that belonging to "Russen" being entirely composed of wire. But if "Russen" could not free himself, he generally managed to gnaw through another dog's traces and set him free. A good deal of time was thus lost in catching the dogs, and sometimes we had to go on as best we could with a smaller team, while the loose dogs followed the caravan at a respectful distance.

Our gloves, too, became stiff and icy, and we had finally to protect our fingers by using wolfskin gloves lined with "senne" grass. We managed to keep our feet fairly warm, but then we took the utmost care of them, making elaborate leg-toilets, both before we entered the sleeping-bag in the evening and when we turned out in the morning. In the evening we took off everything we had on our feet and unravelled the wet "senne" grass, which we put next to our body so as to dry it, till the morning, when we put on the hair- and wolfskin socks or some foot-bandages before putting our feet back into the Lapp boots, which had been turned inside out for the night.

The sleeping-bag was our best friend, but day by day it grew stiffer and heavier with the ice which gradually collected in the hair; now and then we had to turn it inside out and knock the ice off it with our ski staffs. In the evening, when we crept into it, both the bag and our clothes gradually became more pliant. Our poor bodies had first to thaw them up before we could begin to feel warm. The stiff frozen gloves and the wet "senne" grass which we had to wear about us did not improve matters. Still the sleeping-bag was always the goal for which we longed during our march—the moment when we should be able to get into it and get some warm food into our hungry, frozen bodies, whether it was lobscouse, fish-gratin, or Knorr's soups. A cup of warm whey-drink afterwards was our greatest comfort. We would then close the flap of the bag as tightly as possible, creep closer to one another, and compose our weary limbs to rest.

When we awoke next morning, ready for the day's march, our clothes were pliant and damp, and when we opened the flap of our bag and stretched our arms and the upper part of the body, the fine rime frost which had gathered on the inside of the tent fell down upon us in showers, and before long our clothes were freezing again and became as stiff as a suit of armour.

We had a good drink of water every morning, so that we did not suffer from the so-called "Arctic thirst." If at times we began to talk about hot "bock-beer" and such luxuries, we were sure to feel thirsty and suffer not a little; but if we could only leave off thinking of being thirsty, the feeling soon went away. We had taken with us pocket-flasks of ebonite, which we filled with water in the morning and carried against our breasts, but we only used them at the beginning of our journey; besides, I lost mine before long.

The temperature on the night of March 20th was −47°, on 21st it was −43°, and things were becoming worse instead of better. We lost our odometer, but did not trouble to find it again, as we had just had a long delay, all caused by "Livjægeren." We only discovered that he was gone after we had travelled a considerable distance from our last camp, upon which Nansen went back, and found him rolled up in the snow on the very spot which we had left in the morning. This dog gave us a lot of trouble. Twice I had to cut the rope round his neck, when he was on the point of being strangled, and I also had to go back to fetch him on one or two occasions. He had to be killed as food for the other dogs.

Next day the cold was just as bad. The worst of it was that we could not get any sleep at night, the cold and the damp keeping us awake. To-day Nansen took an observation for the first time, and found that we were now in 85° 9′ north latitude. The wind had hitherto been blowing slightly from the north-east. We travelled eight miles, and did not get into our bag until two o'clock in the early morning. The temperature was −48° and −38°. I had been shouting at the dogs so much during the last few days, that I scarcely knew my own voice, and I could feel by my back and my sides that the loads were heavy to get over the ridges and difficult to right after every capsize. We hoisted our flags on the kayaks in celebration of our having passed the eighty-fifth degree.

On March 24th the thermometer stood at 49° below zero. On the day before we had a sharp north-easterly wind, ice in bad condition, and terrible hard work in getting along. We killed "Livjægeren" to feed the other dogs. We used the bear-spear, but he died hard, although he was in a miserable condition. The other dogs did not seem to like his flesh, being, I suppose, as yet too particular. The weather was raw and foggy. This Sunday was the nastiest I had ever experienced. It was an unpleasant and trying day altogether. We were so tired and sleepy that we were simply staggering with fatigue by the time we reached the spot where we encamped for the night.

On the 25th we were in 85° 20′ north latitude. The terrible cold did not seem to be abating. We lost so much time in camping and breaking up, the work being so laborious and slow, that the day was hardly long enough for us. It was a long and unpleasant job to feed the dogs, as we had to dig out the frozen pemmican from the boat-grips with our sore hands, and portion out the food to the dogs according to their deserts. And from time to time we had to take bags of pemmican from the third sledge in order to form fresh supports for the kayaks as the grips were gradually emptied.

We passed on the 28th of March a large hummock, the largest we had hitherto seen, being almost like an iceberg. We were delayed for some time by a lane which opened up after we had got one sledge across, so that we had to make a detour with the others. In the afternoon the sky became suddenly overcast, and the temperature rose from seven to ten degrees. We expected a snowstorm, but for all that we looked forward with pleasure to this change. But it did not come, and the next day was clear and fine, with 64° of frost. Nansen took an observation with the small theodolite, according to which we were then in 85° 15′, which we could hardly believe. There must be some mistake, we thought, or else the drift of the ice to the south must have been unusually great. He took, however, a single altitude afterwards, which showed that we were in 85° 56′ north latitude.

On the night of March 29th the temperature was $-43°$, and on the 30th $-32°$. The barometer was steadily going down, the sky was overcast, and the wind south-easterly, blowing about four metres to the second. A change in the weather now seemed imminent. We decided to keep our course a point or so to the west of due north. We did not finish our work or get any food till six o'clock in the morning, as the cooking apparatus had become disorganized. Nansen had a lot of trouble with it before he discovered why the air escaped, however much he pumped. It was the lid, which had not been screwed on tightly, a layer of ice having got in under it.

We had very rough and uneven ice on our last march, and in one place especially it was very troublesome. We found a deep crack in some old, solid, tightly packed ice, just in front of a ridge. One of the sledges —the one with the provision bags—and some of the dogs fell into this crack, which was about ten or twelve feet deep. One of us had to jump down into it and unload the bags, which we had some difficulty in getting up again. Fortunately the sledge was not damaged. The dogs we hauled up with ropes.

On March 31st I was sitting in the bag, writing this in peace and comfort with my woollen gloves on my hands. What I have written at other times on this tour in my day book was written in the mornings, just before we started from our camp, on my kayak, with big, heavy wolfskin gloves on my hands, the pencil being hardly visible.

We made an excellent start very early in the morning with the wind right at our backs. Suddenly we came to a lane, across which we had just managed to convey one sledge safely, when the ice on both sides of the lane glided away, and Nansen and I with one team of dogs on one sledge stood on the one side, while the two other sledges and dogs were left on the other side. We were standing on the edge of the pack-ice, near the lane, watching the movement of the ice, when suddenly the floe on which I was standing slid away from under me, and I fell plump into the water. Fortunately the floes prevented my sinking deeper than just above my knees. I managed to scramble across to the other side and to drag myself up on to the ice. This was anything but a pleasant situation in a temperature 43° below zero, my clothes becoming at once frozen and stiff. There we stood, one on each side, while the lane gradually grew broader and broader. It was not a pleasant prospect to be separated for the rest of the night; Nansen had the tent and cooking apparatus on his side. I had to run up and down the ice and among the dogs to keep myself warm, while Nansen walked along on the other side of the lane to find a way across, so that we might get together again. We could not use the kayaks to ferry us across, as the ice had torn the canvas into pieces in several places during the many upsets we had endured. Nansen found a way across at last, however, but it was a long and laborious job to get the other sledges across by this roundabout way, the whole process lasting several hours.

The frozen wind-trousers I used on this march became so brittle that they cracked in many places. When we had encamped and I got into the sleeping-bag, I had to put them inside on the top of me while I slept, so that they might be soft enough to be sewn together by the time I woke up. This was the worst piece of sewing I can remember ever having to do, for the trousers became stiff again as soon as I had sewn the least little bit, and I had to put them down alongside me in the bag again. I almost believe it was more trying than having to sew canvas in 72° of frost, a job at which we have also had to try our hands.

During our march on April 1st it struck Nansen that it was a long time since we had wound our watches and when we looked at them I found that mine had stopped, while Nansen's, fortunately, was still going. The temperature had now quite changed, it was −11° during the day and −8° in the evening. A snowstorm from the south-east sprang up, and blew right in our backs during the march. The ice got worse and worse; there were innumerable ridges to climb over, and we did not make much progress in the course of the day, although we pushed on with all our might. It was, of course, always light now in those regions.

JOHANSEN TAKING "BARBARA" TO BE KILLED.

That morning it took us a long time to make a start. A new support had to be put under my kayak, as the contents of one of the boat-grips had been eaten up, and several bags had to be repaired and sewn together, etc., etc., all of which was difficult to perform in the cold with our sore, wounded fingers.

The whole of the previous day and night was taken up with sleep, breaking up the encampment, and marching, and we did not get into our bag until seven in the morning of Wednesday, April 3rd. I was unfortunate enough to fall into a lane again, but I was getting accustomed to this now. Nansen, on ski, and the first sledge had passed safely across, but when I came on without ski, and with the two other sledges, the ice broke under my feet and I went through, but fortunately I held on to the kayak and was dragged out of the water by the dogs. The ice was a little better, but we did not get on very fast. "Russen" was killed to serve as food for the other dogs, but all of them did not seem to like him. They preferred the flesh of the dogs which they themselves had torn to pieces in the good old days on board the *Fram*. The weather was comparatively fine and clear, and the wind a little more easterly.

Notwithstanding the many sufferings we had to undergo during the day as well as at night, there were still bright moments in the routine of our daily life to which we were always looking forward. One of these—it was, in fact, the brightest—was the time when we sat in the bag, hungry, frozen, and covered with ice, waiting for our food. We had to remain in the bag for some time to get warm before we could attend to our feet and change. Our sleep, of course, was not of the best, when we had to lie night after night in the same clothes as those in which we walked through ice, snow, and water every day. The thing was to be able to stand it all. The temperature was now −24°, and the barometer was falling. It had been pretty high up till then. Our observation on April 3rd showed that we were in 85° 59′ north latitude. We had hoped to find ourselves farther north, but the ice had been in such a bad condition of late that we had not made very great progress; in fact, it looked as if things were going to be worse.

I was of opinion that we ought not to venture any farther north, as we might find it difficult enough to reach Franz Josef Land from where we were now in the midst of the drift ice. Nansen was also beginning to have his misgivings about the advisability of continuing to the north, and on April 4th he began to keep more to the west. The difficulty of keeping the dogs in order was increasing. The traces had become knotted and had to be undone many times a day; besides every morning and evening—a pleasant job!

On Saturday, the 6th of April, we had to toil very hard getting over the very worst ice we had as yet encountered —nothing but ridge after ridge and long stretches of old rubble ice with very deep snow and lanes here and there. If the ice was to be anything like this on our way towards land, it looked as if we should want plenty of time to reach it. The temperature was a little milder, $-11°$, the wind was north-easterly with hazy weather. We did not feel quite so cold now; it was the damp from which we suffered most. If we only had dry clothes!

We had not travelled far on Sunday morning, the 7th of April, before Nansen said that he would not proceed any farther. The ice made it impossible for us to make any real progress. Nansen made a short excursion to the north on his ski to examine the ice, but he found it just as bad as ever. We then selected a place for camping, and there made ourselves as comfortable as possible. At this point of our journey—the most northerly that any human foot had ever trod—we prepared a little banquet, consisting of lobscouse, dry chocolate, stewed whortleberries, and whey-drink afterwards. Nansen took an observation from the top of a high, massive hummock close to our tent, and his calculations showed we were in $86° 10'$ north latitude, which, however, when more carefully worked out, proved to be $86° 13'6'$ north latitude.

Thus far and no farther, then, it was our fate to penetrate. Of course, we should have liked to push on more to the north. It was, however, our consolation that we had done what we could, and that in any case we had lifted something more of the veil that shrouds this part of our globe. But as we were now situated—when the eye, strained to the uttermost, could discern only ice of such a nature that it was only with the greatest efforts that we could drag ourselves onward for the very shortest distance each day—we had to bow to the inevitable and turn our faces in the direction of warmer climes.

# CHAPTER XVII

*The Norwegian Flag in the Farthest North—On the Way Home—Our Watches Stop—In the Kingdom of Great Silence—Tracks of Foxes—Mild Weather*

ON Monday, the 8th of April, we turned back, and, having planted a couple of Norwegian flags in this the most northerly camp in the world, we shaped our course for Franz Josef Land.

Curiously enough, our first day's march in the new direction was very satisfactory, the ice here having changed for the better, and permitting of good progress. I was now able to go long distances on ski behind the sledges. Before this I had been obliged to trudge along on foot, pushing and helping the sledges along.

On the night of April 9th and during April 10th we made good progress—indeed, the best we had made as yet. We kept going as long as possible when we once got properly started. On the night of the 9th we were a good deal delayed by having come, after a ten hours' march, to a lane which had lately been frozen over. We managed to get one of the sledges across, and the second had almost reached the other side when the dogs fell through the ice, and the water came rushing up, while the ice yielded beneath the weight of the sledge. We had to set out on the ice on our ski to get the sledge and the dogs turned round and landed on the other side. We eventually succeeded, the ice, however, bulging under our weight all the time.

We tried to get the last sledge across in the same manner at two different points, but with no better result. It was fortunate for us that we crossed over without any mishap. There was, therefore, nothing else for it but to go a long way round to discover some place where we could cross. In this we also succeeded, but not without some difficulty, as the ice-floes drifted away from one another.

Having now got the sledges together we looked for a camping-place, and settled down for the night. It was really a treat to get inside our tent, and get some warm "fish-gratin" inside us.

The night of April 11th was the most comfortable we had hitherto had. It was actually warm in the bag, and the inside of the tent, which lay right in the sun, was free of hoar-frost.

I was sitting writing without anything on my hands. We were in the best of spirits, and were talking about home. When we were hungry, which was generally the case, we discussed what fine spreads we were going to have when we got back. The "Arctic-thirst" had not troubled us much till April 10th, when we suffered a good deal from it. The temperature was $-18°$.

On April 12th also we made splendid progress. The ice was in good condition, and it was seldom necessary for both of us to assist in getting the sledges over the ridges; nor had we met with any fresh lanes to cross. As soon as we had camped, and I had fed the dogs, I looked at my watch to see what length of time we had been on the way, when I discovered that it had stopped. I called out to Nansen, who was busy cooking, to see if his watch were going. No, he said, his had stopped also; we had been travelling so long since we last wound them up. This was not a pleasant discovery. We wound them up again, of course, at once, but Nansen had to take a time observation and an observation for latitude. In the meantime we had to depend upon our reckoning since our last observation for longitude.

"Barbara" was killed on the 12th, and given to the dogs, which were beginning to like the taste of dog-flesh, no doubt because they were getting more hungry. The dog, poor creature, tried to bite my hand when we killed her. I suppose she thought she was too young to die. She was born and bred among the polar ice, and found her death there without having seen anything else of the world but snow and ice.

On Saturday, the 13th of April (Easter Eve), we did not accomplish so much as we had done during the last three days. We came to a lane which it was impossible to cross. Nansen started off to find a place for crossing. He was away so long that I began to be anxious about him. He came back at last, however, after having looked in vain for a crossing, and proposed that we should camp and wait till to-morrow, and make ourselves as comfortable as possible on Easter Eve. Nansen sat in the bag, working out some observations, while I attended to the dogs, and afterwards we had a festive meal in our tent, consisting of fish-gratin, bread and butter, vril food, and a new concoction—lime-juice toddy. I was busy putting our camp in order when the ice began packing over in the lane, which was soon closed up, while in the neighbourhood of our encampment the ice creaked and groaned, so that the dogs became uneasy. Twice of late the dogs attacked our butter-bag. I caught "Storræven" in the act, and although he was an excellent dog, there was nothing for it but to give him a thrashing. We were afterwards compelled to place the butter-bag inside the tent.

Easter Day we spent comfortably in our tent, Nansen being busy with calculations, and I with mending and patching clothes. On the 13th we were in 86° 4' north latitude and 86° east longitude, the variation being 42·5°.

Nansen's watch had stopped about an hour. No doubt the reason we were so far north was that the ice was drifting in that direction. On Easter Day we shaped our course more southerly. A year ago at about this season the *Fram* drifted rapidly towards the north, and probably the same drift was being repeated this year about the same time.

Monday, the 15th of April, was a splendid day. The thermometer showed $-15°$, and the sun was quite warm. About noon, before we got into our bag, after having kept going during the night and the forenoon, we hung up nearly all our belongings on the staffs and ski to dry in the beautiful sunshine. Inside our tent, upon which the sun was shining warmly, we sat enjoying a couple of cups of steaming "Julienne" soup.

We did not make so much progress on our last march as we had expected. Nansen had to go back some considerable distance for the compass, which he had left behind on the ice when he took bearings for our course. A strange feeling came over me as I sat there alone in the solitude waiting for his return. Never before had I felt so deep a stillness. No sound of any kind, near or far, disturbed the quiet around me. The dogs lay as if lifeless with their heads between their paws on the white snow, which glittered in the bright sunshine. The silence made me feel quite nervous; I dared not move from where I was sitting—dared hardly to breathe. Then sleep came upon me, and I dozed till a sharp gust of wind from the south so irritated my nostrils that I woke up. It was clear that it was not summer yet. The thermometer stood at $-15°$. A dog now and then lifted his head from among the sleeping pack and looked round. At last the stillness was broken, I heard the sound of ski gliding over the snow, and soon afterwards Nansen came in sight. He was weary and tired after the march in the unusual heat. We set out again, but did not get on very far before we pitched our tent and had our dinner.

We made a good record on the 16th of April. We set out early in the morning and pushed on for fourteen hours, covering a considerable distance, the ice being in good condition, and the dogs pulling much better, due to the loads having become lighter.

During our march we generally halted midway to have some food. We used to get into the sleeping-bag with some bread, butter, and pemmican between us. At first, when the cold was severe, these halts were anything but pleasant as we lay shivering with cold and gnawing at the frozen lumps of butter, which almost vanished in our immense wolfskin gloves. Later on things improved, but it sometimes happened that we fell asleep while we lay munching our food, and thus lost valuable time.

The apportionment of our chocolate once a day was, of course, a bright spot in our existence. The chocolate had been broken into bits, so that it was not easy to portion it out equally, but we managed it in this way: one of us arranged two portions on the kayak, while the other turned his back upon him and chose his lot by calling out "right" or "left." We were quite fair to one another. Nansen, who was a bigger man than I, never made any difference in the rations. As a rule we had sufficient, but there were days when we thought our allowance rather short.

The day's march began on the 17th in the evening, and lasted till the forenoon of the next day. From the observations taken on 18th and 19th, we found that we were in 85° 37·8′ north latitude, and 79° 30′ east longitude, which showed that we had been getting on fairly well lately. I had been so unfortunate as to have two of my ski broken; the dogs set off with the sledges, which went right over them. "Perpetuum" was killed on April 18th. We thought it would be better to strangle him than to cut his throat with a knife, so we tried that method, but we had to give it up and use the knife after all. The most humane way, of course, would have been to shoot the dogs, but we could not very well afford ammunition for this, as we might find a better use for it later. These slaughterings were rather unpleasant work, but they did not affect me so much as I at first thought they would have done. I soon became so skilled in cutting their throats that they did not seem to suffer any great pain. The poor creatures went quite willingly with me behind a hummock. There they were placed on their side in the snow, and while holding them down by the collar with my left hand, with my right I stuck the knife right through the throat down into the snow. In most cases they died without uttering a sound. The worst part of the work was to cut them up and serve out the rations, so that each dog should get according to his deserts. It was only strict, imperative necessity that, to some extent, made the work more endurable. "Perpetuum" was a lazy, useless dog, but he was in good condition, and furnished the others with a good deal of food. On 18th some paraffin got into the fish-gratin, and next day some got into the porridge, but it all went down just the same.

In the morning we had for breakfast chocolate with bread and butter and pemmican one day, and porridge with whey-drink the next. Repairing our Lapp boots was not a very pleasant job in a temperature which was keeping to about 22° below zero. We felt quite warm, however, when on the march in the sun. I had only been using ordinary woollen gloves since the change in the weather set in.

We marched from four o'clock in the afternoon of the 19th to half-past eight in the morning of the 20th. We got on fairly well, notwithstanding the numerous ridges and lanes. We had, especially, great difficulty in getting across one large, broad lane, full of slush and pieces of ice, but we ultimately succeeded, the ice pressure going on all the time under our very feet. On the other side we found fine, flat ice—a regular "Land of Canaan," as Nansen used to say when he came back from his reconnoitring and had found good ice.

"What in the world is that sticking up above the white ice-floe yonder? Is it part of a ship's mast? Is it the remains of the *Tegethoff*?" These were the questions I asked myself, as we one day caught sight of a piece of timber fixed in an oblique position into the ice. When we drew close to it, we found it was a piece of driftwood, which had probably been raised on end during an ice pressure. It had evidently come from the primeval forests of Siberia, and must have been dancing about up here for ages. It would have provided us with capital fuel, but, unfortunately, we could not manage to take it with us. I cut the initials of our names, and "85° 30′ north latitude," in the log.

"Sjölike" was the dog which had to be sacrificed for the others when we encamped this time. We were obliged to kill the dogs more frequently now, as we had to be sparing with the three to four days' pemmican we had left for them.

From half-past nine in the morning of the 21st to half-past one in the afternoon of the 22nd we got over at least twenty miles, which was our best record. But then the great open plains of ice were in excellent condition, with only a ridge and a short stretch of rubble ice here and there.

The next day we also had good ice, and, notwithstanding a slight fall of snow, over which our ski glided less easily, we managed to cover close upon twenty miles. The sunlight had not affected our eyes as yet, although we had not commenced using snow-spectacles. We merely pulled the brim of our felt hats, which we wore under the hoods, well down over our eyes.

Little "Bjelki," who had not been of much use to us, was killed on April 23rd; but there was not much food in that bundle of wool. We had now twenty-one dogs left, the poorest of them having been dispatched. Nansen broke one of his ski on the 22nd, and we had now only one ski in reserve.

During the 24th and 25th of April the ice was not quite so good, but nevertheless we travelled over a considerable stretch of ground. During the last days the temperature had been $-15°$ to $-18°$ in the day, and about $-22°$ at night. Strange to say, we saw the track of a fox right across our course (S. $5°$ E.), and shortly afterwards we came across another track of the same animal, this time near an open lane which stopped our progress, and upon the side of which we encamped. When we discovered the first trail there were also traces indicating that the fox had had something to eat not long before. But how could it have found food out here in the midst of the drift-ice? According to our reckoning it should not be more than about 120 miles to the west coast of Petermann's Land. The question then was, how far does it extend eastwards?

On the 28th we travelled right on from the morning until ten o'clock at night, when we had to camp on account of the overcast weather and the strong southerly wind. When we began our march we came to a broad, open lane, the ice on both sides of which was in motion. The lane extended from east to west, and we had to walk along one side for a couple of hours before we found a place where we could get over, and then it was only with great difficulty, as we had to wait until the lane closed up in order to get the sledges across.

The ice crashed, crackled, and thundered under our feet, while the ridges grew higher and higher. It was a sound we knew well, but this time we were in the very midst of the fray. After crossing, I had to rush back again to get my ski, which I had taken off while getting the sledges across, and it was only in the nick of time that I managed to pull them out from among the ice-floes, which were on the point of burying them. We felt proud of our achievement in crossing over so safely, and rewarded ourselves with an extra portion of chocolate, which we thoroughly enjoyed as we sat on our kayaks on safe ice, and heard the ice groaning as if with rage at such mites as we managing to escape from its embrace.

After this we had good, flat ice before us, over which we made good progress, although a rather strong southerly wind blew right in our faces, the temperature being 54° below zero. Here again we saw some tracks of foxes. We encamped near an ice-ridge, and fortified ourselves as best we could against a snowstorm, which might last for several days, judging by the appearance of the weather.

The last day of April reminded us of the approach of the beautiful month of May; though it might not bring us much change. We did not travel for more than five to six hours the day before. The beginning was promising, but we came to an immense broad lane, which we followed westward. Nansen then explored farther alone for several hours, but no crossing was to be found, and so we had to encamp.

The weather was fine now, being quite mild; the temperature was 4° below zero. In the tent we felt warm and comfortable, and at night we slept well

# CHAPTER XVIII

*More Lanes—Summer Weather—Another "Seventeenth of May"—A Whale—Where in all the World is Land?*

WE employed the 1st of May in mending our clothes and waiting for the lane to be frozen over. It was a pleasant change to rest and do nothing else but sew. The dogs were becoming ravenous. A pair of reindeer-skin socks, which I had placed on top of the kayak to dry during the night, were devoured by them, probably by "Kvik." I also think it was she who attacked the last half boat-grip of pemmican we had left. "Kvik" would not eat the flesh of the other dogs directly after they were killed. It had to be left out overnight to be frozen through.

During the early days of May the wind was the same as that which used to raise our spirits on board the *Fram*. Now, of course, we were not at all pleased with this south-easterly breeze, for it produced so many open lanes in the ice, and these sorely tried our patience. First of all, we had to find a crossing, and after many detours we might succeed in finding one, when it often happened that the crossing itself caused us many difficulties and troubles.

"Potiphar" and "Kvindfolket" now had to be killed. The whole of the latter was not used at once, but a third part of it was put aside until next day, and this, together with a third of "Ulinka," whose turn to die was come, would form the next meal.

"Pan" and "Haren" had many a heavy pull, and they were now thin and miserable. The dogs that had been the best workers were "Storræven," "Lilleræven," "Icebear," "Suggen," "Baro," "Barabbas," and "Caiaphas." "Sultan" was also a strong dog, but very lazy. "Ulinka" always wanted to keep to one side of the team. She was greatly delighted when properly tethered right in among the traces of another team. Altogether she gave me a great amount of trouble.

On Sunday, the 5th of May, we marched from half-past one in the morning until six in the evening. It was a fine day, and we got on well over long plains of good ice. The lanes were not so difficult to cross, as the floes had been so displaced that we came across several points where the uneven edges of the ice met together, while in other places the lane was frozen sufficiently for us to venture across over the stiffened mass, formed of pieces of ice and slush. We pushed on all we could, and were a good deal fagged when we encamped.

I woke the night before and felt cold; a fresh wind had blown one side of the tent down on to my face. Of late we had not closed the flap of our sleeping-bag, as we felt sufficiently warm otherwise. But the wind had now changed, and was blowing hard from the north, which was in our favour. We were now in 84° 30′ north latitude and 66° 17′ east longitude. We must have drifted a good deal to the north and west on account of the south-easterly wind we had of late. The temperature was 1° above zero.

Our next day's march lasted from five o'clock in the morning till nearly nine o'clock the following morning, the 7th of May. We had, of course, a good many ridges over which to struggle; but there were extensive plains of flat ice now and then, and we made good progress.

The next day the wind, which had been blowing from

the north-east all the time, increased steadily, and in the course of the afternoon it became so intolerable, when the snow began falling, that we had to pull up and encamp before we had intended doing so.

When we had been marching along for about five hours over uneven ice, "Flint," the dog which was to be killed in the evening, tore himself loose and ran off. When once he got away he was a difficult fellow to catch again. He was a strong but lazy and useless animal, and did not mind a thrashing in the least. He was always cross and angry with the other dogs. When we camped in the evening, he put in an appearance to get his portion of dogs' flesh; but he must have been terribly disappointed, for he had to accompany me behind a hummock to meet his doom, and be cut up for the other dogs which deserved to live longer. Poor creatures, they were getting very thin and skinny after all the toil and starvation through which they had gone. But we had to push on, and were obliged to thrash them more than we really liked to do whenever they came to a halt. "Flint," however, was very fat, which was strange, considering the short rations he had had of late. The temperature was about 10° above zero, and we were having splendid summer weather compared with that to which we had been accustomed. Our fingers were still sore and tender, but now we had no need to fear to take off our gloves or other clothing.

The weather was overcast and misty on the 9th of May. After having proceeded for some hours we fancied we saw fine, extensive plains of ice before us, and we congratulated each other on the prospect of good, flat ground again. But the sky became more and more overcast, and the snow began to fall, so that it was impossible to see anything before us. Now and then the weather cleared up for a few moments, and we pushed on for some time, though at last we had to give in and stop. We thought at first that we would have our dinner in the bag, and see if the weather would improve; but the result was that we pitched our tent, made some lobscouse, and lay down to get some sleep in order to be ready to start as soon as the weather

NO LAND IN SIGHT.

should clear up again. The dogs did not get any food that day.

Before we started in the morning we had several little matters to attend to in the camp. Nansen thought of taking off the guard-runners on his sledge, in order to try if it would glide easier on the German-silver plates underneath; but we found that on the ground we now had the tarred wooden runners were the best, so Nansen let them remain. On the third sledge, however, which had no German-silver plates under the guard-runners, I took off the latter, in order to use the smooth, newly-tarred birchwood runners; but we found that one was broken, so we had to fit the guard-runners on again. We should have been in a fix if we had not used these throughout.

The latitude was now 84° 3', and the longitude 64° 20'. We were wondering what had become of land, for which we hoped so much. The temperature was only 14° above zero. We were now obliged to take off some of our clothes during our march.

During the following two days it was difficult for us to find our way, as the whole sky was completely overcast, with the exception of a strip of blue in the southwest, which was visible for about eight hours while we lay waiting for fine weather. But we struggled along, and managed to accomplish a fair day's march after all. The ice was now assuming a different character, which we thought indicated the proximity of land. It was not so flat as the ice we had of late, but we managed to get along somehow. Our march was a troublesome one. From the outset we had to force our way across long stretches of rubble ice and ridges, rendering it more difficult to proceed. The sledges were certainly much lighter, but we had only twelve dogs left. In several places between the hummocks, when we had to help the dogs and sledges across, we often sank up to our waists in the snow. We could not use our ski on these occasions; Canadian snowshoes would have been more suitable. We pushed on from three o'clock in the morning until about half-past eight in the evening, when we encamped and rested, after a day of toil and struggle, covering some ten or twelve miles. The barometer was steadily sinking. We longed more and more for land, although we knew that it would be an inhospitable, unknown land of snow and ice which we should ultimately reach.

On May 13th we had to give up all idea of going on. After breakfast we were talking as usual about making good progress in the course of the day, and were preparing to start, when the weather became overcast and thick, a snowstorm from the north-west setting in at the same time. We then set to work to get rid of one of the sledges, which, perhaps, we ought to have thought of before. The load on this one had now diminished so much that we found it better to divide and distribute it over our two kayak sledges, most of it being utilised as supports under the kayaks, while we put the rest of it inside the latter. Of the three dogs drawing this "condemned" sledge, Nansen got "Barabbas" and "Caiaphas," and I "Storræven." I was glad of this change, as I hoped it would be easier to follow one sledge than two, which had been my task during the sixty days since we left the *Fram*. On turning out, we found that the dogs had been into my kayak and consumed about half of the contents of our bag with the daily rations of liver-pemmican. And at night I surprised my friends "Storræven," "Sultan," and "Barabbas," in the middle of an attack on the same kayak. They suffered, of course, from hunger; but what could we do? We had to get on at all costs.

When we broke up the third sledge, I found that both the runners were broken, and that they had only been kept together by the guard-runners, which had thus done good service. We then commenced to boil our food with some of the pieces of wood we had been dragging along with us on our sledges—broken ski, staffs, and parts of the sledge. We used the empty paraffin can for a pot, and lighted a brisk fire in the opening of the tent where it was hanging; but before long we had to move our fireplace farther away from the tent, as it was in danger of catching fire. By the time the water was boiling, a big hole, about a yard deep, had formed itself in the ice from the heat of the fire, which had consumed a good deal of our fuel. We found that cooking in this way did not pay, so we decided to use the "Primus" for cooking the rest of the dinner, and our fish-gratin tasted as delicious as ever. On May 14th we had a clear sky and bright sunshine. The dogs were fed on half-rations of pemmican.

On May 15th we again had splendid weather, a clear sky and warm sunshine. We had to use our snow-spectacles, which, fortunately for us, had not been much in requisition. We had now only two sledges, with six dogs to each. We were not making any better progress than before, as the dogs were too worn out. Our brave "Baro" succumbed. The other dogs in the team were at last dragging him along after them, so there was nothing else for it but to kill this fine animal, which so long had been the leader of the teams on our journey. We were stopped by an unusually bad lane of great width, which had just formed. We had to follow it for a long way westward before we could find a place to cross. When we stopped for the evening and encamped, we found we had still another lane close at hand to get over. We were now in 83° 36' north latitude, and 59° 55' east longitude, and were crawling along towards the south, but our pace was slow. We were constantly wondering at not having sighted land yet. The land which the Austrians saw from Cape Fligely should not be more than nine miles off from where we were now, but we saw no sign of it. The reason we had not seen any tracks of foxes or any other animal of late might be due to the continuous fall of snow.

## A BIRTHDAY CELEBRATION

It was my twenty-eighth birthday, and we celebrated it in a small way. For dinner we had lobscouse and dessert consisting of "vril" food with bread-crumbs and butter, and warm lime-juice. Nansen proposed my health and wished me "many a pleasant surprise and happy day" in the coming year.

TRYING TO FIND A CROSSING.

Next day we came to a pool of an immense size, extending towards the south-west as far as we were able to see. We walked along it in this direction, but we soon felt misgivings in following it any further, as we could not tell its extent.

It was covered with quite thin ice, which was worse than no ice at all. To turn back and follow it in the opposite direction was our next thought. We referred to our chart, and the result was that we continued our way as we had begun. With the aid of our glass we discovered in the mirage on the horizon signs of ice beyond the extreme end of the pool. We had not proceeded far before we were stopped by a broad lane, which ran in the direction of the pool. We found that the ice at this point was sufficiently strong to carry us, and on examining it further we thought it probable that we should be able to cross the large pool. The ice-floes were here and there jammed up in layers, so that the ice had become strong enough to cross, although here and there were weaker parts and large open cracks, while the whole seemed to be in motion. To our great joy we got safely across at last. The ice showed that we were still drifting westward. Now that we were in 59° 55′ east longitude, this was an unfortunate thing for us. Nansen worked out his calculations again of several observations made from the time our watches stopped. It looked as if we could not quite reconcile ourselves to this stoppage.

On the 17th of May—the Norwegian Day of Independence—we set out about six o'clock in the afternoon in anything but good spirits, although the flags were hoisted on both our kayaks and were waving in the wind in honour of the day. We had arranged, for a change, that I with my sledge should lead the way; but my dogs, which had been accustomed to follow behind the others, would on no account fall in with this new arrangement. They could not understand why they should go first, and their attention was continually taken up with the other team. As I could not very well force them ahead by thrashing them, we gave up this experiment.

Soon afterwards Nansen thought he heard a noise like the blowing of whales in the large pool which we had in front of us, and which we had to cross. I had also heard the noise while busy in the camp in the morning, but I thought it was the ice-floes grinding against one another. But it really turned out to be a whale. We could now plainly see one gambolling on the surface of the water and then disappear. In the twinkling of an eye we were over by the kayaks, seized our guns and cartridges, and got out a harpoon and line. A whale would be worth while getting hold of, as that meant food for a long time. Nansen set off along the pool, fully armed and ready for the fray. In the meantime I was to look for a crossing. Nansen soon came back, however, without having had any success. "They were narwhals," he said, "and they were exceedingly shy."

We continued the journey till dinner-time, the wind blowing hard and the snow falling all the time. The dogs made but little progress, and we had great difficulty in getting along. When we had rested a couple of hours after dinner we thought of setting out again, but we found the weather thick and misty, so we closed our eyes again for another two hours. The weather was then fairly good, and we prepared to start. Nansen, however, first removed the guard-runners from his sledge, as he wanted to try the German-silver plates. They were excellent, and there could be no comparison between the speed which we made now and before.

We therefore took the guard-runners off my sledge as well, and from now the journey proceeded smoothly, so that we came to the end of our day's march in better spirits than when we started.

And now we set to work to celebrate the 17th, although it really was the 18th. We did it in the usual way—by feasting. On this occasion, however, we had a new concoction, which we at first called beer, but later on it went by the name of mead. It was made from frame food, stamina tablets, and lime-juice.

On the 20th of May we were weather-bound by a snowstorm. The day before we did a good day's march over fairly good ground—about twelve miles or more. We saw several large hummocks on the way, but as for land, it seemed that we should look in vain for it for some time to come. It was really pleasant to lie in the tent, while the storm was shaking it and the snow outside was piling up higher and higher by its side. We felt quite safe in the bag, and could let the storm rage as it liked; it did not inconvenience us in the least. It was difficult to say when we should get home. We had just been talking about our prospects. These continuous easterly and north-easterly winds were carrying us farther and farther west, so it might happen that we should not come across any land until we reached Spitzbergen, and we might not get there in time to get home this year. We must take our chance. During this last march we saw tracks of bears in two different places. This, perhaps, might be a sign of land.

On the 21st of May the bad weather still continued, but we could not wait for it to improve any longer, and so set out after having fed the dogs with half-rations of pemmican, leaving three guard-runners behind us. The weather soon became worse, with a strong northerly wind and drifting snow. We could not see very far before us, and, besides, the ice was heavy. Notwithstanding this we fought steadily on till noon, across fairly good ice, in which we met with no lanes. After dinner things grew worse, but still we kept at it. Presently it began to clear up and we came to long plains, across which we proceeded at a good pace. Nansen hoisted the sail on his sledge for the first time, and got along so well, that it was hardly necessary for the dogs to pull at all, but for all that they did not get along any the quicker. However, they did not stop so often, which was all the better for us who were following them. We managed to cross a large pool, although the ice was in violent motion, and that there were places here and there which were not so safe as they appeared to the eye. We were, however, well satisfied with the day's work; it began badly, but finished up well, and we believed that we had now left the eighty-third degree behind us.

# CHAPTER XIX

*More Ridges and Lanes—The First Bird and Seal—
Whitsuntide—Fish—Still no Land—Short Commons
—The First Ferry—A Lucky Shot*

THE 23rd of May was a day of toil and trouble. The number of lanes was terrible, and they could not well have been worse. We had not experienced anything like it before, and neither, I suppose, has anybody else.

Before starting, Nansen set out to reconnoitre along the broad lane which we had seen when we encamped the previous evening. He was away for three hours. In the meantime I mended the tent, which was beginning to get rather the worse for wear. The temperature was now about 10°, so it was not difficult to do some sewing. Nansen proceeded eastwards along the lane, but was unable to find any crossing. The lane branched off into two arms, and he thought we ought to be able to get across in some place or other.

We then proceeded eastwards, partly because we thought we had got too far to the west, and partly because we saw indications in the sky of much open water in that direction. Well, the result was that we did not meet with and cross one lane only, but something like twenty. Such a confusion of lanes and loose ice we had never seen; one minute we wound our way in one direction, and the next minute in another, after having with great trouble reconnoitred and looked for a crossing.

JOHANSEN HAULING THE SLEIGE OVER THE PACK-ICE.

We also passed a number of ridges, the ice being all the time in a violent motion. We were often deceived by the snow-slush which covered some of the pools and lanes, as it appeared like a fine solid sheet of ice to the eye.

The pressure was at its worst in one particular place, just where we were going to cross the ridges; these grew higher and higher, and large blocks began tumbling down from the sides, when suddenly the pressure stopped, and all became quiet. We cleared away the worst of the ice and made haste to get the sledges over, but no sooner was this safely accomplished than the pressure began again. It often happened when we had found a place for crossing that it was destroyed by the time we came up with the sledges, for we took some time, of course, no matter how much we hurried on.

We had, therefore, to set to work and find a new crossing. For fourteen hours we had been wending our way through this maze of lanes, when we at last got over the last lane and the last ridges, and saw a fine plain before us; we rested for a while before proceeding over the even ice, which was a pleasant change, until at length we again came across a lane, just as the weather was growing thicker and thicker. We were now compelled to encamp, so we followed the lane for some distance until we found a suitable place. How grand our food tasted that evening!

A meridian altitude, which we took, showed that we were in 82° 52′ north latitude. We were glad to find that we were so far south, but it was strange that we had not seen any sign of land. This, of course, was our chief concern.

Next day we covered about twelve miles, as far as we could make out; during the first eight hours we had to contend with lanes, but later on things improved. We used sail on the first sledge, thus utilising the strong north wind. Our longitude was now 61° 27' east. We were pleasantly surprised to find this, as we believed we were much further to the west, and were afraid that we might drift past Cape Fligely, for which reason our course had of late been shaped a good deal to the east. Now we were steering due south. We had the misfortune to get our tent torn a great deal, so that I had a regular job in mending it again.

On the 27th of May we were in 82° 29' north latitude. We now took it for granted that we must be a good deal east of land, otherwise we ought certainly to be in sight of it now, especially as we thought we were south of Petermann's Land.

We could not possibly be west of land; in that case we should be about 10° wrong in our observations, which was hardly credible. We were, however, presuming that we were east of land, and were therefore steering in a south-westerly direction. Time would show if we were right, but at present we were really in the dark. We examined our maps, and speculated backwards and forwards about our whereabouts. There was one thing we noticed, during our marches and when encamping, for the last few days—namely, that there was no freshwater ice to be found anywhere; all the ice we passed was salt-water ice a winter old. There must, we knew, be open water where that ice came from.

During the last days of May we went through the same toil and trouble, our progress being greatly impeded by lanes and ridges. On the 28th Nansen saw a fulmar (*Procellaria glacialis*) hovering about above one of the kayaks. It seemed to want to share the remains of "Kvik" with the dogs. Next day we saw several narwhals in a lane, a seal on the ice, and a black guillemot circling round us. These appearances of animal life were a delightful sight to us; they revived us and induced us to believe that land must be near.

The last day of May, and still no land; we only saw clouds on the horizon, and everywhere around us the eternal ice-fields which we had now been gazing at for nearly two long years. At times the sight made us quite depressed. Time seemed to drag so heavily so long as there was no sign of land; and then what sort of land would it be? A desert, cheerless, ice-bound coast in the far north, where no human being could desire to live; it was for this land that we were now and had for long been wearying. Day after day went by, and yet we never seemed to reach it. But we must get there some time, and then we hoped we should be safe; but it must come soon, for the number of our dogs was diminishing at a terrible rate. On the 30th we killed "Pan," who formerly used to pull for three dogs, but had now become a shadow; and "Kvik," who at last took to eating her canvas harness, had also to meet her fate. Nansen was quite out of sorts on the evening when "Kvik" was killed. She was the only one of our dogs who had been in Norway. Nansen had had her in his own house, where she was a great favourite. I took her quietly away, and had killed her before he was aware of it.

Our marches, as well as the times for resting, were now much shorter. We were trying to get a regular amount of work and rest into each day, so that one should not encroach upon the other. The dogs were oftener fed, as we thought that by so doing we should be able to reach land the sooner.

We no longer took our midday meals and rests in the sleeping-bag; we placed a sail on the snow and sat down on it to eat some bread and butter. We found the fresh tracks of three bears at the foot of a hummock; they led to a lane, but we were not prepared to follow them up. We were now in 82° 21' north latitude, which was rather satisfactory. An unpleasant, strong, southerly wind was now blowing and shaking the tent, although we were in the lee of a group of hummocks. Among these we found some fresh-water ice. On the other side we had a view of an open lane—quite a picturesque spot, considering that we were in the midst of the polar ice. To the east we had the "leaning tower of Pisa," an unusually large ice-floe, which had been pressed on end into an oblique position.

On the 1st of June we crossed a lane on a loose ice-floe, which every moment threatened to capsize, as smaller floes were getting under it, and the whole lane was in violent motion. No sooner had we hurriedly managed to get across with the dogs and sledges than the floe broke in pieces, and made any further crossing impossible.

When the weather was clear and bright it was a fine sight to see the coal-black lanes running away between the unusually white masses of ice, while the ridges and hummocks glistened in azure blue among them.

In vain does the eye attempt to pierce the bottom along the wall of ice. There are immense masses down there, and it is no wonder that everything they get into their embrace is broken and ground to pieces when the current and the wind crush them against one another.

For seven days in the beginning of June we were obliged to remain on an island of ice surrounded by lanes on all sides. We set to work to repair our kayaks, taking off the canvas covers and mending them, and relashing and splinting the frames, which had fared badly over all the bad ice which we had encountered. All this took time, but it had to be done now—we should have to face the lanes and bid them defiance. We would now, of course, prefer to get as much open water as possible, so that we might continue our journey in our kayaks, which would be easier for us than the toil and trouble which we had hitherto had.

On Sunday, the 2nd of June, I find the following entry in my diary:—

"This is Whit Sunday! To us, however, it is just like any other day; Sunday and Monday are just alike. This Whitsuntide, alas! we cannot rejoice in the summer, 'with all its wealth of foliage and flowers.' But we shall be glad to see it all again when we get home to those we hold dear—yes, glad beyond all compare."

It was most depressing to be compelled to remain here, unable to get on, and still more depressing to think of the long way we had still to travel before we could reach Spitzbergen, there to begin our search for some ship to carry us home. It was terribly depressing on a day like this, when, in my thoughts, I saw them all at home enjoying themselves in the lovely summer weather and revelling in the beauties of nature. It was at such moments that our imprisonment on the ice seemed most dreadful; but—

> "Though the night seem never so long,
> Morning oft may break with song."

And so, no doubt, it would to me, also, long and dark though the night has been. Yes, welcome should'st thou be, thou blessed, glorious morn!

During the succeeding days we had a bad time of it, and things began to look more and more serious. Our rations were being daily reduced, and we had to be most sparing with our fuel. The dogs were getting thinner and weaker, the sledges with their loads were still heavy, the ice became worse and worse, and the days passed by, but no land appeared. But still we must push on. Although we had both a good stock of patience, it had been put severely to the test on more than one occasion.

I think my readers will best understand what we

had to go through if I quote a portion of my diary at this time:—

"*Thursday, June* 11.—We have just partaken of our rations of aleuronate bread, butter and chocolate, and are ready for our day's march. It is not an easy matter to keep up one's spirits as one should do situated as we are just now. It will soon be impossible for us to proceed any further. The snow is melting and is soft all through; we are, in fact, wading through a sea of slush, and the poor dogs, of whom only five now remain, sink deeply through it at every step.

"We shall soon have nothing but water to walk in. Progress is rendered more difficult than ever by the innumerable lanes and the bad state of the ice. We do not know where we are. The land which we have been steering for so long we have almost given up all hopes of finding. It is the open sea which we now long for, but it is far away, and it will be difficult enough to reach Spitzbergen across it. We shall have to depend upon our guns for subsistence. At times we cannot help feeling disheartened. It was at one such moment yesterday that Nansen said, 'Just fancy what it will be to be able to rest our limbs and say, "It is all over, there is nothing more to be done."'"

The day before we covered about three miles. After dinner, which consisted of three and a half ounces of pemmican and three and a half ounces of bread, the sun appeared at times between fantastic clouds, dark or almost black in hue, while others near the horizon were quite light. The ice-fields were white as the driven snow, the water in the lanes was a deep black, and the horizon to the south was yellow and red, while dark, cumulous clouds were continuously drifting up from E.S.E., darkening the sun from time to time. This was a wonderfully beautiful sight, which we greatly enjoyed, and which revived our spirits.

Nansen found a small dead fish (*Gadus polaris*) in a narrow lane. If we could get fish we should be in no danger; at night, therefore, we set a line in the lane close by, with the fish as bait. We did not, however, catch any fish.

Sometimes we had to make bridges of ice-blocks which, with the aid of bamboo-poles, we floated into their place; and we had often to take leaps, of which no acrobat need have been ashamed, from one floe to another.

Before we broke up our encampment on June 14th, Nansen took a single altitude, and afterward a longitude observation. Of late we had very seldom seen the sun. The weather was as nasty as it could be, and our prospects were no better. The observations showed 57° east longitude, and 82° 23′ north latitude. We had consequently drifted 4° westwards since the last observation. I did not know whether this was for good or ill; it might mean that we were west of land, for our watches could scarcely have been so incorrect as not to justify us in expecting to see land now, even if we assumed that we were a good deal to the east.

If we were to the west of land, there would not be any great prospect of finding it soon. We should then have to face this interminable drift-ice. And if so, what about food? Where was it to come from? Hitherto we had not succeeded in finding much. If things did not improve, our outlook would be bad enough. If we were really east of land—which, perhaps, was now more improbable—it could not be far off, and then we should be able to procure food. The fact that we had drifted to the north was certainly a sad business to us.

Our marches were now pursued in the following manner: Nansen went on for some distance in front to find a way, while I followed behind with both sledges, one behind the other, until I fell in with Nansen on his way back after having found a passage, when we each took our sledge. It often took both of us to get the sledges over the ridges or across the lanes and over the loose ice.

OUT RECONNOITRING.

Now that the ice was in as bad a state as it possibly could be, we made but slow progress. All our hope of reaching land rested on the prospect of meeting with "slack" ice with plenty of lanes running in a south-westerly direction, through which we might proceed towards land in our kayaks after having killed our last dog, whose flesh we must ourselves be prepared to eat.

We considered whether we should use only one kayak, making this larger with materials taken from the other, leaving behind everything which we could possibly do without, and then push on with all our might. The temperature was keeping just below freezing point.

It was during this march, while Nansen was away reconnoitring, that I killed "Lilleræven," who had fallen down in front of the sledge. "Storræven" kept up until the evening, when he, too, met his sad fate. Nansen made our suppers from his blood. Were I to say that I liked it, I should not be telling the truth; but it went down, and that was the main thing.

On Sunday, June 16th, there was no wind. The stillness of Sunday seemed to rest over the ice; for some time I had not felt as if it were Sunday, but to-day it seemed to be more like one. My mind was at rest and in a peaceful mood, and with a feeling of sadness I longed for a Sunday at home.

We had now made ourselves harness for pulling the sledges, and were obliged to use all our strength to get on at all.

On June 20th we were obliged to encamp near a lane and begin looking for game of some kind.

Nansen's kayak was launched on the water, and we saw some seals, but could not catch any. Nansen also tried to catch some small marine animals with the aid of the net we brought with us for this purpose, but we had no better success.

"We are practising starvation as best we can until our stomachs groan with pain. When this becomes intolerable, we take about two ounces of pemmican and the same quantity of bread. We have had only one meal in the course of two days and a half, and this consisted of two sea-gulls, which, confronted with our appetites, seemed to vanish like dew before the sun. On another occasion our meal consisted of two ounces of bread and just as much pemmican, and our next of two ounces of aleuronate bread and one ounce of butter. But now we are going to have a proper meal before we start again."

We set out again in the evening on the 20th, after having vainly made many attempts to shoot a seal. Nansen had been out reconnoitring and told me that some distance off there was a large pool, where we should have an opportunity of trying our kayaks. On the way there we came to the conclusion that, in order to make any real progress, we should have to put wooden grips under the kayaks, and take the loads which he had on the sledges into the kayaks, so that we might float the whole load across the lanes and pull the sledges up again on the other side, and so continue our journey without any loss of time. And we must also get rid of everything which we did not absolutely want.

Before reaching the pool we saw a seal in one of the cracks in the ice; Nansen fired, but missed it. As soon as we came to the pool we prepared for our first ferrying. The kayaks were placed side by side on the water and tightly bound together, with the ski stuck through the straps on the deck of the kayaks, while the sledges were put right across the kayaks, one forward and one aft. The dogs went on board readily enough and lay down quietly, just as if they had been accustomed to this mode of transport all their lives. We got the pumps ready and, with the guns between our knees, we set off and began paddling across the pool. Here we were, with all our worldly belongings, at the mercy of the glittering waves. Our gipsy-like turn-out was certainly a curious sight, but to us it was a welcome change in our mode of travelling. We had to use the pumps frequently, my kayak especially being very leaky. As soon as we came to the other side of the pool Nansen jumped upon the ice with his camera and took some shots at our floating conveyance, while my kayak was gradually being filled with water and drifting away from the ice. All of a sudden we heard a great splash in the water behind us.

"What's that?" I shouted.

"A seal," replied Nansen, and began pulling the sledge ashore which was lying aft on my kayak, whereby the water rushed in and filled it right up to the gunwale, where the cover had not yet been sewn together. It was no use pumping, I was simply sitting in water. Another splash, and up came the big, shining head of a seal; it struck a couple of blows with its flappers against the edge of the ice and then dived under the water again. We did not think we should see it any more, but I took the harpoon which was lying on my kayak and threw it across to Nansen, in case he should want it. In the meantime the water rose more and more in my kayak, and something would have to be done to get it on to the ice at once. There was another splash, and the head of the seal again appeared, close to the edge of the ice. I quickly seized my gun and fired at the seal just as it was disappearing under the ice. It made one final splash, and then lay floating in the water, which was coloured red by the blood flowing from its shattered head. Nansen came running like the wind to the place with the harpoon and threw it into the seal. The harpoon was small and slight, so Nansen thought it best to plunge his knife into the seal's neck in order to make sure of it.

Now followed an exciting scene. Both the kayaks began to drift away, mine being kept afloat by the other, while the sledge which we had been trying to land was half-way under the water.

The dogs now began to feel uneasy, and no wonder. I sat fixed in the kayak and dared not let go the sledge, nor could I venture to stand up and attempt to pull it up on to the kayak.

Over by the edge of the ice lay Nansen, not daring to let the seal go, for it meant abundance of food and fuel to us, who were so sadly in want of it.

Finding that the seal kept afloat, he came rushing up just in the nick of time to save me and my sinking flotilla. I and the dogs were safely got ashore, and the sledges with my kayak were dragged up on to the ice while the other was left to itself, whereupon we both ran off to secure our precious prize; but it was no easy task for two men to pull a big, fat seal out of the water. While we were busy with this, our attention was again turned to our other effects, as we noticed Nansen's kayak adrift some distance from us, while our cooking apparatus was having a trip of its own, floating away lightly, high out of the water. After having rescued our property, we returned to the seal, which we finally succeeded in pulling out of the water, after having fastened a rope to it by its lower jaw.

There it lay on the ice at our feet, a sight which gladdened our hearts, as there was now no danger that we should starve to death for the present; now we should have food for a long time, not to mention fuel, and we could now rest and wait for the ice to loosen still more.

There was, however, one important matter to be considered. Had the ammunition, which lay in my kayak, been damaged by the water? And the matches? Bread and pemmican there were also in the kayak. We were very anxious about the ammunition, as we spread the wet cartridges out on our sleeping-bag. Nansen tried one of the shot-cartridges on a couple of Arctic gulls, which appeared on the scene to share in our catch, and it went off all right. The matches were also found to be fit for use, our principal stock having been kept in hermetically-sealed tin boxes.

Nansen then started to cut up the seal, collecting the blood that was still left in it. I set to work to find a place for our tent, to collect all our things, which lay spread about on the ice, and to bring them to the tent, where I then unpacked all the wet things.

In the meantime, Nansen had cut up our find nicely, and the flesh and skin, with a mass of blubber, lay temptingly in the pure, white snow. It was all brought to our camp, where we began preparing a really square meal.

We had made up our minds, just before we caught the seal, to lie for the coming night in our blankets only, to see whether we could do without the sleeping-bag; but we used both the blankets and the bag after all, and settled down first to eat and next to sleep. The pot was filled with the flesh of the seal, which tasted remarkably fine, along with the raw blubber. It was now more than twenty-four hours since we had had anything to eat.

Thus all our anxiety with regard to food was at an end for some time to come. We might, perhaps, soon become tired of living only upon seal's flesh for a month, but it could not be helped; the main thing was that it was food. The wind, which had now shifted right about, was blowing freshly from the north, and I took a walk to look at our surroundings.

The flesh, the blubber, and the skin of the seal lay round about our tent, while the gulls at times cruised about over it. Some distance away stood the sledge, with the three dogs at a respectful distance from the flesh. Poor creatures! they vomited after having been fed with the intestines of the seal.

The open water in the pool, where we intended fishing and hunting, became considerably reduced in extent by a pressure in the ice, though it was still of quite a respectable size. Two fish-hooks which I had set with blubber as bait for the sea-gulls had been completely cleaned. The gulls were too clever to swallow the hook, and we did not care to shoot them now that we had got out of all our troubles about food.

# CHAPTER XX

"*Longing Camp*"—*St. John's Eve Illuminations—Three Bears—A Long Sleep—The White Cloud-bank—Land!—In a Bear's Clutches*

WE remained for a whole month on the same spot where we had shot the seal; we called it "Longing Camp." And the spot was well named. It tried our patience to the utmost, as we lay there waiting for the snow to melt and make the ice passable, and enable us to proceed towards the unknown, unseen land which we felt could not be far off. It was strange, however, that we should not see it. I thought of Welhaven's poem:—

> "Bright, 'mid the skerries of the western sea,
> An island rides upon the wave. Yet none
> May know its beauty; for if mortal ship
> By chance should drift too near th' enchanted shore,
> A curtain of dark mist enshrouds the isle.
> No eye can see its brightness, and no foot
> May leave its prints upon the golden fields.
> 'Tis best in fancy he who dwells ashore
> May picture in the longings of his dreams,
> This fairy jewel of the western sea."

And I could not help laughing when I thought of the difference between the fairyland which the dweller on the shore, according to the poet, was longing for, and the land we were yearning for. Still, I think that we did not yield to him in the sincerity of our yearnings, although they were not directed to any fairyland.

During this time we lived on the flesh of the seal, which we boiled or fried over our train-oil lamps. Nansen had been among the Eskimos in Greenland, and had had great experience in living as a wild man, by which we greatly profited both now and later on. The lamp consisted only of a small bowl made out of a plate of German silver which we had brought with us to repair the mountings of the sledge-runners, and for wicks we used some of the canvas of which our provision bags were made, or the soft, antiseptic bandages, which we had in our "medical-bag," and for which we could scarcely have found any better application. Several of the doctor's things came to be used in quite a different and much more pleasant manner than was originally intended; thus some plaster, intended for use in the event of a collar-bone being broken, came in most usefully, for we discovered that the adhesive matter with which it was coated was a most excellent putty for making the seams in the kayak covers watertight. For this purpose we also used some water-colours which Nansen had with him, and which we scraped into fine shavings and made into a kind of putty with train-oil.

The kayaks were thoroughly overhauled and repaired while we were in "Longing Camp"; we made some paint for them out of soot and train-oil and daubed it well into the canvas with a brush made of bear's hair.

One day we resolved to treat ourselves to pancakes made from seal blood for supper. Nansen began frying them over a splendid fire, the flame of which was produced by several wicks; everything went all right until he was engaged on the last pancake but one, when the heat became alarmingly great, as the pieces of blubber which were put in the bowl to provide oil for the wicks caught fire while melting. The tent being crowded with boxes and utensils, it was not an easy thing to put out the fire, so Nansen took a handful of snow from the floor of the tent and threw it into the flaming bowl, expecting to put out the fire with it, but apparently it did not like such treatment, for the flame leaped high up into the air against the sides of the tent and set fire to one part of it; we jumped out of the bag and made a rush for the opening of the tent, bursting off the buttons on our way through it, and so got out into the open air. The fire, which had confined itself to one corner of the tent and burned a hole through it, was soon out, and we had to use one of our sails to patch it.

This happened on St. John's Eve, and so far the conflagration was quite opportune[1] as our contribution towards the usual festivities on Midsummer's Eve. We swept up the floor of our tent and bestrewed it, not with fresh juniper or birch leaves—of which there is rather a scarcity in those parts—but with snow, which is plentiful there even in the midst of the summer.

We found that, in spite of the wind having been westerly and south-westerly of late, we had drifted not a little to the south, as the meridian observations on the 22nd of June showed that we were in 82° 4' north latitude; nor had we drifted eastwards, as the longitude was 57° 48'.

One day (the 25th) I lay asleep barelegged and in my shirt-sleeves on the top of the sleeping-bag, with my legs sticking outside the tent, the weather being so fine and warm—the best, in fact, that we had hitherto had. I was suddenly awakened by Nansen calling out, "Johansen, here is more seal-steak for us." He had been out and had shot a young seal.

On the 28th we were in 82° north latitude.

---

[1] In Norway it is an old custom to light bonfires on the hills on St. John's Eve.

We must now have been drifting towards land, for this strong wind would most certainly force the ice to drift much more rapidly if there were not something to keep the ice back. The temperature was just above freezing point; it was raining pretty constantly, sometimes we had wet snow and hail.

The ground was now becoming too wet to lie on; we had to put our ski and staffs under the sleeping-bag to keep some of the wet off; sometimes the water dripped from the sides of the tent right into the bag, and we had to use our drinking cups to ladle the water out; but for all this, we preferred it to the fearful cold we had had.

The north wind blew, on this day, at the rate of six to seven metres in the second, but notwithstanding this I went outside the tent and made grips for the kayaks. It was an unfortunate day. I broke the saw in my knife, likewise a screw-driver, and our last quicksilver thermometer; but I was in the best of spirits for all that, probably because I was looking forward to my supper, and we were going to have dessert that night.

The month of June went out with fine, bright weather; the air was still and warm, but it was seldom quite clear. We preferred the warm mist, however, for then the snow melted most rapidly, and we were able to get nearer to our goal.

We could now lie on the top of the sleeping-bag, where we made notes. With the aperture to the tent quite open, while a gust of wind moved its sides from time to time, throwing shadows across my note-book, I imagined myself at home under the pines and birches. It is wonderful what things one's imagination can conjure up.

We now had our meals twice a day: in the morning boiled seal's flesh and soup, and in the evening seal's flesh fried in train-oil. The blubber we generally ate raw. Our appearance had changed considerably; we were quite black with the smoke and soot of the train-oil, and we scarcely recognised ourselves when we saw ourselves one day in the artificial horizon, which we used for a mirror.

On July 3rd we killed "Haren," which was the only event of any importance. Poor creature, I thought him the best of all the dogs! How he worked from first to last, even after his back had become a little crooked! It was not a pleasant task to cut his throat, especially as I could not finish him so quickly as I had wished; but he was so thin and skinny that it was difficult to find the arteries at once. Now we had only "Suggen" and "Caiaphas" left of the twenty-eight dogs.

Nansen tried to manufacture some paint with ground bone-dust, but it was too coarse, and with our appliances it would have taken a year to grind it as fine as it should have been. The temperature was just below freezing point, while the wind was westerly.

On July 5th the weather was bad, with sleet and easterly wind, which carried us westwards. The wind shook our tent, so that the damp which collected on the inside dripped down upon our good friend, the sleeping-bag, in which we sat, while waiting for supper, which invariably consisted of fried seal's flesh.

At such time on this particular day, we were both very quiet, and when we did talk about anything, it was of course mostly about our return home, and the treat it would be to get there. We also talked about wintering on Spitzbergen or Franz Josef Land, and how pleasant it would be if we could fall in with the Englishmen on Franz Josef Land. We thought they were sure to be there then, as they were to start the year after we left. And then the problem constantly arose—what was our exact position?

Nansen now painted our kayaks with a kind of soot-paint which he made, and I cut up some seal's flesh in strips and hung them up to dry. I also began to weigh the remainder of our provisions; of pemmican we had twenty-two pounds, and of fish-meal seventeen and a half.

When the evening approached, Nansen used to fetch flesh and blubber from our stores, and I fresh and salt water. I also fed our two dogs, put things straight in the tent, took the temperature, wind, etc., after which we both crept into the tent and waited till our food was ready. On those evenings when we had dessert, which consisted of one spoonful of "vril food," half an ounce of butter, and one ounce of bread, we seemed to enjoy our existence most. Then when the night set in, we would forget all about "Longing Camp," and in our dreams find ourselves at home.

Next day the weather was excellent; the rain came pouring down steadily the whole day and made short work of the snow; we only wished the rain would keep at it like this every day for some time to come. The weather being so favourable, we thought we would treat ourselves to something nice, as a change after our meat diet, and Nansen lit up and began making some chocolate. I had had one cup, and Nansen, having accidentally upset his, was waiting for another to be ready, when we suddenly heard the dogs barking in an unusual manner and guessed at once that something out of the common was in the air. We rushed out of the tent, Nansen first and I after him. A huge bear was standing sniffing at "Caiaphas." Nansen seized the gun, which was standing at the entrance of the tent, and fired, but the shot could not have struck a vital part, for the bear at once took to his heels, leaving traces of blood behind. Nansen fired another shot at it, this time also without result. I now got hold of my gun, and both of us set off after the bear. Suddenly we saw

IN "LONGING CAMP."

the heads of two cubs looking over the ridge of a hummock. The hunt now began in earnest; the ground was in a terrible state, covered as it was with deep snow, lanes and hummocks. Now and then we gained on the bears, but we wanted to be well within range, as we had not many cartridges with us; out of mine Nansen had two. We then came to a point where they had turned off in a different direction. Nansen followed their tracks, while I made a circuit, thinking that we might thus succeed in approaching the bears from opposite sides; but after I had proceeded some distance in the deep snow I was stopped by a lane, and Nansen and the bears got right away from me. This was most irritating, but the spirit of the chase was upon me, and I flew across some floes, only just sufficiently large to save me from a cold bath. I had not gone far on the other side when I heard a shot fired, followed immediately by another. Shortly afterwards, when I got up with Nansen, I found the three bears lying among some nasty drift-ice close to a lane, one of the cubs being quite dead, while the mother and the other cub still showed signs of life, although they were bleeding profusely. The mother was finished off with a bullet, and the cub received a shower of shot in the head.

We cut up the bears, and then returned to the camp by an easier way than we had come. The lamp had gone out and the chocolate was now cold, but Nansen lit up again and we finished our interrupted meal.

We then took both the dogs and a sledge and fetched one of the cubs. "Suggen" also seemed now to be done up; he was no longer able to walk, and we had to put him on the sledge. At this he began howling and making a terrible noise, for he was evidently highly indignant at this treatment. I think we made a mistake in killing "Haren" and letting "Suggen" live.

We had now three splendid bearskins to lie upon

instead of the bag, which had now become hairless, and through which we were beginning to feel the sharp edges of the ski.

Next evening we lay very comfortably indeed, and for supper we had pancakes made with blood and whortleberry jam.

This was the last of the whortleberries, which, by this time, had become pretty well soaked through with both salt and fresh water. We lay down to sleep at eight o'clock in the evening, and when we woke up we found it was six o'clock. We thought, of course, that it was six o'clock in the morning, but just then the sun suddenly burst forth, and, appearing as it did in the northern sky, we began reflecting and soon discovered that it was six o'clock in the evening. This you may call sound sleeping, if you like, particularly when it is remembered that our bed was upon the ice.

The dogs were now given as much food as they could eat, and they seemed to thrive well on the nourishing bear's flesh; we also ate a great quantity of it ourselves, both morning and evening. Any housewife would pray Heaven to preserve her from having guests like ourselves, if she could but see the meals which we managed to get through; but then, of course, there was a considerable interval between each meal, generally twelve to fourteen hours.

In clear weather we were always on the look-out for land from the "observatory hummock." We noticed that to the south a white bank of clouds always kept over the same spot, and we could not but think that it must be standing over the land.

Later on, however, it turned out that it was not clouds, but land itself, at which we had been gazing; the bank of white clouds was really nothing else but the inland ice on one of the islands of Franz Josef Land.

One day, when out in my kayak to try if it was watertight, I found a dead fish in the water. It was as long as a herring, but thin and slender, with a long snout and fine scales, something like a garfish. But neither Nansen nor I could tell what sort of fish it was.

It was getting to be time for us to continue our journey, for the state of the ice had now considerably improved. We got rid of everything we could possibly do without, such as a lot of little things which separately did not weigh anything to speak of, but which collectively amounted to a great deal—plaster of Paris and other kinds of bandages, cotton, the reserve cock for the paraffin can, the reserve burner for the "Primus," various articles of clothing, Lapp shoes, a photographic lantern, a sailmaker's glove, some of the contents of the tool and sewing bags, a water flask, etc., etc. The sledges had been lightened of some of the extra supports, the kayaks thoroughly overhauled and caulked, the boat-grips being provided with cushions made of foot-bandages and bearskin. The dogs were in good trim and high spirited; "Caiaphas" was as broad across the back as a barn-door. We ourselves were only too eager to see the last of this place, which had kept us back so long and had taught us what patience meant.

We left the sleeping-bag behind, as we intended to sleep in the kayaks, but after trying the latter we had to give it up. We then made a bag of our two blankets, which turned out to be quite sufficient.

On the 22nd of July we packed up and said good-bye to "Longing Camp." After having divided our baggage into two heaps and drawn lots for them, we started off. We had lashed some bamboo rods to the sledges to serve as shafts in addition to the drag-rope fastened to our harness.

We took with us some dried meat and about sixteen

pounds of blubber. Everything went satisfactorily—in fact, better than we expected. Although the ice was in as bad a state as it could be, we managed to get along with our sledges all the way with one dog to each.

Nor was it necessary to use our ski all the time; sometimes we came across a belt of snow, when we could dispense with them and walk.

DR. NANSEN GETTING HIS GUN TO RESCUE JOHANSEN FROM A BEAR.

Altogether we were well satisfied with our first day on the "homeward journey," and the way in which we had now arranged matters.

On Wednesday, the 24th of July, I find the following entry in my diary: "At last the longed-for event has happened! We have sighted land, and apparently it is only a couple of days' journey distant. It was, however, a most difficult land to sight, for it was covered with ice, just like that on which we are travelling. It was a black, oblique stripe on the horizon, evidently composed of bare rock, which enabled us to discover it. I saw this stripe yesterday about noon from the top of a hummock, while Nansen was out reconnoitring, but I did not think it was anything but one of the usual black streaks on the ice caused by mud, of which we have lately seen a good many. I mentioned the matter to Nansen, however, and towards evening he saw the same oblique stripe from the top of a ridge, and after having taken the glass to examine it more closely, he exclaimed, 'Yes, you must have a look at it, too; it is certainly land!' And sure enough the black stripes were rock, that we could plainly discern—rock projecting through the ice-sheet with which the land was covered. To the east of the two smaller black stripes we saw that the horizon was bounded by ice—probably inland ice—of the same colour as that we are travelling over, but arched in form and sharp in outline, with a little irregularity on the top. It was the same outline which I noticed from the observatory hummock at 'Longing Camp,' and which I had thought to be the clouds lying over the land.

"Later in the evening I also noticed to the west of the black stripes a similar mass on the horizon, but much smaller, and this too, I think, must be land." This, we discovered later, must have been Crown Prince Rudolf's Land.

"So the blessed land for which we have been looking so long is there at last! We shall soon be able to say farewell to this drift-ice we have had so long beneath our feet. We shall be able to push forward on the channels near the shore, or along the shore-ice to Spitzbergen, and thence to our 'promised land.'

"We are delighted; a new chapter in our adventures is now opening. It is a pity that we remained a month in 'Longing Camp' with land, so to speak, next door to us. But what else could we have done? We could not make any progress, and we could not see any land! There was nothing for us to do but to wait for better times, which have at last arrived. Our prospects are now bright, although we do not know what land this is. Now we can understand why we always remained on the same spot in spite of the wind, and why we saw so many 'little auks' passing to and fro some time ago.

"We are making fairly good progress, in spite of the general bad state of the ice. It is gradually being ground to pieces against the land by the continuous northerly wind. It is a great advantage to us not to be obliged to use our ski; we can proceed on foot, pulling the sledges behind us. When we came to lanes, we simply waded right into the water and up on the other side. Once or twice we let loose the dogs during these crossings. 'Suggen' seized upon the opportunity to run away, and followed up the old track to 'Longing Camp,' remembering, no doubt, all the fine bear's flesh which we had left behind there. I had to use my legs properly to catch him again, as he set off at full speed whenever I gained upon him; but he, poor fellow, was not quite himself and could not get clear away.

"Last night we celebrated our safe arrival within sight of land in grand style. For dinner we had lobscouse, made from dried bear's flesh, bear's tongue, pemmican, and dried potatoes, and for dessert breadcrumbs fried in bear's fat and 'vril food,' finishing up with a piece of chocolate.

"Everything seems now to smile upon us; we have sighted land, and hope to reach it in a couple of days, so near does it appear to be. The idea of wintering up here, which of late has more and more forced itself upon us, must now give way to thoughts of an early return home. Of this we now feel more sure, seeing that we have the land before us—a land which, although it is doubtless as barren as can be, is still land all the same."

At this time we saw several specimens of the rare Ross's gull. Lightly and gracefully, silently beating their wings, they came flying about us, and were not at all afraid. They floated right over our heads, so that we could see the pink colour of their breasts. Perhaps this is the country where this mysterious bird lays its eggs?

"We are not likely to reach land to-morrow, but certainly the next day," we said to one another, as we began our march towards land. Alas! it took fourteen days before we had worked our way up to the wall of the glacier on the shore.

This was partly due to the land being farther away than we thought it to be, and partly to the ice being in such a state that it was almost an acrobatic feat for a person to get on by himself; how much more difficult, then, when encumbered with a sledge and kayak! At times the lanes and pools were filled with small floes, too small to carry a man, but large enough to prevent us using our kayaks. We had then to jump from floe to floe and pull the sledges and the kayaks across after us by a rope. Our gymnastic skill, indeed, stood us in very good stead. And, most unfortunately for us, the ice was in motion and drifting away from the shore, while we were making our way across it towards land. When we encamped in the evening we could see that the blue wall of the distant glacier was nearer to us than when we began our march in the morning. On turning out next morning it was again farther off; and to make matters worse, Nansen was taken ill with pains in his back, probably lumbago, and was almost helpless for some days. He was only just able to limp along with the aid of sticks after the caravan, which, however, did not make much progress, as I had to see to the sledges alone through this abominable ice. It was a sad job to have to help Nansen off and on with his clothes and "komager" evening and morning; he suffered great pain, but he did not complain, and dragged himself on as best he could instead of giving in. Fortunately he got better at the end of three days, but this experience was sufficient to make us understand what it would come to if one of us should break a limb or fall ill in real earnest.

On Wednesday, the 31st of July, I wrote in my diary: "Our progress yesterday was much the same as on the two preceding days. Nansen still suffers in his back, so I have to get over all our obstacles all by myself. Yesterday the weather was cold and bitter, the barometer standing at 723 mm. A strong south-westerly wind was blowing, accompanied now and then by snow squalls, so that, in spite of our hard work in getting along, we had to dress as if it were the middle of winter. But we should not have minded all this if only the wind had not altogether destroyed our chances of getting on; it had loosened the ice all round the lanes, so that these were completely filled with slush and small pieces of ice, which is the worst hindrance we can have. We have not noticed such a movement in the ice before. When, after much reconnoitring, I had found a way, it was generally destroyed by the time I got back to it. We had then to make fresh attempts, taking short stretches at a time. When, in addition to this, I say that Nansen is quite helpless, it would seem that one could hardly have more difficulties to contend with than we have already.

"But, notwithstanding all this, we saw we had really made progress when we encamped last night; the edge of the distant blue ice by the land is now much nearer—so near that we hope to reach it to-day in spite of all hindrances. We have now no more food for the dogs; I shot a couple of ivory gulls for them yesterday. 'Suggen' ate his with evident relish, but 'Caiaphas' does not like the flesh of the birds. Yesterday we also saw some of Ross's gulls. The dogs will not cross the lanes by themselves if they are ever so narrow, and they often fall in.

"Last night we felt the cold severely in our thin blankets, and we are longing more than ever for the time when our life up here will come to an end. That is still far off, however, so we must have patience. With this we may conquer everything, and we shall be certain to reach home."

On the 2nd of August we were in 81° 36' north latitude. We had then got the north point of the land due west of us, and had consequently drifted eastwards. We were in the same latitude as the land; this must have been from twenty to twenty-five miles distant when we first sighted it, but this distance is no small matter with such ice.

When we were unable to shoot birds for the dogs, we had to give them a small piece of blubber. 'Caiaphas' went several days without food; he could not eat gulls, although he was much interested in the shooting of them. One day he ran after a wounded fulmar across the flat ice, with sledge and kayak after him, but as for eating it—no, that was quite another matter. We heard the breakers now, but saw no sign of water except the indications in the sky. Nansen tried several times to shoot some seals in the lanes, but was unsuccessful.

On the 4th of August we passed over the worst

drift-ice we had ever seen or encountered, and consequently we did not get on very far, but our comfort was that we now saw that all our trouble would soon be at an end. On the 3rd of August we saw with the glass the open water in front of the edge of the glacier.

It was on this march that I just escaped being eaten by a bear. It happened in this way. On August 3rd when we set out the weather was very foggy, and presently it got worse and worse; the ice was impassable; it was all struggling up mountains and down valleys and through deep snow, with lanes, some wide open, others nearly closed, and still others full of the most impenetrable brash. Just as the fog was at its thickest and the ridges at their highest, we were stopped by a lane, which we prepared to ferry over. We generally did this in the following manner: we put both the sledges with the kayaks side by side close to the edge of the water, and placed our ski and staffs across them, the whole being securely lashed together. This floating arrangement was then ready to be launched on the water.

Nansen had just brought his sledge to the edge of the water and stood holding it, as the ice inclined down towards the water. My sledge and kayak were standing a little way back, and I went across to fetch it. I leant down to pick up the drag-rope, when I suddenly observed an animal just behind the kayak. I thought at first that it was "Suggen," but the next moment I discovered that it was not he, but a bear sitting in a crouching position ready to spring at me. Before I had time to get up from my stooping position, it was right upon me, pressing me backwards with its two legs down a slight incline to a fresh-water pool. The bear then dealt me a blow on the right cheek with one of its powerful fore paws, making the bones rattle in my head, but fortunately it did not stun me. I fell over on my back and there I lay between the bear's legs. "Get the gun," I shouted to Nansen, who was behind me, while at the same instant I saw the butt end of my own loaded gun sticking out of the kayak by my side, my fingers itching to get hold of it. . I saw the bear's jaws gaping just over my head, and the terrible teeth glistening. As I fell I had seized the brute's throat with one hand, and held on to it for dear life. The bear was somewhat taken aback at this. It could not be a seal, it must have thought, but some strange creature to which it was unaccustomed—and to this slight delay I no doubt owed my life. I had been waiting for Nansen to shoot, and I noticed the bear was looking in his direction. Thinking that Nansen was taking his time, I shouted to him as I lay in the bear's embrace, "Look sharp, or you'll be too late." The bear lifted one of its paws a little, and strode across me, giving "Suggen," who stood close by barking, and watching us, a blow which sent him sprawling and howling over the ice. "Caiaphas" was served in the same way. I had let go my hold of the bear's throat and, taking advantage of the bear's inattention, I wriggled myself away from between its paws. Getting on my legs I seized my gun, when Nansen fired two shots and the bear fell down dead beside the pool.

Nansen had, of course, made haste to my assistance, but when he saw me lying under the bear and went to get his gun, which was lying in its case on the top of the kayak, the sledge with the kayak slipped right out into the water. There I lay under the bear, and there stood Nansen, and out on the kayak lay the gun. His first thought was to throw himself into the water and to fire from over the kayak, but he soon gave up this idea, as he might just as likely hit me as the bear. He had then to begin and pull the whole concern up on to the ice again, which did not, of course, take up much time, but to me, situated as I was, it was an age. The bear fell down dead at the first charge, which happened to be small shot. In the hurry of the moment Nansen had cocked the shot-barrel, which was the nearest to him. To make sure of the bear he fired the other barrel containing the bullet into its head.

I bore no traces of the bear's embrace except some white streaks on one of my cheeks, which were quite black with the soot and smoke of "Longing Camp," and two small wounds in my right hand. Fortunately we could now afford to make merry over these trifles. No sooner had the bear fallen to the ground than I suddenly caught sight of two more bears, which were standing on their hind legs behind a ridge close by, and had been following the whole incident with great attention. They were two cubs about a year old, evidently waiting for their mother—the bear which had attacked me—to bring them food. I set off to shoot one of them, for the flesh of the cubs is better than that of the old bears; besides, my blood was on fire with excitement, but they took to their heels and I gave them up. While we were busy cutting the flesh off the bear—we did not give ourselves time to skin it—we saw the cubs again, and I started off in pursuit once more, but could not get within range of them. I fired a ball at one of them, however, and a terrible howl told us that it had taken effect, but not mortally, for they both ran off. We saw them again several times afterwards, but could not afford to waste any more shot on them. The blood was running down the sides of one of them, bellowing all the while like a bull. They went round about the spot where the mother's carcass lay, in a circle, and we heard the bellowing of one of the cubs a long time after we had left the spot.

The dogs were allowed to eat as much as they liked; they were both uninjured, "Caiaphas" having only got a scratch on his nose. We also had a good meal; we cut up thin slices of raw meat and placed them on the snow to cool, and then ate them with great relish. Bear's flesh was a welcome addition to our stock of provisions; we took both the hind legs with us as well as some of the inside fat, which would be useful as fuel.

It is, no doubt, a rare thing for an ice-bear to make straight for his enemy as this one did, that is to say, when it is a human being, for it is then generally very shy; but this one must have been ravenously hungry.

I took the claws of the paw with which the bear gave me the blow, and Nansen the claws of the other paw. We could not very well drag unnecessary things with us, but we thought we ought to have some memento of this incident about us.

On our journey, further on towards land, we saw numerous tracks of bears in all directions. Here, it seemed, were plenty of bears, but we did not now trouble ourselves about them. One of them had been right up to our tent while we were asleep.

## CHAPTER XXI

*Farewell to the Drift-ice—"Suggen" and "Caiaphas" must Die—Under Sail at Last—What Land is this? —Attacked by Walrus—The Fog Lifts—We Cut our Sledges Adrift—A Snowless Land—Drift-ice Again—Plenty of Bears and Walruses*

AT last, on Wednesday, the 7th of August, we reached the goal for which we had been striving; on the last night we slept on the shore-ice at the foot of the glacier which we had seen so long before us. It was no longer a delusion; we could now hear the thunder and the roar of the glacier itself.

To our great surprise and joy we found a great improvement in the state of the ice on the last stretch of our journey. It was much more even and there were hardly any lanes, and our day's march was as good as several of the previous days combined. We pushed on with all our might. The edge of the glacier gradually came nearer; soon we could see it from the ice without mounting any hummock, and at last we stood by the edge of the drift-ice, a large open channel with drifting floes lying between us and the glacier, which fell precipitately into the sea.

Nansen stood by the edge of the ice wiping the sweat off his brow and waving his hat at me, who followed a little behind; I waved my hat in return, and the first hurrah on the whole expedition now rang out clearly across the open water.

We looked back triumphantly at this drift-ice, which had tried our patience and our endurance for such a length of time. We rewarded ourselves with a piece of chocolate for this our last exertion.

And now we should have to depend upon the water for making progress. We tried to take a sledge on each kayak and proceed separately; but this we found impracticable, and had to lash the kayaks together as before. We could no longer take the dogs with us—ungrateful creatures that we human beings are! After these dogs had toiled for us and suffered such cold and hunger that it was a wonder they held together at all, we rewarded their fidelity and devotion with death now that we believed we could get back to a life of civilization amongst men again. It was a heartrending business to be obliged to kill them; but, unfortunately, it had to be done. In order to make it less painful to us, Nansen took my dog and I took his. Poor creatures, they followed us quite quietly as we went each our way behind a hummock, when two shots soon announced that "Caiaphas" and "Suggen" had ceased to exist. We had become quite fond of them, and could not kill them in the same way as the others, so we sacrificed a cartridge upon each of them.

We now said farewell to the drift-ice and set out in our kayaks. The weather had become somewhat foggy, but we had the wind right at our backs, so we rigged up our sails and could now sit at our ease and in comfort, while at a fairly good speed we were approaching the glacier, which we soon saw emerging out of the fog. It was a long time since noon, when we had had our last meal, so we had one in the kayak which, considering the hour, might have been called either breakfast or supper.

What a sudden change from our life on the drift-ice —to sit at ease and have our food while at the same time travelling onwards!

We could not land on the glacier, as the edge formed a solid wall of ice, about fifty feet high, in which we could clearly see the various strata. The current flowed in a westerly direction, the same as that in which we were journeying. So we steered westward, and at last found the floe on which we spent the night. In all probability

A PARTING LOOK AT THE BEAR WHICH NEARLY KILLED ME.

we drifted westward with it while we slept. There was great commotion in the ice around us.

August 7th was our first day at sea, and everything went excellently. In the morning we had to haul our kayaks and sledges over some floes, by which we had been surrounded, and which were continually grinding against us, giving us now and then a friendly push and preventing us from getting out into the open water, of which we could catch glimpses to the west of us in the thick fog. At intervals there came from the glacier great crashes like cannon-shots, occasioned by large masses of the glacier breaking loose and falling into the sea.

We settled down on a large floe near the edge of the ice to make paddles from a broken ski, which we lashed to our ski-staff, as the canvas blades we had brought with us turned out impracticable. We then set off again in our kayaks, lashed together as before, with our sledges across us, on the splendid open water. Unfortunately the sky was so overcast that we could not take any observation.

After having paddled along the wall of ice for some time, we had to shape our course towards the north, as we were met by the shore-ice; we were probably in a bay between the large glacier and the land with the black rocky mountains. Later on, when the fog lifted a little, we could see these, and before long we had them right in front of us.

There were plenty of seals about here to keep us from anxiety about food. We began our journey at six o'clock in the morning, and paddled on until the same hour in the evening, when it began to rain, whereupon we encamped on the shore-ice. The temperature was about the same as we had usually had of late—about freezing point.

The next morning we had again to haul the sledges and the kayaks over some ice which had collected in the course of the night in front of the shore-ice. After having got into open water we sailed before a north-westerly wind for six or seven hours at a fairly good pace.

It was wet work sailing in our kayaks; my clothes were still wet, and during the night of August 8th I felt the cold not a little; but we were getting on quickly, so we did not mind any bodily discomfort. The weather was again foggy, and we could see very little round about us, but at last it cleared up sufficiently for us to discern some fresh land just inside the edge of the ice along which we were sailing. This was a small island covered with ice and snow, like the two other islands we had just passed; and opposite this island, farther to S.S.W., we saw some other land which was much larger.

SAILING IN OUR KAYAKS.

Altogether we had thus four islands. It was this group to which Nansen later on gave the name of "Hvidtenland" (Whiteland).

We were still at a loss to know where we were, when, on August 8th, as we proceeded, the course became more and more southerly; and at times we steered due south in broad open waters as far as we could see. Perhaps we were off the west coast, and in that case we were pretty certain of reaching Spitzbergen in time to catch one of the whalers. If we were off the east coast we were probably in a deep large bay which cut into the country, and we should then have to proceed north again in order to get further homewards.

On the morning of the 9th we ascended the glacier on the small island where we had camped; the fog lifted sufficiently to enable us to take bearings of the islands we had hitherto seen. We had looked forward to a fine race on our ski down to the shore, but the incline was so slight and the state of the snow so bad that it did not go off well.

After having rigged up our kayaks we sailed away from the four islands in bright, sunny weather and with a fair wind across the sea, which, as far as we could see, was quite open. We were thoroughly comfortable in our craft. We made our dinner of cold boiled bear's flesh and three ounces of bread, while we were being swiftly carried along by the wind.

Towards evening we encountered some flat ice, which was in violent motion. The current then was evidently on the turn, and we had to take to the ice with our kayaks, lashed together as they were, the ice pressure beginning just behind us.

At noon we took an observation near our tent, and another while on our way across the ice. We hauled our sledges across a flat floe, on the other side of which we came to open water; but the current was by this time so strong that we found it best to remain and encamp where we were. Shortly afterwards the ice closed in upon us from the opposite direction and pressed against our floe, forming ridges here and there as it collided. The floes, however, were very large and flat, and we felt sure that they must have something to do with land. Yet to us there was something mysterious about it—open water and flat fjord-ice, but no land.

The next day, after proceeding some distance over flat ice, we came to open water which extended in a southerly and south-westerly direction. In one place we saw a herd of walruses lying on the ice, but we did not trouble ourselves about them, as we had sufficient food for the time being. A nasty, obstinate fog prevented our seeing anything; we proceeded at haphazard across waters which never have been traversed by human beings before.

Eventually we steered due south, and we were wondering where and when we should meet with land, when we came to the edge of the ice, which turned out to be shore-ice, and which extended in a westerly and later in a more southerly direction. It appeared that in the fog we had got into a bay and had now to get out of it again; but we now had the current right against us, while some thin ice was beginning to form on the water, so we were obliged to seek the shore and proceed along it on the ice.

Wherever we had to pursue our journey on the ice, whether it was on floes or on the shore-ice, we saw numerous tracks of bears. A good many bears must have been dancing about around our encampment in the night, and as we were expecting a visit from them some fine night, we had our guns standing ready against the tent-pole.

Our one wish now was to know our whereabouts; if it would but clear up we should, no doubt, see land close by, and according to the direction in which it extended we should know whether we were on the west or east side of Franz Josef Land. At present we were just as wise as ever on this point, but in any case we were making good progress towards the south.

One Sunday (August 11th), while Nansen was ashore on a hummock inspecting the water ahead of us, an unusually big walrus suddenly lifted its unshapely head out of the water close to us, and lay puffing and staring angrily at us.

"Look at it," said Nansen, "it's a regular monster." The next moment the animal disappeared; Nansen came back to his kayak, and we continued our journey. But all of a sudden the walrus came up again quite near to us; it then dived under and came up again several times, always nearer and nearer, until at last it was close to our kayaks, when it raised itself on end out of the water, snorting and shaking its immense tusks at us. We were afraid it would sink our fragile canvas craft there and then, and we seized our guns; but the next moment it disappeared, only to come up again, this time almost touching my kayak. I sent a bullet straight into its ugly head; it uttered a terrific roar, gave a violent sprawl, and disappeared, colouring the water red with its blood.

We thereupon proceeded on our way, and soon forgot all about the walrus. Suddenly I felt myself and the kayak lifted right out of the water by a violent shock against the bottom of the latter, and the next moment a head with long tusks appeared right alongside of me, so that the water splashed straight into the kayak. We again saw the walrus's ugly face, the hole made by my bullet in its head being plainly visible. We instantly seized our guns; Nansen fired a bullet into its head from the front, as he could not get a shot at its neck from behind, which is the most vulnerable part of the animal. Fortunately, Nansen's shot settled it this time. Its body lay floating in the water, while the gulls began cruising about around it as we began with great difficulty to cut a hole in its one-inch thick hide, and to cut some flesh and blubber off the carcass. While we were occupied with this the knife entered the lung, upon which the air came whistling out, while the water rushed in. The carcass became heavier and heavier and more difficult to keep afloat with the paddle, and at last we had to let it go. We could see it sinking through the water in circles towards the bottom, while the gulls made a terrible row because they had been cheated of a share in the catch.

We now talked about making the sledges shorter, so that we might get one on each of our kayaks, and then proceed singly in them. In this way we thought to get on more quickly than when both were lashed together.

In the evening of this Sunday we were closed in by the ice, and the weather being very foggy, we encamped for the night on the shore-ice, and began cutting the sledges and making ourselves proper kayak paddles. In the course of the night, while busy with this, the fog, which had so persistently enveloped everything around us and depressed our spirits, gradually lifted, and little by little we discovered land in front of us, extending from S.E. to W.N.W., covered with glaciers and precipitous mountains. In the west there appeared to be a sound. As this veil of mist was gradually drawn aside, we watched from a hummock with the keenest interest the gradual unveiling of the land throughout the entire night. It was, of course, very satisfactory to see so much land, but unfortunately we had to admit to ourselves that it was to all appearance the east coast, and with this our hopes of reaching home this year must vanish. But, as the poet writes—

> "If a hope or two is blighted,
> A new one gleams in the eye."

Since shortening our sledges we proceeded singly in our kayaks at the greater speed·which we had anticipated, but we had not now so much opportunity of getting on by water as we had before. We were obliged to haul our stumpy sledges over the ice a good deal again, but in a way we were making progress after all. On the night of August 15th we lay down to rest without pitching our tent and without cooking any food; in fact, we lay down without tasting a morsel. We were waiting for a current, which was preventing us from proceeding by water, to turn. But the current turned without bringing about any change, and we had to set out, hauling and pulling steadily and laboriously at our sledges the whole day. On the way we passed an iceberg, about fifty feet high, which we tried unsuccessfully to ascend. At last we reached the island, and had for the first time bare land under our feet, and slept on granite sand.

It was a strange, indescribable feeling we experienced in setting foot on *terra firma* again—to let our feet feel that it really was land, and not ice, they rested upon. At first we walked most carefully over the hard granite blocks, our feet touching the ground almost lovingly; and our feelings on finding moss and flowers among the rocks! We sat down, each apart by himself among the rocks, overwhelmed with thoughts.

What a strange influence land has upon us human beings! We hoisted the Norwegian flag in honour of the day. To the west of us there was an island with comparatively high mountains, whence we heard the merry twitter of the little auks.

For the last few days, since the paraffin came to an end, we lived upon dried food. Once, indeed, with the aid of train-oil, we cooked a good meal of lobscouse among the granite blocks, and used up the last of our potatoes.

Next day we set off in the direction of the alluring island in the west. Nansen went on in front to examine and measure the coast-line. As I was pulling along across the ice, I saw a bear coming towards me; it approached me steadily and briskly, in the customary way of polar bears, while cruising up against the wind. I got ready to receive it, but before it came within range of my gun, it stopped and scented the air carefully, and then it suddenly turned right about and trotted off as fast as its legs could carry it. There must have been a great number of bears here, judging by all the tracks we passed daily.

HAULING IN A WALRUS.

There was plenty of life on the island; the snow buntings flew chirruping from stone to stone, and the little auks set off in flocks for the open lanes, and then returned to their nests. The merriment of these little birds was quite infectious, and put us in good humour. High up on the pointed crags sat the black-backed gulls, anxiously guarding their young ones, their melodious, flute-like notes floating down towards us. At the foot of the mountain, the surface of the snow was coloured a beautiful red; it is a kind of algæ which grows on the snow and gives it this appearance. The scene before us was altogether charming. We climbed up the mountain with our photographic apparatus, but did not succeed in getting to the top, as we were overtaken by the fog. We saw, however, that there was plenty of open water down the sound we were making for, with a number of large floes here and there.

We set out again in our kayaks, but could not proceed far on account of the floes and the thin new ice on the water. So we took to the ice, pulling our sledges and kayaks along until at last we stood by the large open water which extended from the sound down to a promontory covered with ice which ran out from the land. Behind this promontory we should learn our fate. If the coast trended towards the south, we must be on the west coast; but if we found more land in a north-westerly direction, then it must be the east coast.

At last we reached the promontory, and to our great joy we found that the coast was trending southward, with open water along it. We made good progress, first along the lofty wall of ice, and later, along a mountainous country with a remarkably sharp ridge of torn and jagged basalt. In the middle of the mountain there was a deep gap, with a steep declivity on both sides. We crawled up along this gap to get a view of the coast-line along which we had to proceed. Here we saw two foxes fighting over a bird they had caught. They did not seem to be troubled by giddiness, those fellows, for they were struggling at the very edge of the precipice. The open water seemed to extend south as far as we could see; so, although we were tired and worn out, and it was time to rest, we agreed to proceed, especially as a fair wind was blowing freshly. We thought it better to go on sailing as long as it lasted. After a meal of raw meat and blubber, pemmican and bread, we set out and sailed all night until the wind went down. At last we became so sleepy that we sat nodding in our kayaks; we then rowed ashore and

BIRD MOUNTAIN, NEAR CAPE FLORA.

encamped on the shore-ice. Nansen afterwards called this part of the land "Brögger's Foreland."

"For luck, it often changes," says the old ballad, and we certainly experienced the truth of the saying often enough during our roving life. Only lately we were full of hope that we should be able to return home this year, having the open water before us. Now we had been stopped by the ice, which was packed tightly against the coast, and we had not been able to stir for a week. We supposed, therefore, we should have to say farewell to our brilliant hopes; that we should in all probability have to spend another polar night in those regions, and that it might prove the worst of the three for us.

We set out in our kayaks, in bright, beautiful weather, not unlike a spring night at home, after having made allowance for the cold, and we were making good progress along the shores of the new land we had found. Then we came to a promontory, outside of which there was a number of small islands, and here we encountered the ice. We tried to find a path close along the shore, but could not get on, owing to the slush and thin ice, whereupon we lay down on the ice to get some sleep, without pitching our tent, intending to wait for the turn of the current and then proceed upon our way. But before we settled down here we had another adventure with a walrus.

As we were paddling our way among the floating pieces of ice, Nansen in front and I behind, I saw the water under his kayak violently agitated, and the next moment the kayak was lifted out of the water. I thought it was a floating hummock, which had "calved" as he passed it, and had struck the bottom of the kayak, but I had not made many more strokes before a huge walrus rose to the surface just in front of the kayak, shaking his long tusks and snorting angrily.

I backed suddenly and felt for my gun, which I had laid down in the kayak. The animal dived and came up on the other side of me. Fortunately I was not far away from a floe, on to which I managed to scramble out of the kayak, and was glad to feel the solid ice under my feet. I stood ready with my gun, waiting to get a good aim at the walrus, which now gave up the chase after me and set off after Nansen, who had paddled up to a floe and was just getting out of his kayak, and setting his foot on the edge of the ice, when it gave way. Fortunately, the walrus was not near just at the moment. For some time afterwards it swam round about, us, going from one kayak to the other, while we had our dinner on the floe. At last it disappeared altogether.

We then lay down on the floe, without pitching the tent, to get some sleep and to wait for better times. Before long we were awakened by the wind, which must have changed, as we were no longer sheltered from it, and the ice had packed tightly around us, while we ourselves were adrift on our little floe, which had broken loose from the shore-ice. It was an unpleasant awakening, especially as I had just been dreaming that I was at home eating cherries in the garden. We had now to make haste and scramble across the floes on to the shore-ice again, where we were at the moment of writing this paragraph. A dreary and unpleasant time it was for us, with dark prospects before us.

On the third day Nansen shot a bear from the tent; it had been right up to it, and might have turned out an ugly customer if it had been of the more ferocious sort, but it hesitated and turned round.

We both lay awake in our sleeping-bag. Nansen heard something pawing about outside, and looken out through a hole in the tent, when he caught sight of the fellow. He lost no time in snatching up his gun, and sent a bullet through the hole right into the bear's breast. It fell forward, but raised itself again and was going to straddle on, when it received another shot in the side, whereupon it dragged itself, in the agonies of death, over to some rough ice, where we had some difficulty in getting hold of it. That bear came at the right moment, for we had not much food left just then, and this was an unusually big monster.

We regretted that we had not shot any seals on our way, as there were plenty of them. One day I saw a kind of seal which I had not seen before. There was a whole herd of them—one after the other came up to the surface of the water. Nansen told me they were young Greenland seals.

On another occasion we went reconnoitring along a promontory—a most unpleasant spot, with irregular and impassable ridges of ice in front of it, which Nansen called "Helland's Foreland." We looked round for a place, in case we should eventually decide to winter here, but when we left it we both hoped that this would be our first and last visit to this region. The south-westerly wind blew hard day and night, and our tent was badly sheltered against it.

But on August 24th we got the wind from the opposite quarter, N.E., and stronger than ever. The ice had cracked and was opening between us and the land, and we were consequently no longer on the shore-ice; the lane was gradually increasing, and we were soon adrift with the ice. We could not launch the kayaks on the water, as the storm was dashing the waves high up above the edge of the ice; for the time we had to submit to the inevitable and let ourselves drift out to sea with the pack-ice, while we saw the land vanishing before our eyes more and more.

On Monday, August 26th, however, we were safe again on the shore-ice close to land. We had now got a good bit past Cape Athos, as we called the promontory; it was this point we had been so anxious to pass for so many days.[1]

It was on Sunday, the 25th, that we got away from the drift-ice; before this the wind had been blowing harder than at any previous time on the whole expedition. After having speculated as to the best means

OUTSIDE OUR HUT IN SPRING.

of getting on, we settled down for the night; but after a few hours' rest, we had to take the tent down, as it was impossible to find a sheltered place for it. We then laid it over us and went to sleep. When we awoke we discovered that the wind had gone down

[1] Nansen did not give this promontory any name later on, as he thought that the English sledge-expedition from Cape Flora in 1895, under Mr. Jackson, had, in all probability, discovered it before we got there.

considerably, and that we had now drifted a long way from land; we then turned out at once and got ready to start. When we reached the edge of the ice, the wind began to blow just as hard as ever, carrying with it much loose snow from the land, which greatly inconvenienced us. We walked for hours along the edge of the ice, looking for a chance to launch our kayaks. Nansen set out in his first, to try how it would weather the seas. It was with the greatest difficulty that he got free of the loose ice and floes, but the kayak answered very well. When Nansen came back I seized the opportunity and tried my kayak, which also did very well. Nansen then started out again in his, and we began paddling towards land. But we soon found that we could not keep on in this way, for the kayaks were too heavily laden in front with the bear's flesh we had taken with us, and leant so heavily over to leeward that we could only use one oar-blade, and could therefore make but little headway. We then landed on a floe, had our dinner, lashed our kayaks together, and rigged up our mast, as we thought we could now venture to set sail, the wind having gone down somewhat. We got on capitally in the high sea, Nansen steering and I looking out for the floes, so that we could steer clear of them. We sailed merrily along for a considerable time, but for my part I must admit I did not altogether escape sea-sickness. We began to be afraid that our craft would not hold out, especially if we should venture to set the double sail. A squall, however, soon compelled us to lower one sail hurriedly and proceed again under single sail.

Both we and our baggage got a soaking, and when we encamped for the night we had to wring out the sleeping-bag, which was drenched; but we had reached land, and that was the chief thing. We were glad to be able to creep into our tent, although we were as wet as rats and had nothing dry to lie upon. We had a violent snowstorm, which again soaked the tent and the sleeping-bag. I had to get up in the night and wring out my socks. The bag was lying in a pool of water.

When we awoke in the morning we found we had encamped on a beautiful spot. We climbed up along the mountain side over the loose, slippery stones to take a look around us. The mountain behind us was composed of basalt which rose in tall slender columns, and upon it a multitude of birds—little auks and gulls—kept up a terrible noise, which resounded with redoubled loudness along the torn columns which extended beyond the mountain itself.

In front of us the shore was blocked with ice, which had drifted towards it in the course of the night; but farther on, beyond a promontory lying about S. by W., there was open water. It appeared as if a great fjord ran eastward into the country, while westwards out to sea the ice was everywhere visible. Far out in this direction we discerned some islands, but the atmosphere was misty and we could not see them clearly.

On Monday evening, August 26th, we left our encampment by the lofty basalt mountain with all the birds. It looked as if we should have some difficulty in getting on, but we managed to get over the ice into the open water, and shaped our course towards the promontory in a S. by W. direction. As there was every appearance of a fair wind, we landed on a small island in our course and rigged up the kayaks ready for sailing; but when we got away again the wind began to go down and to blow from the opposite quarter. We then took to paddling, each in our own kayak, and had fairly good weather during the night.

But very soon the wind began to blow so hard from the south-west that we had to steer for land, and thus we arrived at our encampment.

As soon as we landed Nansen took a walk along the shore, but came back almost immediately and asked me if I wanted to have a shot at a bear which was coming along. "Yes, of course I did." We crouched down behind the kayaks near the shore, and, sure enough, there came the bear trotting along towards us at a quick march; then it stopped and sniffed at Nansen's tracks not far from us. "Bang!" went the bullet into its shoulder and felled it to the ground. It was not, however, mortally wounded; its back was broken, so that the hind part of its body was paralysed and refused to act. It kept pawing with its fore-legs and trying to get along, and then it sat down and began biting furiously at its paralysed hind-legs, after having first tried to tear away at the wound. It growled and scowled at us who were standing close by; we then sent a bullet through its skull and put an end to its sufferings.

It was an unusually fat young she-bear; we afterwards existed on its flesh, and its skin became our couch.

There was a great number of walruses here; there was one spot on the ice in our neighbourhood where they assembled and lay grunting, fighting, and sleeping on the floes for hours, safe in their greatness, afraid of neither bear nor any other animal, and still less of human beings, whom they had never seen before.

While lying asleep in our tent one night we were awakened by a strange wailing sound outside, near the place where we kept the bear's flesh; and on looking out we saw a she-bear with a cub standing over it, and actually wailing over the loss of their comrade. Nansen seized his gun, but, shy and timid as these animals are, they noticed we were awake and ran away scared.

It appeared that there was sufficient food here. We now abandoned the tent, which, in such a wind as we had had of late, was only like a thin veil, and afforded no shelter. We moved into a stone hut which we built, with the sail and the tent above as a roof.

# CHAPTER XXII

*Obliged to Winter—Our "Den"—Hunting the Walrus—Adrift Again—A Hard Struggle for Land—Awakened by Bears—Hunting Bears in the Kayak—An Inquisitive Walrus—Birds and Foxes—Our Implements—The "Hut"*

WE were now at the end of August, and the winter was at hand, and still we were just as wise as ever about the country we had reached. We had to prepare to winter here; there was no help for it. We had entertained a faint hope of getting farther south before wintering, for if we were on Franz Josef Land we felt that we ought certainly to find the place where Mr. Leigh Smith, the English Arctic explorer, had wintered. The possibility had, of course, great attraction for us, and we were sorely tempted to try and find it; but we were stopped by the ice, and our experience told us that we should only just have time to build ourselves a hut, and provide food and fuel before the winter set in.

We resigned ourselves to our fate, and set to work to make ourselves as comfortable as possible. As matters stood we thought it would be a nice change to get a proper rest in a good, cosy hut, after all the hardships we had undergone on our march across the drift-ice.

One might think that it was with a feeling of despair and misgiving that we began our preparations for wintering; this, however, was not the case, even if the work with the hut was allowed to rest now and then, and although we gazed with longing eyes over the ice-fields towards the south in the direction of the home which we were not to reach that year. We were, however, always full of hope, especially as we had found that we could subsist on bear's flesh alone. But our patience would be sorely tried; in fact, the sledge expedition was from the beginning to the end a splendid schooling in the virtue of patience.

As I have already mentioned, we built one night a stone hut, which we called the "den." It was but a poor place; it was so low that I could hardly sit upright, while Nansen had to lie down at full length. We used the tent and the sail for a roof; later on we used bears' skins for this purpose, but we were then always visited by gulls, which annoyed us greatly by their continual screaming and their pecking away at the roof. We lived for a month in the den while we were building the hut, and went hunting to provision ourselves for the winter.

On the 28th of August we prepared for a walrus hunt, but we could not discover one on the ice and had to go out to the open water. Before we got out I caught sight of two bears—a she-bear and its cub—coming along the edge of the ice towards land. We seized our guns and set off to meet them, but when they got to the shore they followed it along the fjord, and finally began to ascend the mountain slope. We ran after them and hid ourselves behind a hummock. The bears were then at rather a long range, but I was fortunate enough to hit the mother in the side from behind, the bullet passing through her chest and out on the other side. She roared in the usual way, bit at the wound, staggered a few steps, and dropped down dead. The cub could not understand what had happened to its mother, which lay there motionless; but on seeing us it set off up the mountain slope and almost immediately afterwards came back and put its head across its mother's neck, glaring defiantly at us. Nansen sent a shower of small shot into its head, and the cub sank down on top of its mother. We skinned and cut up the two bears and covered the flesh over with the skins to protect it against the gulls.

We then set out in our kayaks, which were lashed together, to look for walrus; there were plenty of them out in the open water. We soon got within range of one, and Nansen fired a bullet at it. It turned over and got under the kayaks, while the water was whirling around us. We backed as quickly as we could to avoid getting the canvas on the bottom of the kayak ripped up by its long tusks. Shortly afterwards we again saw it, apparently quite uninjured. We each fired two or three shots into its head, but it was always facing us, so that we could not get a shot at it sideways; we noticed, however, that it was bleeding freely. Just then Nansen's gun went off accidentally, just as he was laying it aside to take the paddle; the bullet passed through the deck and the fore part of the kayak, fortunately just above the water-line. The walrus dived and came up several times and received on each occasion more shots; its breathing became more and more laboured, and its eyes more and more dim; the water around was dyed red with its blood. Another bullet put an end to it at last, but it sank before Nansen had time to throw his harpoon into it. We were terribly annoyed at having thrown away so much ammunition to no purpose, and paddled ashore in rather a despondent mood.

Before long we saw two walruses getting on to the ice some distance out on the fjord. We gave them some time to settle down while we fetched the flesh of the two bears we had shot. We then approached the walruses cautiously, treading in each other's footsteps like Red

Indians. We had to go some distance across the flat ice before we came up to them. The walruses now and then turned round, so we had to remain motionless while they were looking back; but finally we succeeded in getting close upon them unnoticed.

Nansen first shot the one lying in the most advantageous position. With one shot he killed it on the spot. The other started up from its sleep, but the next moment I had fired a bullet into its head, which, however, lodged too far forward. It was the same with the next shot which was fired by Nansen. It was a monster walrus; the blood streamed from its nostrils and mouth, spurting all round about as it dug its enormous tusks into the ice in its efforts to get into the water again. The third bullet hit the right spot at last, and the shapeless mass of flesh lay motionless. We felt we had now made up for the cartridges we had spent on the walrus that had sunk; for our four cartridges we had got two walruses. But the worst part of the work—the skinning—had yet to be done.

We fetched our sledges to bring the catch home. Nansen thought we had better take the kayaks with us as well, and it was fortunate for us that we did. Before we began skinning the animals a strong wind from the south-east sprang up, which gradually increased in strength and made us afraid that the ice on which we were standing would get loose and drift out to sea with our catch. This fear proved only too well founded, for we had scarcely skinned half of the biggest walrus before we discovered that we were adrift. We saw we could not save the whole of our catch, but hoped to secure half of the hide with the blubber, so we set to work with our knives, cutting away at the thick hide with all our might. We had, however, to give up the idea of saving half of the hide, and to rest satisfied with a quarter. We hurriedly took a few pieces of the flesh, flung them into our kayaks and set out. To our great chagrin we saw the sea-gulls take possession of our splendid catch; some of them sat closely packed on the half-skinned carcass, at which they pecked away vigorously, while the others flew around uttering their hoarse cries. These creatures did not mind the storm or the bad weather, but were only too glad to get a trip out to sea in company with so much food. We intended to cross over to the edge of the floe on the windward side, and thence to set out for the shore-ice and work our way to the land. In the meantime the wind increased rapidly and loosened a number of small floes. We could not make any progress with the kayaks lashed together, so we had to separate them and paddle ahead, each in "his own canoe." We did not, however, reach the shore-ice; it proved, in fact, to be a very long way off, for the storm had broken it up far in towards the land. We had to let go the quarter of the walrus-skin with the blubber, which the sea-gulls at once attacked.

Now began a hard struggle towards land: sometimes on the water between small floes, with the sledge aft on the kayak and the spray dashing over us; at other times across half-melted floes with the kayaks on the sledges, drifting, however, constantly to the north-west, past our store of bears' flesh and the den. It seemed only too probable that we should once more drift out to sea amidst the hateful drift-ice. At length we came to a considerable stretch of open water in the direction of land, and embarked for the last time in our kayaks. Nansen paddled ahead first, and I followed in his wake. I took off my gloves, as I was afraid of losing the paddle if I kept them on. We had the seas right on one side, which was rather awkward as far as my kayak was concerned; at the best of times it generally heeled over to the port side, while now it was canted over still more by the walrus-flesh and my gun, which had shifted over to the leeward side inside the kayak.

Nansen looked back now and then to see if I was all right. It was a hard pull, but we were glad to see that we got nearer and nearer to land, although our pace was slow; and at last we succeeded—thoroughly fagged out and wet through as we were—in scrambling up on the shore-ice to the north-west of our den. Here we chipped off small bits of ice wherewith to allay our burning thirst. We then proceeded along the shore-ice and safely reached the bare shore, where we pulled up the kayaks and wrung the water out of our clothes. We then crept into our bag, ate some bear-steak, and soon fell asleep, tired with the day's exertions, and pleased at having also got safely through this adventure.

We had not been long asleep, when I was awakened by hearing a strange, moaning sound just outside the door, and a similar sound answering some distance off. "That's a bear," I said to Nansen, who was now awake also. We at once turned out and caught sight of three bears. After several shots Nansen killed the mother, while her two somewhat large cubs vanished between the boulders, only to appear afterwards, side by side, out on a small ice-floe, which was hardly big enough to hold them and keep them above water, their heads alone being visible. It was of no use to try to shoot them under these circumstances; I therefore waited until they should swim ashore, and lay in ambush for them; but they drifted out to sea on the floe before the wind, which had now gone down considerably. We let them drift on, as we should have to hunt them from the kayaks in any case. So, drenched as we were from our last expedition, we got ready to get into our kayaks again, taking our "duliker"[1] on us, however, in order not to get more drenched. But what should we find when we got to the kayaks but the dead body of a walrus lying floating

[1] A kind of waterproof sealskin jacket with a hood.

close to the edge of the ice! Here was a prize for us, so we lost no time in securing it and making it fast. It turned out to be the walrus which had cost us so many cartridges, and thus we got it after all. It had risen to the surface again, and had been drifting along the shore.

The bears had been rummaging terribly about in the kayaks; Nansen's had been thrown into the water. They had been right into the kayaks and dragged out the walrus-flesh from them, and after having torn and eaten some of it, had scattered it all over the place; they had evidently been having a fine time. While thus occupied they had done some damage to my kayak by splintering some of the bamboo stretchers in it, but fortunately it was still fit for use.

The two bears had now drifted so far out to sea that they were almost out of sight, but we set out and soon gained upon them. Some walruses came to the surface quite close to the kayaks and snorted at us, but they left us in peace. We were now close upon the bears, and made a circuit round them, as we wanted them to leave the floe and let us drive them towards land, where we might then shoot them. This, of course, would give us least trouble in securing them. And, sure enough, as soon as we made for them, they slipped off the floe and began swimming towards land. An interesting chase now began; each of us went in pursuit of one bear and drove it before us in the direction we wanted it to take. They growled and showed their teeth whenever we came too near them with our kayaks, and exerted themselves all the more to get away from us. Nansen's bear was a better swimmer than mine, which was very broad across the back; he therefore soon got ahead of me. I had to stir up mine from time to time, when it would hiss angrily at me, but swim on all the quicker.

Nansen was now close under land and fired. I saw him throw his harpoon into the bear to make sure of it, after which he towed it ashore. I steered my bear towards the shore just outside the den where our meat was kept. When we were close to the edge of the ice I fixed the paddle by the strap, took the gun and sent a bullet through the head of the bear, just as it was making some hasty strokes to get ashore.

We now had all three bears, the mother lying farther east along the shore. We skinned them and added their flesh to our other stock, after which we crept into our bag and slept long and well the sleep of the just. We had not had much sleep of late, so now we took the rest we needed so much.

Our precious walrus lay securely moored to the shore-ice in a long, narrow bay, close to a place where the glacier precipitated itself into the sea. Here we hoped to be able to draw it ashore and skin it. We did not take the flesh into account; it was the hide we wanted most, in order to get a good roof for our hut and blubber for fuel. It was a troublesome and nasty job to get the walrus skinned. With the implements at our disposal our strength was not sufficient to get it landed; we had therefore to skin it in the water. Half a sledge-runner, which we had been carrying with us since we cut the sledges, came in most usefully as a handspike, both now and afterwards. We cut notches in the ice with our hatchet for the handspike, and another short piece of ash-wood—also from a runner—we fixed in the ice. To this we fastened one end of our rope, while the other was passed through a loop which we cut in the thick walrus-skin and tied to the handspike, whereby we got a kind of tackle which enabled us to exert greater power.

One of us had to use the handspike while the other was skinning, and in this way we at length finally managed to secure the hide; but it was an exceedingly nasty job. We had to lie across the greasy carcass of the walrus while cutting away the skin down in the water; our clothes were thoroughly soaked with fat, and we had no means of getting them cleaned, but had to use them in this state all the time.

While Nansen was cutting away the "inch-thick" skin and I was working with the handspike, I discovered an unusually large walrus swimming into the narrow bay straight towards us, evidently to see what we were doing with his comrade. "Just look at that fellow," I shouted to Nansen; "hurrah, here is another prize for us!" Nansen seized his gun, which, needless to say, was our constant companion, cocked it, and stood ready waiting for the walrus to turn the back of its head towards us. It was not the least afraid of us, but examined us in a minute and leisurely fashion. I should say it would have been anything but a pleasant job to tackle a creature like that in a kayak. Nansen now fired, and the walrus tumbled round into the water, where it lay motionless, but it soon showed signs of life again. Nansen fired a second time, and once again it lay stunned; this repeated itself several times, and after having received three or four bullets in the head it still attempted to get away, so after turning our pockets inside out I had to go to the den for more cartridges.

These animals seem to be exceedingly curious and gifted with excellent sight. They often came right up to the shore to us, hooked themselves fast in the edge of the ice with their long tusks, and remained quietly staring at us until their curiosity was satisfied. It was perhaps this feeling which prompted them now and then to caress our kayaks when we were paddling. Unfortunately, we were not in the mood to appreciate these caresses—they were too dangerous.

We now gave up skinning the first walrus, and set to work on our new prize, which was much bigger and fatter; one, in fact, which was a source of great joy to us. It took several days to get these animals skinned,

but at last we got through the work. We took the flesh of the last walrus and piled it in a heap on the shore, and spread the skins with the blubber still adhering to them over the heap.

There was plenty of bird and animal life over in the little bay where the walruses were moored. The big gulls (the glaucus gulls) took entire possession of the entrails and lungs, etc., while the pretty, snow-white ivory gulls fluttered angrily about because they had to be content with the leavings which the larger birds would not eat. The ivory gull, though so pretty, utters a most disagreeable scream; it is very petulant and bad tempered, and much more importunate than the dignified and majestic glaucus gull. The kittiwake looks with contempt upon these carrion birds; it will not have anything to do with food which it has not caught itself, as long as there are crustaceans in the sea—and of them there is plenty in these regions. These birds fly in flocks lightly and gracefully along the edge of the ice, looking with their keen eyes for food, and now and then darting like an arrow at the surface of the water and appearing immediately with a small shrimp in their beaks. Suddenly one of them would dart upward in a great fright; a large dark bird would be seen throwing itself upon it with a screech, and pecking at it with its beak. This is the skua, or "Thieving Joe," as the Norwegians call it, which lives upon what other birds catch. It pursues the kittiwake, with its hoarse cry, pecking away at it, until the kittiwake lets go what it has in its beak, which the robber, swift as lightning, then catches and devours. We often paused in our work to watch this struggle for existence.

Suddenly the whole flock of birds rise with a screech right up into the air. What can it be? Ah, there is the explanation! Just round the corner by the glacier appear some foxes; they approach at full gallop and take possession of the entrails and pluck as unconcernedly as if no human beings were near. If we sit quiet, they come right up to us and wonder what sort of new boulders have appeared upon the scene. They then set to work at the carcasses until tired out, when they take to their heels and race one another till they hardly seem to touch the ground. Then they come to such a sudden stop that their bodies appear bent up into a curve; then back they go again at lightning speed to the carcasses. Yes, there is indeed life up here, at least as long as the summer lasts.

On the 7th of September we began in earnest to build our winter abode. We chose a piece of flat ground covered with soil and moss close to where the cliffs projected from the glacier, and where there were sufficient stones among the steep talus for building materials. Here and there small arms of the glacier had found their way down among the *débris*. The area on which we built our hut measured six feet in breadth, and nine to ten feet in length. We dug the same distance into the ground as the height of the walls over the ground, which we built with stones from our quarry. The entrance was at the south-western corner, where we dug a passage in the ground and covered it with stones, ice-blocks, and snow, so that we had to creep out and in just as the Eskimos do.

It was not an easy job to build our hut without tools and implements, and with no other wooden materials than ski and ski-staffs. We had no difficulty about the walls, but we could scarcely make the roof without spars or planks of some kind; the stones were not suitable for building a vaulted roof.

But one day Nansen fortunately found a piece of driftwood of suitable dimensions frozen fast between the boulders, in the neighbourhood of the den, some distance from the shore. This we decided to use for the ridge-

## BUILDING A HUT

pole, and then roof over the hut with the walrus-skins. For tools we had nothing but a sledge-runner, a bear-spear, a miniature hatchet, and a ski-staff with an iron spike. We made a spade out of the shoulder-blade of a walrus and the cross-tree of a' sledge, together with the remains of a ski-staff; but this soon came to pieces after we had dug for a time in the hard-frozen soil. The bear-spear and the iron-shod ski-staff served as a pick-axe, till Nansen struck a tusk off one of the walruses, for which I made a handle out of another cross-tree.

OUR FIRST ENCAMPMENT ON OUR MARCH SOUTH.

Sometimes the weather was so mild that the water came trickling down to us from the melting snow and ice, but at other times everything was frozen quite hard. The soil which we dug out we used, together with moss, to fill up between the stones in our walls. It did not take us long to get the walls up, but the roof gave us a deal of trouble. The log which we were going to use as a ridge-pole lay frozen fast with its thickest end, the roots still adhering to it, deep into the ground. We had to cut it in two where it was lying. One fine morning, after having sharpened our hatchet with the two small files we had brought with us, I set to work; but it was evening before I had cut it through, although I stuck closely to the work, and cut and chopped away all the time. Next day we took one end of the log at a time and dragged it over the boulders to a place higher up where there was a kind of a plateau, and from which it could easily be rolled over to the hut. We had to exert all our strength to get the heavy log rolled on to the top of the low, slanting walls. The weather was now becoming so cold that we had to get ready our walrus-skins by freeing them of their blubber, and fortunately we had mild weather for one day, so we got through this work fairly well. It was no easy matter to get these thick, heavy skins transported to the hut. The skins were in four halves, to the first of which we fastened a rope at each end, dragging it across the boulders all the way. The second we put on a sledge and dragged it for some distance along the shore over some very bad ice, and the rest of the way we carried it on a ski and a bamboo pole. The third we carried the whole of the way, and after that we could do no more that day.

When we went to fetch the fourth half-skin it was quite frozen. There was nothing else to be done but to place it in the water under the ice, so that we might get it sufficiently thawed to handle it.

# CHAPTER XXIII

*An Uninvited Guest in our Hut—Walrus in Abundance—The " Water Bear"—Two Motherless Ones—The " Lean Bear"—We Change our Quarters—The First Night in the Hut*

ONE morning, as we were walking along the shore on one of our usual excursions between the den and the hut—I with a bucket and gun in my hands—I saw Nansen, who was some distance ahead of me, suddenly stop and then begin to step back cautiously. A bear was standing sniffing at the fourth half-skin, which it had pulled out of the water, where we had placed it to thaw. Nansen went off for his gun, but as I had mine I began to steal a march upon the creature under cover of some large boulders. I soon came to open ground between me and the bear, and could not therefore proceed any farther. As the range from where I stood was too long, I lay down and waited quietly until it should approach me, for it was facing me and seemed as if it would proceed in my direction. Apparently, it had not as yet seen me; but it set off across the boulders towards the hut, which made it still more difficult for me to get within range. As soon as it arrived at the hut it began sniffing at the roof, when, to my great surprise, I saw another bear appearing in the opening in the roof, where it had torn down the skins. It was standing on the stone bed, growling and hitting out with its paw to keep the new arrival off.

By this time Nansen had returned, just as the first bear was beginning to walk towards the shore again. I called Nansen's attention to bear number two, which had now completely emerged from the hut. There was nothing else to be done but to go ahead and fire at as close quarters as possible. Nansen was to see to the one by the shore, and I to the one by the hut. We rushed out simultaneously from our cover towards the bears, which were greatly frightened by the sight of the two-legged creatures running towards them, and both took to their heels. Nansen hit his bear in the hind-quarters, and soon afterwards I saw him some distance off in full pursuit of the wounded animal. In the meantime my bear made a long detour out on the ice, where I could not very well follow it. I therefore confined myself to watching its movements from behind a hummock on the shore. I noticed that its attention was greatly engrossed by its comrade and Nansen, and soon it began gradually to approach the shore, where there was blood upon the ice and where the traces of the hunt began; it evidently wanted to examine the tracks of the strange beings, who had so suddenly appeared upon the scene. By this time it had come near enough to the place where I lay hidden to enable it to meet its doom. My first shot hit it in the spine, and my next in the head,—the latter shot, however, not before the bear had managed to drag itself along the smooth ice to a larger and safer floe.

I began at once to skin it, and was nearly ready when I saw Nansen coming quietly along with his hands in his pockets and his gun slung across his back. As I had not heard any shot from him I thought at first he had had to give up the pursuit, so when he came nearer I said, "It was a pity we did not get the other one also." "Oh, yes," said Nansen, "we have got it sure enough; it was a beast of a bear, but now it is lying dead up in a snowdrift at the foot of the glacier farther inland." He then told me that after a time the bear had made for land again, and had lain down in the snow some distance up the glacier. Nansen intended to finish it at his leisure at close quarters, but the bear came rushing at him, so that he had to make quick work of it and shoot it.

ALL DOGS KILLED AND EATEN: OUR SOUTHWARD JOURNEY IN THE SPRING OF 1896.

Thus we had secured both the bears, which we transported to our large meat-store outside the den. They were really fine young bears, and their flesh was excellent. But unfortunately they had damaged the roof of the hut, so that we had to take down all the skins and put them into the sea to get them thawed again. It was a difficult job to get the hut roofed over again. We were unable to get the skins properly stretched over it, so we cut thick strips of skin, and with these we fastened big stones to the ends of the skins, which were thus weighted down over the edges of the wall on both sides.

One morning, towards the end of our stay in the den, I discovered, as I turned out to read the temperature, a herd of walruses lying on the ice not very far out in the fjord, which was now covered almost entirely with ice. The walrus, however, easily manages to make a hole in it, even when it is of considerable thickness; it dashes its massive, unshapely head against the ice from beneath, the noise being heard a long distance off, and up comes the walrus amidst a shower of water and ice-splinters.

I stood for a time watching these animals. There were constantly new arrivals, which, after having dragged themselves up on the ice, were received with grunting and digs from the tusks of the largest one on the floe. We had noticed this before, and we had now again an opportunity of seeing the peculiar manner in which these animals receive their comrades. Among the walruses on the floe was a large bull with long tusks. Now and then it lifted its head in the air, and struck about with its tusks to right and left, evidently to show that it was master; and to this the others seemed to submit without a murmur. Among the latter, moreover, the stronger and bigger animals would, in their turn, administer blows to the weaker ones with their tusks. Every time a new arrival appeared at the edge of the ice with the intention of getting up on the floe, the old bull exerted itself to the utmost by force of grunting and swaying of tusks round about him to impress upon the visitor that it was he alone who could give permission to strangers to be admitted to the circle; and after this introductory ceremony the new arrival would very meekly settle down on the outskirts of the herd.

I had been standing for some time watching them when Nansen came out; we counted eleven walruses, and more were continually arriving. We decided to shoot two of them, especially if we should find any young ones in the herd. For some distance we managed, under cover of some pack-ice and hummocks, to steal quite unperceived upon the monsters; but the latter part of our way was open ground, so that the animals soon discovered us and became somewhat uneasy, shifting nearer to the water's edge. We discovered several young animals among them, and we each shot one. Mine, which was lying at the very edge of the ice, just managed to jump into the water after it had been hit by the bullet, and the one Nansen shot did the same; but the next he fired at was shot dead on the spot. The others plunged, one after the other, head foremost into the water, grunting and making a terrible noise; the old "chief," in particular, was in a great rage. Two of the "grown-ups" remained on the ice, and evidently did not want to leave it. I shot one of them dead on the spot, the other remaining quietly while I advanced towards it with my gun raised. Nansen availed himself of the opportunity, and photographed us in this position. The walrus looked at us and at its dead comrade, and could not understand what could be the matter with it, seeing that it did not seem inclined to go back into the water. At last it set off by itself to join the others. At one moment the surface of the water would be smooth and still, the next it was a sheet of foam, as heads of the brutes with their long tusks and ugly, bloodshot eyes appeared all around, and looked angrily at us. The "chief" dug his tusks furiously into the edge of the ice, and raised himself up over it; the next moment he slid back into the water, and dived under the ice.

We heard him butt his head against the ice under our feet, but fortunately the floe on which we were standing was an old and solid one, otherwise it would very soon have been broken up into small pieces. Gradually they disappeared out at sea. We were quietly skinning our two victims when suddenly the head of the "chief" appeared close to us with a terrible roar that made us start; evidently he could not easily forget what had happened. He came back twice more, after which he disappeared altogether.

We took all the skins and blubber we could get off the walruses, as they lay, without troubling to turn them over on the other side. Altogether we had two sledge-loads, and with these we set off for the shore with a feeling of great satisfaction as darkness set in. This happened on the 24th of September.

After this great catch we had more than sufficient skins for the roof of our hut, but they had to be thawed in the sea before we could use them. While we were busy doing this in a hole near the shore, a walrus broke through the ice some distance farther out. As soon as it caught sight of us it vanished, but appeared again in our hole as if to see what we were doing. I seized the broken sledge-runner, our indispensable implement, and was going to deal the walrus a blow with it; but it got frightened of the runner, and dived under the ice and vanished.

On the 26th September we shot a bear, which we called the "water bear." Nansen had gone across to the walrus carcasses in the morning to fetch some sinews which he had cut out of their backs, in order to make thread, when I saw a bear coming sneaking along between the hummocks in the direction of the newly formed ice. I whistled and gesticulated to Nansen, but he was so engaged in searching for the sinews, which the foxes had stolen and run off with, that he neither heard nor saw anything. It looked as if the bear also wanted to pay a visit to the carcasses, and as Nansen had no gun with him, I took mine and ran towards him. But the bear set off across the new ice for some distance and along the edge of the old ice, and at last lay down leisurely at full length. Nansen now went to fetch his gun, and we decided that he should take a large circuit round the bear to prevent it getting farther out, while I was to keep to the shore and receive it there, if it should come in my direction. But it did not seem to be in the least afraid; it got on its feet and walked straight up to Nansen, who lifted his gun and began to take aim; but the bear speedily changed its mind and walked slowly out over the newly frozen ice again. Nansen had now to fire, although the range was long. One shot passed over it, but the next took effect. I saw the smoke and the flash from the gun, and the bear gave a start and took several violent bounds along the ice, long before the sound of the shot reached my ears. But the thin ice was not strong enough for such a heavy fellow to cut capers upon, and down through the ice it went. I could no longer see what took place, but Nansen was shouting and calling to me, and at last I gathered that I was to bring ropes and sledges. When I came up to him I found the bear dead and floating on the water; it was a big fat monster with a splendid white coat. It had been breaking up the ice all around it in its attempts to get on it again. One of its forelegs was shot through, but Nansen did not want to spend any more shots on it, hoping that it would have dragged itself on to the ice. But it expired during these attempts, and now we had to try and get it up. It proved no easy matter; every time we had got part of it up, the ice broke and we were just as badly off as ever. While Nansen was waiting for me, and the bear was floating in the water, he saw that it suddenly received a violent push from below, and the next moment the well-known head of a walrus appeared. It stared for a while at Nansen, but did not take the slightest notice of the bear. It appeared at last to grasp the situation and vanished, and we saw it no more.

In order to get the bear up on to the solid ice, we had to cut a narrow creek in the thin ice leading to an old floe. We tied one end of the rope round the bear's neck, and by letting it pass through the narrow opening in the ice, we were able to drag the bear along under it until we reached the safer ice.

We had a good deal of trouble in securing the "water bear," but it was well worth it. It was late in the evening and rather dark when we approached our great meat-store outside the den, each of us with a heavily laden sledge. But I was just able to discern no less than three bears standing eating away at the heap of blubber from our first walruses.

I whistled softly to Nansen, who was some distance in front with his load, and pointed ahead, when he also saw the bears. To tell the truth, neither of us had any particular inclination for any more bear-hunting. We had already made up our minds that what we wanted most at present was the sleeping-bag and a good pot of meat. We could not, however, let them go; we took the guns off our backs and got ready for the bears, which turned out to be a she-bear and two cubs. But they scented us and disappeared before we got within range of them, and for this we were not in the least sorry.

Nansen began cutting up some meat for supper, while I fetched salt-water and fresh-water ice for cooking, took readings of the temperature, etc. (it was now about 36° of cold), when we again saw the forms of three animals out on the fjord-ice, making straight for the heap of blubber. We stole quickly across to our stores and got there before the bears. We sat like statues behind some large boulders, and when the mother passed, Nansen fired at her, aiming as best he could in the darkness. She gave a roar, threw herself over and made a few jumps out over the ice and then fell down. The young ones pulled up, but fled as soon as we approached, and we could not possibly get within range of them. We made haste to drag the mother to the shore and get her skinned, when we at last settled down in our miserable dwelling, after having done full justice to the splendid meat of the "water bear."

Next day we found that during the night the two cubs had been over to the place where the mother had been skinned and had eaten some bits of blubber which they had found in the mother's stomach. Shortly afterwards we saw them trotting backwards and forwards far out on the new ice. We thought they would return again to where the mother lay, and this they shortly did; we stole upon them, but could not get properly within range of them. Nansen fired a shot at one of them, but without any effect, for they set off and we could hear them tramping over the ice like a pair of horses.

We then went over to the hut, which was now approaching its completion, and worked at the roof and the entrance. Once more the two young bears came in sight, but they had now become so shy that it was impossible to get near them.

We made a window, or, more correctly, an opening, in the hut in the south wall, which looked out over the fjord. While we were at work on the hut, we often thought how glad we should be to move into it; it was quite a palace compared with the den. Nansen had been looking forward to the time when he should be able to sit down and write his account of our journey, as he would have plenty of time on his hands during the coming winter. We ought to have a window, he said, so that we might keep an eye from the interior of the hut on any game that might appear out on the ice as long as there was any light, and afterwards, when the polar night was over, and the sun appeared again. It was not easy to know what might happen; in any case we could not afford to lose the chance of securing anything.

But the window did not come to anything, after all; we were only too glad to fill up the hole as tightly as possible to keep the cold out, after having had to give up the idea of making a kind of pane from the peritoneum of the bear's stomach, or from the intestines.

The last time I turned out of the den to read the temperature on the morning of the 28th of September, I caught sight of a bear over at our store of blubber, and thought at first that it was one of the young bears which had come back again, but I soon saw it was an unusually big fellow. I told Nansen, who was still in the den, and, taking my gun, I approached it cautiously in order to get as close upon it as possible. But it did not appear to trouble itself about me; it lay in the middle of the heap of blubber, eating away quite unconcernedly. It just lifted its head when I put up my gun, and the next moment I fired. I had aimed at its head, and thought it would have dropped down dead on the spot; but afterwards we found that the bullet had gone right through the beast's throat just below the brain. But no one would have thought that it was hit at all, for it got up from the blubber quietly and leisurely, gave me an angry look, and began to walk most majestically out towards the ice as if nothing had happened, when I sent another bullet, this time into its shoulder, so that its spine was disabled. This put a little more life into the fellow. Nansen had now come upon the scene, and he fired a couple of shots at the beast, and I another. At last a final shot in the brain settled it. It was of an enormous size, the largest we had yet seen; but it was terribly lean. It had eaten so much blubber, however, that just then its stomach was fully distended. It could not have tasted food for several months; goodness knows where it had been wandering about, perhaps it had come from the North Pole itself! In the death-struggle it vomited a good deal of the blubber upon which it had been gorging; the great, heavy beast was thawing the ice as it lay, and was now on the point of sinking through it. We had therefore to drag it over to a safer place on the thick ice.

There was not a trace of fat on the carcass, and we therefore called it the "lean bear." But for such a coat as it had, one would have to search long and in vain. It had fine, long, glistening hair, and socks on its paws.

"That skin is worth 1,200 kroner," was Nansen's remark. We afterwards used it as an under mattress on our stone bed throughout the winter. Besides rummaging about in our blubber-heap during the night, the bear had been otherwise engaged. Away down by the shore, between the hummocks, we found one of the two cubs lying dead, and on the following day we found the other also lifeless and stiff. Apparently the cubs had, under cover of the night, again approached the blubber-heap and the place where the mother was lying, and had then met with the old bear, with whom, no doubt, they had tried to strike up an acquaintance. But the old fellow evidently did not want any competitors now that he had found a regular treasure-trove of blubber, and had simply given them a blow with his terrible paw. By the tracks we could see he had actually taken the trouble to pursue one of them out on to the ice.

While engaged in skinning the bears we had shot, I had often been forced to admire the wonderful muscular strength of the forepaws of these animals; but when I examined the paws of the "lean one," my admiration knew no bounds. Such a conglomeration of gnarled muscles and sinews right down from the shoulder-blade to the long, crooked claws I had never seen. It was not to be wondered at that the young bears lay there with their heads smashed; the monster might have smashed anything he came across; in fact, it was a terrible beast, for it did not mind even a rifle-bullet through its throat and jaws.

In the evening of the same day we at last moved into our new palace. The final piece of work we had been engaged upon was the stone benches upon which we intended to sleep. We thought it would be a fine thing to have a bed each, so that we should be independent of each other, and might toss and turn about at pleasure; hitherto we had been obliged to turn round both at the same time, whenever we wanted to lie on the other side. We therefore ripped open the sleeping-bag so as to have a blanket a-piece. We also used the skins from the roof of the den, as well as some of those which we had not yet freed from blubber, for making our beds. We also lighted a couple of train-oil lamps, but we felt terribly cold at night on the frozen, hoar-frosted skins, and we were glad when morning came. We lighted a fire and prepared a plentiful breakfast of bear's meat. It did not seem as if we could get enough blubber and boiling-hot bear-soup down our throats. We had not experienced such cold since the coldest days in the drift-ice, so the first thing we set to work at in the morning was to sew the blankets together again for a sleeping-bag, making only a few stitches here and there, as thread was now becoming a scarce article. By means of the ski-staffs and some driftwood which we had found along the shore in a very decomposed state, we managed to construct a single bedstead between the two benches, and were glad next night to creep into our bag again, although our bed was hard and uncomfortable. We did away with the woodwork we were lying on, and built the foundations of our bed of stone instead.

We did not get much heat from the train-oil lamps, except close under the roof, where the walrus-skins began to thaw and hang down in large bulges, so that they slid apart from one another where they were joined together. At these places the snow therefore melted, causing a constant drip, and filling the bulges with water. We stretched the skins again, and mended the joints with bits of skin and pieces of driftwood, but before long things were just as bad again. We had then to begin lining the roof with bearskins. The frozen skins, which were lying outside the hut, were then taken inside to be thawed before being used on our couch; while those we had hitherto been lying on were fastened up under the roof with small nails and the remnants of the tent. It was sad to have to treat these valuable bearskins in this way, and the job was a long and nasty one.

On each of the main walls inside the hut a ski was fastened with straps, which went right through the wall between it and the roof. Between these ski we stretched the skins which were to be dried, and they had to hang for weeks before we could take them down and hang up new ones.

Besides the large ridge-pole proper, we had to support the sides of the roof as well as possible with ski, bamboo-rods, and our two paddles, and when the cold finally set in thoroughly, the whole of the roof froze into one solid, stiff mass, with a thick layer of snow on the top.

In the south-eastern corner of the hut we built a hearth, with a bearskin for smoke board; the smoke issued through a hole in the walrus-skin and a chimney which we built of snow, bears' bones, and walrus-meat. When the fire was out on the hearth, we put a piece of bearskin in the hole to keep the draught out. It happened sometimes, of course, that our chimney began to melt, especially when the weather was less cold than usual, or when we made a big fire to cook a first-class beefsteak, and then the sooty water would drip into our frying-pan; but we were not very particular about such trifles.

In the south-western corner, a bearskin hung from the roof in front of the opening which led to the passage out of the hut. Through this we had to creep on all-fours, and up through a hole over which we laid a bear's skin, which formed the outer door, so to speak.

It was often difficult to get out in the mornings; when the wind had blown the snow over the hole into a hard drift in the course of the night, and it weighed heavily on the skin across it. Nansen had special difficulty in getting out; being tall, he could not manage to bend himself sufficiently in the narrow passage, so as to get into such a position as would enable him to lift the skin off with his back; he had to loosen the snow along the edges of the skin with a knife or ski-staff, before he could manage to get it up.

# CHAPTER XXIV

*Life in the Hut—Our Domestic Animals—Fox Traps, but no Foxes—A Kayak Adrift—Open Water—Christmas once more*

A MONOTONOUS and dreary life now began for us during our third and worst polar night; but, after all, it might easily have been worse. It was a great satisfaction to know that as far as food was concerned we had sufficient, whatever should happen; our larder outside the door was well stocked with bear-flesh—legs, shoulders, and whole carcasses of it being buried in the snow round about the hut. The little we had left of the provisions from the sledge expedition we had also placed in the snow and covered with stones to protect them from the foxes. We resolved not to touch these provisions until we should set out again in the spring, unless we found it necessary to use them medicinally in the event of either of us becoming ill, from the sameness of our flesh diet. Fortunately, however, it agreed with us remarkably well the whole of the time.

We lay in the sleeping-bag most of the time, both night and day, and slept as long as we could. In the mornings we had boiled bear-flesh and bouillon, and every evening fried steak, also of bear-flesh; in the middle of the day we had no meal. We took it in turns to be cook for a week at a time. By the head of our bed stood the train-oil lamps, which burned day and night; the saucers to hold the oil we had made of some plates of German silver, and for wicks we used plasters and bandages from the doctor's bag; the blubber we melted in a pot made out of one of the paraffin cans.

He whose turn it was to be cook lay outermost in the sleeping-bag, and it was his duty to attend to the lamps night and day; consequently we did not use many matches. The cook had to take in a leg or a shoulder, sometimes even a whole bear, when it was a small one, and put it near the hearth, so that the meat should thaw until it was about to be used. Of course it became black and dirty with the soot, but we did not mind that very much.

He who had not the cooking to do, had to keep the hut provided with fresh and salt-water ice, or by preference salt water, if it were possible to find any. We had no salt; the little we took with us from the *Fram* (it was only a small quantity of table salt in a mustard box) had been used long before we got away from the drift-ice. There were weeks at a time during which we had no salt of any kind, either in the form of salt water or salt-water ice. The salt which is found in flesh must therefore be sufficient for the human body, even if the food is entirely animal.

We had always a pot, made out of half a paraffin can, filled with ice, hanging over one of the lamps, so as to have water for drinking whenever we required it.

In the course of the winter we did not go out of doors more than was absolutely necessary; it was too cold for us in our greasy, much-worn clothes, and there was generally a bitter wind blowing, which went through our bones and marrow. But when the weather was fine, and we had the Northern Lights and moonlight, we defied the cold, and kept running up and down outside our hut.

The foxes used to walk about the hut like domesticated animals, gnawing away at the carcasses of the bears; but we did not mind this, as we had plenty of meat. They used to come in parties of two or three,

ON A SHOOTING EXPEDITION.

and tramp about on our roof, which we did not at first like, as every little sound was so loud in the intense cold. We used to knock at the ridge-pole, in order to frighten them away; but this was of no avail! It was just as much as we could do to get them to go when, after creeping through the passage and throwing the door-skin to one side, we suddenly appeared before them as if we had risen from the ground. They would then shriek loudly, as if with surprise and vexation, the shrieks resounding most unpleasantly through the stillness of the Arctic night; and no wonder, for it must have been a strange sight for a fox to see a two-legged creature rise so suddenly out of the ground. And what right had human beings in their domain, of which they have been in sole possession, along with the ice-bears, for thousands of years! Was it any wonder, then, that all the foxes, both white and blue, gave vent to their indignation at such an apparition?

These foxes used to steal everything they could get hold of, even articles for which they had no use whatever, but which were of no small importance to us. Nansen had put several things in the silk bag net, which we used for catching marine animals, and had hidden it close to a big stone, but the foxes managed to steal from it a harpoon-line, a small bag with specimens of stones, which Nansen had brought with him from the first bare land we encountered, and, worst of all, a ball of twine, which we intended making into thread. They were especially fond of the thermometer, which they had twice dragged away with them, but which we found again. On the third occasion when it was stolen, they must have dragged it off to their den, for we never saw it again. We had now only one thermometer—a minimum one—left, and this we lashed securely to one of the sledges, which did service as a thermometer cage. This thermometer was a large one, marked with clear and distinct graduations, the column being metaxylóe and red in colour, so that it was possible to get a fairly correct reading, even when the light was bad. We had often thought of making a lamp or torch for this purpose, but it was never really needed. We were sorry that we could not afford ammunition to shoot the foxes, which kept walking about the hut, making themselves quite at home. The fur of the blue foxes, too, was most costly. To us, however, it was of no value, for it was only the flesh of the animals which we set any value upon, and there was too little on the carcass of a fox to make it worth our while to spend a cartridge on it.

On one occasion, however, Nansen did shoot two with one shot, and on another he was obliged to shoot one which he found it impossible to drive away. We thought that the white foxes were prettier than the blue; they were as white as the driven snow, and their fur was so soft and fine that we thought it a pity to touch them. We found some use for them, however, before we left the hut; we cut up the lovely skins and used them to cover the train-oil buckets, in order that the oil should not run out on the way.

On New Year's Eve, in the bright moonlight, I went close up to the glacier to look among the boulders for a flat stone, which I should be able to use for a foxtrap. I found one which I thought would do, and got it moved down to the hut. I fixed up the trap on the roof with props made from a piece of ash-wood, which we sacrificed for the purpose. My fingers were nearly frost-bitten before I got it fixed up, but at last it was ready, with a tempting bit of scorched blubber as bait, while Nansen and I lay down in the sleeping-bag and listened, for we were sure that a fox would be there before long. And sure enough, there was one. Bang! Down came the stone on the roof, but the fox seemed to have got away. I went outside to see; the trap was down, but the fox was gone. The stone was evidently too short, and the fox had managed to get away before the stone fell over it.

I then tried what I could do with a walrus-skin which was frozen stiff. This was large enough, and when I put the stone on the top of it, it ought, I thought, to be heavy enough too. But the fox only amused itself with the whole arrangement; the props I found down on the ice near the shore. The fox was evidently not satisfied with the blubber alone, but thought it ought to take the props as well. And so I gave it up!

Nansen liked the flesh of the fox very much. On one occasion, when I was doing the cooking, I remember I roasted the whole back of one for him. I also tasted it, but I did not like it so much as bear's flesh. There was, of course, a great difference in this also. Altogether we shot nineteen bears before leaving the hut, and yet our stock had nearly run out when we left. On board the *Fram* and in "Longing Camp" we had disposed of thirteen, and before we got to the hut some more had been consumed. As soon as we began upon a new bear, we generally passed our opinion as to the quality of the flesh, and we could easily discern the difference in the taste of the various animals. The flesh of the "water bear" was most delicate, as was also that of another bear, which we called the "fat bear." But best of all were the two "kayak bears"; one of them was therefore reserved for Christmas. The legs of the "lean bear" were not so bad as we imagined they would be. The ribs of the young bears were excellent, especially when boiled.

Sometimes when cutting up the bears we took the stomach, turned it inside-out, and filled it with blood, which then froze into a solid mass; this we afterwards cut into pieces and fried in the pan. The best part of the bear, in our estimation, was the brain, which we also fried, and which was really a most delicious dish.

The cook for the week had also to act as waiter. When the food was cooked, we both crept into the bag, after the pot had been placed on the stone bench by our bedside. We then brought out our tin cups, and the cook had to fish up the pieces from the pot, and so we set to work, using our five fingers and eating long and heartily. Last of all we drank the bouillon in long draughts, after which we lay down to sleep away the time that separated us from spring and the light.

Now and then I was awakened by a dig in my back; Nansen would say I had been snoring, and get me to change my position in order to put a stop to the disturbance.

Inside the hut the temperature was not very severe; I put the thermometer by the head of our bed on one occasion, and it showed 19° below freezing point. Near the walls, however, it was very cold, especially when there was a wind; the whole inside of the hut was then white with hoar-frost. When there was a change in the weather, this began melting up near the roof, and ran down the walls into our berth, so that the skins froze fast to the stone wall, while down by the floor and half-way up the wall a thick crust of ice was generally formed.

Our clothes were very greasy, and stuck to our body; we had hoped to get new ones made from bearskins, but we had to give up this idea, as it took such a long time to prepare the skins. We only managed to get sufficient for a sleeping-bag and gloves, as well as some pieces for repairs. When the spring came, however, we made ourselves a suit of clothes each out of our two woollen blankets.

Our hair and beards grew long and shaggy, and our faces and hands were black and greasy, so that we looked quite like savages. It was a great nuisance to have to handle so much blubber, and have nothing on which to dry our hands now and then. Whenever we shot a bear it was an easy matter; we then washed our hands in its blood, and they became beautifully clean and shiny. In the hut we used the remnants of the tent as towels; when this was used up we had to be satisfied with moss, which we cut from beneath the snow with our little hatchet, and thawed over the fire. We found, however, that the best way to clean ourselves was to scrape our bodies with a knife. Nansen almost scraped the skin off his legs in trying to get rid of all the dirt that had accumulated. Now and then he had to melt some ice in a cup and take a rag from the doctor's bag to wash himself with. Oh, how we longed for clean things! Oh, for some soft woollen clothes instead of the heavy greasy ones which were sticking to our bodies! As for soap and warm water, to say nothing of Turkish baths, we dared not even think of such luxuries!

Here I may, perhaps, be permitted to break away for a moment from the course of events to reproduce a picture of the dwelling of certain other human beings, whom we were to meet later, and who were that very winter living on the same group of islands as ourselves, but almost a month's journey farther south.

I refer to the English expedition under the leadership of Mr. Jackson. The eight members of this expedition were quartered in a well-built log-house, well supplied with light, warmth, and suitable food, with plenty of soap, water, and clean clothes. They were cosy and comfortable, and did not trouble themselves much about the Arctic winter. They had also a good library, a thing we were very much in want of. We had only a nautical almanack, in which we could read all about the Royal Family and the treatment of the apparently drowned, and I was longing so much for the last volume of Heyses' novel, which I had not managed to get through on board the *Fram*.

But although those men were not far away from us at that time, none of us knew anything about each other.

One morning, in October, we heard some heavy steps

on our roof, quite different from the light tripping of the foxes. Soon afterwards we heard something rummaging about and gnawing at our blubber-heap just outside the hut, and close to our heads, and then we guessed it was "Old Bruin" himself who was about. One gun stood inside and another just outside the door. We put on our Lapp boots with all possible speed, and Nansen disappeared through the passage, but before he got the door-skin thrust aside, the noise outside had ceased, and no bear was to be seen. It had, no doubt, been scared as soon as it discovered there was something alive under the ground. We could see from the tracks that it was a small bear.

With the reader's permission I will now quote some extracts from my diary, written from time to time in the course of the winter.

"*Wednesday, December 11th,* 1895.—To-day my week for cooking is over, and I shall have time to attend to my diary. During the last few days we have had stormy weather, with south-easterly wind, which pierces through the snow and in between the stones in the walls, so that they become coated with rime; the lamps flicker and a cold blast sweeps over our couch. The storm has broken a ski made of maple, which had been fixed on end in the snowdrift outside the hut; while my kayak, which has been lying buried in another snowdrift, so that scarcely anything could be seen of it, was carried away by the wind—heavy as the kayak was and full of snow—about a hundred yards off, among the boulders just below the glacier.

"I had a long search in the darkness before I found it, and I expected it to be a good deal damaged; this we shall be better able to ascertain when the light returns. Both the kayaks had been lying side by side, mine being on the weather side, and it was fortunate that Nansen's was not blown away also, for we should then have undoubtedly lost all the photographs we had taken on the journey, and our apparatus as well, for all these things had been stored in Nansen's kayak.

"This week I have made an excellent snow-shovel out of walrus-skin; in the cold weather this skin becomes as hard as iron, although inside the hut it could be easily worked, and, in a thawed condition, given any shape. With this shovel I set to work, covering the roof of the hut with snow again.

"*December* 11*th*.—To-day it is already the eleventh of December. The time seems to pass rapidly here after all, which is a blessing. The old year will soon come to an end, and the new, from which we hope so much, will soon be here.

"For a while the sun must still go farther and farther away, leaving us in darkness; but towards the end of the month it will gradually return to us again, bringing with it greetings from those regions where mankind dwells. At the end of February we shall one day see its beaming face over the mountain ridge on the other side of the fjord yonder, in the south, and we will creep out of our den, and welcome the beloved guest right heartily to our out-of-the-way corner of the world. Its rays will thaw our limbs, and make the blood course more rapidly through our veins; our hearts will beat more quickly, and our bosoms swell with the thought of our approaching journey towards freedom, light and life. Ours is a great goal, and the thought of it exalts one's being.

"*Thursday, December* 12*th*.—It is a change to get outside and have a walk, although it is dark and bleak. It braces up the mind to get out of our rime-covered hut and stretch our stiffened limbs, even if we do now and then feel cold. To-day the weather has been fine and clear, and the Northern Lights have been playing across the sky. We walk up and down outside the hut, each occupied with his own thoughts. Over to the south and south-west we can just discern a dark streak, where the starry sky and the ice meet. This dark stripe is the open sea; the late storm has broken up the ice out there, which has drifted out of sight, goodness knows whither! It is the same ocean which washes the shores of our native country, and it awakens strong longings in my breast—longings for the life of light down there in the south, where warmth and love dwell. We have now been away from the world for about three years, and for nine months we have been living like the wild animals found in these inclement regions; for nine months we have not had the clothes off our backs either night or day, and we have suffered much from cold and from many other hardships. But at certain moments gentle thoughts steal into the mind, bearing with them the glow of home and the promise of a life better than any we have known before, free from all that is evil, full of everything that is good. And with the summer it will come!

"*Tuesday, December 24th*, 1895.—Christmas has again come round. I do not suppose there are any other human beings in the whole world who are celebrating this festival under the same conditions as we are. Here we lie in our stone hut in the midst of the Arctic regions, enshrouded in the polar night, far away from the world, and deprived of everything that belongs to civilization. We have, however, made some preparations for the occasion, modest though they be. We have still some remnants of our provisions from the sledge expedition left, partly damaged, such as fish-flour, and a little bread, sufficient chocolate for one meal, and two portions of Knorr's soup. This is not so bad after all, and we have kept a tender young bear for

Christmas. It had not been cut up, but had been placed, frozen into a solid mass, against the wall of the hut, and so had lain half buried in the snow along with the other bears' flesh.

"I put it on the ground, one end of the carcass resting on a stone, and then went over among the boulders, and in the dark found a large stone with a sharp edge. With this I managed to cut the carcass in two in the middle, and now we have the hind part of it inside the hut to thaw. For to-day we have saved some splendid blubber from the last bear we used, to mix with the fish-flour and fry the bread in. We have also laid in a good supply of fresh and salt-water ice to save ourselves the trouble of fetching it during Christmas.

"Our clothes have also undergone some changes, although nothing very startling. 'Cleanliness is a virtue,' as the old woman said, when she turned her shift on Christmas Eve. This is just what we have done; that is to say, we have taken our outer shirts to wear next to our bodies, as our under ones were beginning to stick to us. I have also put on the camel-hair jersey instead of the anorak, and am now sleeping upon the latter; it is not easy, however, to say which of the two is the greasier.

"Nansen has let his long, blackened locks grow; but one day I took the scissors, put back the hood from my head, sat up in the sleeping-bag and cut off some handfuls of my hair, after which my head felt much lighter. We are, indeed, badly off with regard to clothes and food, as well as light and fuel; but no doubt the time will come when we shall be able to celebrate Christmas in a way that will make up for all the hardships we undergo. 'With pain man must buy his future happiness.'

"After this long, dark polar night, one hopes for a

bright and happy morning, with sunshine and the singing of birds, the fragrant scent of the flowers, and the dewdrops on the fresh grass.

"The time passes quickly enough. Yesterday, the sun ceased descending, and has now again begun to rise;—higher and higher it rises, bringing with it light and warmth. It will melt the wall of ice which separates us from the world, it will melt the icy armour round our breasts, and shed light into the darkness and into our minds; it will greet us, beckoning us towards the warm, smiling world, and we shall not be tardy in responding to its summons. It is the sun which is the great life-giver; we, who have been bereft of it so long, can fully comprehend this.

"*Wednesday, December 25th, Christmas Day.*—We celebrated Christmas Eve as well as we could. We boiled fish-meal and some maize-meal together with train-oil, and then fried it in the pan. It did not taste as well as we had expected, but the bread fried in bear's blubber tasted excellent.

"This morning we had chocolate and aleuronate bread and blubber—a grand Christmas morning breakfast! In spite of everything, we are doing very well; we are satisfied with what we have got, and enjoy life so much, that there are, perhaps, many who might envy us. We have just had our usual walk up and down the promenade, in weather which we shall long remember, and which we are not likely to experience again another Christmas. When we crept out of our hut and got our heads above the ground, the whole of the heavens was ablaze with Northern Lights of every possible colour, which rushed like a whirlwind through the zenith, and then drew towards the northern sky, where they remained for some time; while in the southern sky the moon shone brightly.

"It seemed as if the elements had combined to make

it as pleasant a Christmas for us as they could. The wind, which of late had been blowing somewhat strongly from the east, covering our walls with hoar-frost, had now gone down considerably; while at intervals we even had a dead calm.

"The temperature was not very high, generally about 20° below zero.

"This wonderful weather awakens quite a solemn feeling within one, and then the moonlight—this strange Arctic moonlight, which makes everything so soft and peaceful—seems almost to caress the hard, unlovely nature round us. This contrast between the harshness and bleakness of the scene, and the softening, soothing moonlight is indeed wonderful. It seems to penetrate and melt the heart—filling the mind with peace and goodwill, and stirring one's better nature. One feels happy as one goes up and down outside the miserable dwelling, shivering with cold, far from one's dear ones, while the Northern Lights flash and tremble, as if controlled by an invisible hand, filling the soul with their sublimity.

"*Thursday, December 26th.*—This is the second day of this remarkable Christmas-tide. This evening I have just finished an important piece of work; I have cut a piece out of a bear's skin to mend one of the knees of my trousers, in which there has been a large hole for some time. I was busy with this, while Nansen was making 'pastry'[1] and washing his feet with a little water in a cup. This is not exactly the sort of occupation one is accustomed to in the Christmas holidays.

[1] This is the name we gave to the thin slices of blubber, which, after the oil had been boiled out of them, shrivelled up and became crisp. We were very fond of them, and took a good deal of trouble to make them really good. Much depended upon their being boiled carefully.

"At home, I suppose, they are dancing and amusing themselves to their heart's content. Here, there are no people dancing merrily, but, instead, the fiery tongues of the Northern Lights dance incessantly across the bright vault of the heavens.

"*December 27th.*—The Arctic winter has assumed a new garb to-day, and there is an end to the fine weather; evidently it thinks we have had enough of it. The moon is hidden by threatening clouds, and a snowstorm is beginning to blow from the south-east. Again, we can see the dark stripe in the south-west, which tells us there is open water in that direction. The Northern Lights have disappeared; I suppose they have gone to still more northerly climes. It did us good to-day, however, to take a walk and let the wind beat the snow right against our faces."

## CHAPTER XXV

*The New Year—The Sun Reappears—Spring—Running Short of Blubber—The Bear which Wanted to Get into the Hut—Preparing to Start Again—The Land of the Ice-bear*

> "Sleep, uneasy heart, sleep!
> Forget the world's joys and sorrows;
> No hope thy peace disturb,
> No dreams thy rest!"

THESE lines by the Swedish poet, Runeberg, often came into my mind, as I lay and tossed about on the hard stone bed. To be able to sleep and forget everything, to sleep and not awake until the summer came, when we should be able to rise from our hard couch, harness ourselves to our sledges, and set out for the south. And when I crept deep into the bag and pulled the hood over my head I used to wish to kill as much time as possible in sleep. It is a good thing that time never comes to a standstill.

On the last day of the old year Nansen proposed that we should begin to say "du"[1] (thou) to one another. Hitherto we had called each other "de" (you).

On New Year's Eve I relieved Nansen of his duties as cook. Instead of the usual bear-steak, we had a grand supper of maize porridge with train-oil. It was really a nice change to have a meal of farinaceous food.

[1] A sign of intimate friendship, like the French "tu."

The breakfast on New Year's morning was equally grand; it consisted of fish-soup made from fish-flour, a packet of Knorr's lentil soup, and some stock made from bear's flesh, as well as aleuronate bread fried in bear's fat—a splendid breakfast indeed! Our last packet of Julienne soup was used a few days later. The first days of the New Year were very cold, the thermometer showing 82° of frost, so it was anything but warm to walk about in our greasy clothes, which became as stiff as leather, as soon as we got outside the door. But it is marvellous what one can accustom oneself to, and, at any rate, we deemed ourselves fortunate to have a dwelling, such as it was, to protect ourselves against the extreme cold, which caused the glacier to contract to such an extent that it cracked with loud reports like cannon shots and shook our hut to its foundation; or against the wind as it howled across the snow and the boulders, causing our palace to tremble, which however lay safely protected beneath the ground. For some days we had been having snowstorms from the south-east; on January 8th the barometer stood at 717·8. Then there was a lull for a time, after which the wind began blowing again from the north-west, with renewed strength, the barometer rising all the while. The sledge, which we used as a thermometer-cage, was carried off by the wind, but I found it lying in a dangerous position among some big boulders below the glacier, and, fortunately, the thermometer had not been damaged.

The storm from the north continued to rage till January 11th, when the temperature was 74° below freezing point, and it was almost impossible for us to go outside. Inside it was so cold that water froze in a cup standing between the two lamps on the hearth. A week again passed,—one week less to wait, one week nearer our goal,—for we began to see the dawn of day over yonder above the mountain ridge. We had now only about 36° of frost, so we had many a good walk. It was cheering, in our monotonous existence, to turn out and have a look at the small bright stripe on the southern horizon, announcing that daylight was on its way to succeed our last Arctic night. Day by day, week by week passed, the one just as monotonous as the other. Our conversation turned daily upon home, and the time when we should be able to begin our journey thither. We made a sleeping-bag out of bearskins, and could now lie down at night without our trousers, and without having so many bandages round our feet. This was a pleasant change to us, who for nearly a year had our clothes on continuously both night and day. We also shortened our stone berths, the projecting ends of which we had now no use for; they had frozen into solid masses, which had to be knocked to pieces, bit by bit. We began to fear that we should run short of blubber towards the end of the winter, but we hoped to be able to get some bears in the spring.

We now discussed the advisability of crossing the ice to Spitzbergen, instead of following the coast southward. The question was, whether we could manage it with the outfit we had, especially the short sledges, in case the ice should be very uneven, for the loads would be heavy. And how about food? Still we should be able to get to Spitzbergen earlier, and this was, of course, a great attraction for us.

Now and then we had to mend our rags. We chewed the fat out of bits of bearskin and sewed them on our trousers with thread, which we manufactured by untwisting pieces of string. We sewed the pieces of skin to our Lapp boots and gloves with thongs made from bearskin, which we found very serviceable. We were very cosy and comfortable in our sleeping-bag while the storm was raging outside, and we discussed the drift of the *Fram*. It might be that she had got home before us, and in that case we imagined there would not be many who believed we were alive.

Up to Thursday, February 13th, I had written nothing in my diary. The reason was that I had to be cook for two weeks at a stretch, as Nansen was suffering with his back, and was obliged to keep to his bed day and night. He was now all right again, and resumed his duties as cook. The time passed quickly, and day by day it became lighter; soon we knew we should have the sun itself. We were now much occupied with the plans for our journey and our outfit, and with discussing our chances of quickly reaching North-East Land or Spitzbergen; we were confident that it could be done. We were still in a fog as to our whereabouts; that is to say, we knew we were in 81° 27′ latitude, but the longitude? We felt sure, however, that we were a good bit to the west. During the two weeks I got through a good deal of work. I dug out our blubber-heap, which had been buried in a hard snowdrift, and now we could easily take stock of our supply of flesh and blubber. We had made great inroads into it, but we thought we had sufficient left. I took a bearskin into the hut, scraped off the blubber, and hung it up to dry; we were going to use it for gloves and socks. The chimney on our roof had melted away and had to be built up again with snow. It was a fine thing to go out in the middle of the day now, when the weather was clear; it was so light that we could see our surroundings just as they were before the Arctic night set in. There were not many bright spots in our landscape, but we welcomed them all the same, whether they were ice-hummocks or projecting rocks; there they stood in the bleak scene just as they did before; but now we looked at them with wondering eyes, for it was light.

On Tuesday, February 11th, I slung my gun across

my shoulders and climbed up to a bare crag in the glacier just above us. The weather was fine and clear and, being in the middle of the day, it was fairly light. I stood there for a long time looking about; there was so much that was new to see, no longer merely the four ice-covered walls of the hut. Down below I saw the heap of snow, under which we two had fought through the long, dark winter. God be praised, I said, it will soon be over, and before long we shall say farewell to the hut and give it up entirely to the foxes. No one would believe that human beings had been living under that heap of snow, especially throughout an entire Arctic winter. But we had done it, and we had not fared so very badly after all; one gets accustomed to so much in this world. On Sunday, February 16th, we had delightful weather, with only 22° of frost, but it was blowing pretty hard. In the course of the night there had been a fall of snow, but not of the sort we were accustomed to,—fine, dry and cold,—but snow which reminded us of the kind we had at home. Next day we had 63° of frost and a strong, biting northern wind; so changeable can the weather be here.

On February 25th we saw the sun's golden light reflected on the clouds above the ridge beyond us, while the sky above it was grandly illuminated in all sorts of colours. While we were walking about rejoicing at the return of the sun, I suddenly saw a flock of the little auks coming flying from the south and following the land northwards, and shortly afterwards Nansen also saw a flock flying in the same direction. They were the early harbingers of spring! "Poor little birds!" I thought; "what do you want so early up here in the cold north? Return to milder climes!" And again, like last summer in the drift-ice, I envied the small creatures their wings, which carried them so quickly wherever they wanted to go. My own course, however, should be to the south, and I should not have been long on the road, had I been one of them!

We made another push forward (till March 10th) before I again wrote in my diary. It had been somewhat dark of late, but now it had cleared up again. We had been talking about leaving here in April, but we were obliged to give up this favourite plan of ours, as we were running short of blubber. We should not have sufficient of it for food and fuel on the journey; and, moreover, we should not be able to get any flesh dried by boiling it in train-oil, as we originally intended to do. A material reduction had to be made in our consumption of blubber, and now we could only afford to boil food once a day, and burn a lamp just long enough to melt blubber for oil, and ice for water. We were in the same straits as the Eskimos; when they are badly off, they cannot afford to burn lamps at night, and are therefore obliged to sleep in the dark, to which they have the utmost aversion. Fortunately, we had lately had lovely, mild weather; only about 6° of frost. This want of blubber rather damped our spirits; we did not at all like the frozen meat for breakfast in the mornings; besides, the best parts of the meat had by this time been consumed. We had to rely on the bears, and we were not disappointed in this hope.

On Sunday, March 8th, I had a proper cleaning out of the hut, which consisted in raking the ashes out of the hearth and in scraping together all the remnants of flesh and blubber on the floor, which sometimes accumulated to a considerable extent.

There was the backbone, pelvis, and skull of a bear, which we had just finished, also to be cleared out; and I had got these as far as the passage leading out of the hut, and had crept over them to throw the door-skin aside, when I discovered, just outside the opening, a regular monster of a bear with a white, shiny coat which almost blinded my eyes, so unaccustomed was I to the light. In less than no time I tumbled along the passage back into the hut, where I seized my gun from under the roof and told Nansen the great news. After seeing that the gun was loaded, I crept out again into the passage and found the bear standing over the opening, with its head and neck far down into the passage, its broad, flat skull presenting a most tempting target. I cocked the gun and put it up, but had to put it down again, as I discovered a large tuft of bear's hairs in the muzzle of the gun. At this movement the bear pulled back its head, but began scratching with its forepaws at the edge of the opening. It was now high time for me to fire, if we did not want the bear in the hut; but nothing except its paws were visible, and I could not get a proper aim at the animal in the narrow passage. I therefore placed the barrel of the gun in a slanting position towards the opening, so that it should point right at the chest of the bear, and fired. A furious roar announced that it had been hit. During all this Nansen had been busy putting his things on In any case, of course, he could not have been of any assistance in the narrow passage. The whole thing took place in a jiffey.

I put my head out of the opening and peeped round, when I discovered the bear some distance off, over by the glen, with heavy traces of blood behind it. I had only one more cartridge left in the gun after I had fired the shot, and with this I set off after the bear, which increased its speed when it noticed it was pursued.

I was surprised at being able to run as well as I did, for we had had hardly any exercise during the winter. I followed up the bear along the shore in a northerly direction, while a fresh southerly wind, with drifting snow, was blowing, thus enabling the bear to have a continuous scent of me. Now and then I caught a glimpse of its back over among the hummocks along the shore. After some time, I found the tracks led up along the steep shore, beneath a high mountain with a glacier at its foot, while still farther down were large pieces of rocks and boulders. I thought it would have taken refuge here, and I crept cautiously up the side of the mountain to reconnoitre; but I soon discovered its tracks again down on the ice. At this point of the bay, which had a background of lofty mountains, the wind blew in my direction, and thus the bear could no longer scent me. I set off quickly after it, keeping myself well hidden behind the hummocks along the shore.

At last I got within range, and fired my only bullet at it; it fell to the ground, lifted its head, and then let it drop again. I threw the gun across my shoulder, and set off towards the hut as quickly as I could, feeling sure that the bear had had its quietus. Presently I met Nansen, who was fully dressed in his wind-clothes, and had his gun and a good supply of cartridges; he had also brought with him my gloves, which in the hurry I had forgotten. I told him where the bear was lying, and he said he would go and skin it while I went to fetch the sledges. We were some distance from the hut, and when at length I came back to the spot I saw neither Nansen nor the bear. I could now see by the tracks that the latter had got on its legs again and gone off. I followed the shore for some distance, and then heard Nansen shouting to me from among some large blocks of rocks at the foot of a steep incline overlooking the bay.

It appeared that when Nansen arrived at the spot to skin the bear, he saw it trudging off in front of him, as lively as possible, on three legs. It was evidently making for the interior; it crept across an arm of the glacier, and began ascending the steep talus just beneath the lofty, precipitous mountain side above.

Nansen was afraid it would settle down up there, for in that case we should hardly have been able to get at it; he therefore expended a bullet on it, although the range was rather long. Whether the bullet hit or not, he could not say; but the report gave the bear such a start, that it slipped over the edge of the hard-frozen snowdrift, and down the slope it went, rolling head over heels on its downward course. Nansen stood behind a large piece of rock, reloaded his gun quickly, and, when the bear came to a momentary stop, fired at it once more, and down it rolled again, until it landed up against a big rock, where it expired. This bear was a tough customer—"one of the right sort"—an unusually large he-bear; one of its forepaws had been broken by a bullet close to the shoulder, and its chest had also received some injury from the first shot, which was fired without any aim being taken; but none of the vital parts had been touched. It was very fat, and this rejoiced us most.

We had great trouble in getting it cut up and carried down to the sledges on the ice at the foot of the talus. The wind blew so hard all the time that we were nearly thrown over by the gusts. We each took half of the bear on our sledges, but could not get on with such a heavy load; a quarter of the animal was almost more than we could manage. The skin, with the blubber and some of the flesh, were left behind, and fetched away afterwards. We longed to get back to the hut, which was a long way off; but we were now so little accustomed to dragging loads, that we found it a hard job to reach home, which we did about midnight. We took one of the legs, and filled the pot with flesh, crept into our bag, and very soon did full justice to the fresh meat. That bear came just in the nick of time; we had now a good contribution of blubber towards our journey, and the fact that the bears had again begun to make their appearance put us in a good humour, although now we ourselves had to be the bait instead of the walrus carcasses, which had hitherto been the attraction; they were now completely buried under the snow.

On the morning of the 10th of March I was outside our hut at six o'clock, and saw an extraordinary large number of little auks arriving, in unceasing flocks, from the north, and flying in along the fjord. The same day, in the afternoon, we saw flock after flock flying back again. Nansen also saw two black-guillemots.

On the 16th of March the sun appeared in all its glory, and I availed myself of the opportunity to make an excursion nearly to the top of the mountain. I had to go on all-fours up the steep talus and, at intervals, across small glaciers. I finally reached a kind of terrace on the mountain side, from whence I had a splendid view, although no open water was to be seen. Far away, at the bottom of the fjord, rose a glacier just behind the "Little Auk's Mountain"—a mountain which we believed to be the haunt of the little auks. Between the promontory lying S.S.W., from which we were to set out on our course along the coast, and the large glacier in the east, which I have just mentioned, I could not discover any inlet. This landscape of frozen desert, the white surface of which was bathed in the strong sunlight, was a magnificent sight; fjord, ice, and glaciers extended as far as the eye could reach. The little auks flew close to me as I sat almost motionless. They are most beautiful birds,—in the sunlight they look so velvet-like and stately. We were certainly having better times than we had a year ago, when we were struggling with the cold far north among the drift-ice.

Now we had a busy time before us in the hut, getting ready for our journey southwards. There were many things which had to be looked to, but, worst of all, were our ragged and greasy clothes. Fortunately, we had the two blankets, and, after much measuring and calculating, we found we should just be able to get a pair of knee-breeches and a jacket for each of us out of them; but it was a long time before the solemn moment came when we dared to insert the scissors in the blankets and actually cut them up. We were no longer afraid of running short of thread, for we had discovered that the cotton threads in our canvas provision-bags did good service. For weeks we sat side by side in the sleeping-bag, sewing at our new clothes. We had to make new soles for our Lapp boots out of walrus skin, which we pared to a suitable thickness, and then dried over the lamp. I even managed to make a pair of Lapp boots from the skin of the "lean bear," but the hairs were so long that I had to cut them, in order not to slip when walking. Nansen, while skinning the bears, had left sufficient of the skin on the hind paws of some of them to enable us to use them as "natural" socks. We turned them inside out, cleansed them of all fat, and hung them up to dry, intending to use them as foot-gear, just as they were, after they had been turned inside out off the bears' paws. He was not, however, able to get them properly dried, and they became so sooty and nasty that we had to give up all idea of using them.

Our wind-clothes were all in rags, but we did not give in until we had got them sewn together and mended, so that they could be used again. The trousers were cut off by the knee, and the odd pieces, as well as the provision-bags, were used as patches. Pieces of bearskin were scraped, chewed, and dried, and made into gloves and bandages for our feet. We were not well off for ropes, so we set to work and made some of walrus skin, and some thinner lines from bearskin. But our new clothes interested us most of all; we looked forward like children to the pleasure of trying them on, but it was slow work. No doubt Nansen was right when he said we should soon starve if we tried to get our living by tailoring when we got home. But here patience brought us through also, and one fine day we were able to show ourselves on the promenade outside our hut in our brand-new clothes, made of the very latest material, the pattern being a most peculiar one, with large checks and a few spots of train-oil here and there. The latter had been caused by our occasionally upsetting the lamp while we were at our tailoring, and which we had not been able entirely to wring out or chew away.

The clothes, however, were strong and good, the trousers being lined outside with our old drawers. The sealskin leggings which we had brought with us from the *Fram*, and which had been made by Eskimos, were as good as ever, so we were able to use them, and leave off our grey "vadmel" leggings.

While we were busy with these preparations for our journey, our conversation most usually turned upon the well-stocked woollen drapers' shops at home, in which we hoped to revel when we got back. We were constantly returning also to the topic of the whalers at Spitzbergen. We discussed what sort of provisions and clothes they were likely to have on board these vessels. Sugar and bread they were sure to have, and butter as well, so that we should be able to have some fried "Dænge"[1]; and, no doubt, they would be able to spare us some clothes—and soap! And when we got to Tromsö—we always supposed we were to fall in with a Tromsö vessel—we would buy all the cakes we could get hold of! Yes, we would have a regular good time of it! Our under-garments we took and stuffed into our biggest pot—or as many of them as it would hold—and boiled them on the hearth. In this way they became so "soft" that we could scrape off the worst of the dirt with a knife. The stuff we thus scraped off we were able to use as fuel in "Primus the second," as we called the train-oil lamp on the hearth. Nansen also tried to

---

[1] A fried mess of bread-crumbs, butter and sugar.

wash in the Eskimo style, but without success. Nor were we able to make any lye from the ashes of some wretched driftwood, which we had found, and had been using as firewood. To scrape off the dirt with a knife was, no doubt, the best method.

Our kayaks,—and especially mine,—which had made the aërial journey during the winter, wanted repairing; of the poor wooden materials we had, we made proper high boat-grips, which we lashed to the short sledges so that the ends of the kayaks should run clear of the ice. We used straps cut out of bearskins as lashings. Our precious sails were patched and mended and scraped free of fat, for we were going to use them for our tent on the journey. We also made a sleeping-bag of some light, fine bearskins. Now and then we were visited by bears while we were at work.

On the 2nd of April we heard a noise outside the hut, which we at first imagined was occasioned by a bear; we thought it was more likely to be a fox, since the noise was but slight. It was my week at the time, and, when I went outside to take the meteorological observations, I saw at once that it was a bear, which had been making a tour round the hut; but, apparently, it did not like the sight of all the bears' carcasses there, and had trotted off to the ice. And, sure enough, down there I discovered Bruin, just as he had scented the walrus carcasses which lay buried under the snow, and there he began to scratch and dig, so that the snow flew about his ears. We were so busy with our clothes, that we scarcely took any notice of the bear; but at last it was decided that Nansen should go after it. He set off, taking with him my gun, as his was out of order. I stood outside the hut, and looked on. The bear had by this time dug his way a good bit into the snow, for the fellow knew how to use his paws. It neither saw nor heard anything, apparently feeling quite secure.

Nansen walked at his usual pace across the flat ice right up to the bear, which was greatly surprised, and threw himself right round, the same moment receiving the bullet in its face. It ran a few steps, shaking its head, so that the blood spurted about, and then stopped. I could see Nansen had some difficulty in loading his gun again, and it seemed as if the bear intended to go for him; but I soon saw that he was all right. Nansen had to fire five shots before the bear succumbed in earnest. I was not at all happy, standing as spectator with a useless gun in my hands. I could so well understand Peder's feelings every time his gun refused to "burn."

On another occasion Nansen was standing outside the hut, taking a time observation with the theodolite, when, on looking down towards the ice, he discovered a bear standing there quietly staring right at him. He went inside for his gun, but, when he came out again, the bear was beginning to walk away, so Nansen let it go in peace. The next morning we awoke on hearing a bear rummaging about among the blubber, and Nansen rushed out and pushed the door-skin aside—the opening of which had been covered up with the drifting snow—and fired at the bear, but did not hit it, as his eyes were dazzled by the strong sunlight.

On Wednesday, May 6th, we were still hard at work with our outfit. When the weather was very clear, we could see land, or what seemed like the looming of land, to the S.W., which we thought was the North-East Land itself; and all the blue sky, which always kept to the same spot, indicated, we thought, open water,—open water along the coast of the North-East Land, or perhaps nearer. Three days before, when I was busy digging out some flesh for our housekeeping, I saw a bear out on the ice, making straight for a bay to the north-west of us. I set out to look for it, and, when not very far from the hut, I discovered fresh tracks of three bears, but did not see any of them. I went home again; we had a cold breakfast, and began our work, and had forgotten all about the bear, when we heard a skin being dragged along the ground, after which everything was quiet. I stole outside with the gun, pushing the skin cautiously aside. The strong light, as usual, blinded me; but, fortunately, the bear was ravenously hungry, and did not notice me. I soon caught sight of its head behind the snowdrift near our store, where it was busy chewing away at the blubber of the bear which had wanted to get into our passage. I put up my gun, aimed, and shot the greedy bear right through the skull, without its having seen me; and down it fell on the spot in the midst of the other carcasses. Nansen was sitting in the hut, sewing at the new sleeping-bag for our journey. The bear was very lean, but it came in very well for our stock of provisions for the journey; it saved us taking some of the frozen meat into the hut and thawing it.

A couple of days later we received another visit from a bear. Nansen fired one shot into its head and lamed half its body, and had to spend another shot upon it before he killed it.

Of our provisions left over from the sledge expedition, all that could be used was some maize-meal, fish-meal, aleuronate flour, and bread. The latter we fried in train-oil, partly to dry it, and partly to make it keep longer. Besides the principal stock of our provisions, which consisted of raw flesh and blubber, we also took with us some meat boiled in the ordinary way and some boiled in oil. The silk net was filled with "pastry"; we generally got a lot of this from all the blubber we melted for train-oil, and we had altogether three zinc buckets full of it. With the remains of the old cooking apparatus we knocked together a fairly good stove, and out of the lower part of the real "Primus" we made an excellent bowl for melting blubber in.

There was no longer any difficulty about bears, but we did not trouble ourselves any more about them. A she-bear, with a very small cub, made her way towards us the night before the last we spent in the hut; the mother stopped and looked at us in surprise, as we were busy getting the kayaks ready, while the cub began sucking its mother. We had to chase them away in order to be left in peace during the night, and we pursued them for some distance. The mother was angry, and hissed at us as she made off, trying to get the cub to follow her quickly. Nansen fired a shot to frighten them, but to no purpose; he then pursued them again, the mother being in a great rage all the time; she could not get the cub to follow her fast enough. At last Nansen was close upon them, when the mother set off at once up along the steep glacier, growling and snorting all the while, while the young cub crawled up the glacier in its mother's tracks. They then vanished, and we never saw them again.

The last thing we did was to lift up the roof of the hut, so that we could get hold of our precious ski, staffs and paddles, which had been supporting it during the winter. Nansen availed himself of the opportunity, now that the light could penetrate into the hut, to take a couple of photographs of the interior. A short account about the expedition was then written and put into a small brass tube which had belonged to the air-pump in the "Primus," and this tube was hung up under the ridge-pole.

## CHAPTER XXVI

*Farewell to the Hut—Across the Icefield on Ski—Weatherbound for Fourteen Days—Open Water—Sailing on the Ice and at Sea—Where are we?—A Swim for Life*

ON the 19th of May we were at last ready to start for the south.

> "In spring the mind awakens
>   To longings full and free;
> Spring breaks the bonds and fetters
>   That crush the heart of me;
> Her light pierces the darkness;
>   To spring, then, welcome be!
>
> "Oh, Spring! with hearts of yearning
>   We ever think of thee;
> With wistful eyes of greeting
>   We gaze across the sea.
> The Ice-King's grip has held us
>   Three years: Oh, set us free!
>
> "The soft wind from the southward
>   Whispers of spring to me;
> She beckons us towards her,
>   To life, and joy, and glee;
> No longer let us tarry,
>   But springward, homeward flee."

The lines which I quote above I find on the last leaf of my diary. They can scarcely be read for soot and train-oil. I think, however, they will give the reader some idea of our longing for light and warmth and the coming of spring. Spring,—well, it had come at last; we were now going to say farewell to this inhospitable shore, over which so many severe storms had swept; we were to say farewell to the glaciers, the basalt mountain and the talus, to all the bones and skins of the bears we had lived upon, and to our hut with the hard stone bed, and leave everything in the sole possession of the foxes.

It was, indeed, with strange feelings that we set off late in the afternoon with our heavy loads in the direction of the mysterious promontory at which we had so long been gazing. Unaccustomed as we were to marching and pulling, we did not do too much at the start, but encamped before long on the flat ice and settled down for the night for the first time under our new tent arrangement, glad that we were actually on the way home. With the kayaks as walls, and the sails as a roof, and having buried ourselves pretty deeply in the snowdrift, we had quite a comfortable dwelling, which Nansen thought should be immortalized. On this journey along the coast we took it in turn to do the cooking, one day at a time.

On the 21st of May we reached the promontory, tired and worn out after our unaccustomed exertions. Nansen took the glasses and went up the mountain to have a look at the surroundings, while I looked after the encampment. He came back and told me that he had seen plenty of open water not very far from us, behind the island just outside the promontory; the blue sky we had so often seen in this direction was now easily explained. He had also seen two new snow-clad islands, but a promontory, somewhat like the one where we now were, stretched itself farther out to the south, and hid from us the coast-line farther on.

On the morning of May 22nd, while we were having breakfast, it began to blow and snow, and the storm went on increasing after we had got outside and were preparing to break up our camp. When we set out it was just as much as we could do to push ahead. In such a snowstorm it would hardly have been wise to proceed, and we had therefore to remain where we were, build ourselves a proper house, and take things easily. The south-west storm lasted the whole day and night; it has now gone down somewhat, and the temperature was only about freezing-point, so that the sleeping-bag was quite wet. We remained in the same place on May 23rd, and made an excursion in a southerly direction, and saw that the land trended still farther to the south.[1] We also saw open water, but not to the extent that we did on the first day of our arrival here. We could not, however, see the two snow-clad islands which Nansen had sighted in the south-west. Otherwise, we had been busy mending our paddles, caulking the seams of our kayaks with stearine, and repacking our things for the sea voyage. On Friday morning, while busy cooking our breakfast, we discovered a bear quite close to us, walking about and sniffing some tracks made by me in the snow on the previous day while on an excursion in search of ice. The bear, however, did not scent us, and went its way; we might easily have shot it as we lay in the bag, while "Primus the second" was burning away under the breakfast pot by our side in the snow. We had sufficient food for the time being, however, and let the bear go in peace.

On Sunday afternoon, May 24th, we broke up our

[1] On this excursion we were, as we afterwards discovered, within a few yards of a depôt of provisions which the Jackson Expedition had, on their visit to this place in the spring of 1895, deposited in a narrow ravine. Nansen went into the ravine and cut off some pieces of the rock to take home with him, but saw no sign of any depôt; but we learnt afterwards from the Englishmen's description of the place, that we had been on the very spot.

encampment on the promontory, and set out for the island just outside it, in order to reach the open water beyond. A slight easterly wind was blowing, and we hoisted sail on our sledges. We reached the island during the night, when suddenly a storm blew up from the south-west, and we had to make for land in hot haste. I had to stop to save the mast and the sail of my kayak by lashing them securely to the deck. In the meantime, Nansen had got a good way ahead of me, when all at once I noticed his sledge and kayak at a standstill, but there was no sign of Nansen. I thought to myself that he must have slipped on his ski and fallen, which happened to us now and then when we had to get over the big snowdrifts; but the next moment I discovered him lying in front of his sledge. I was now ready to start; but what could have happened to Nansen? He remained lying on the same spot; it was strange that he did not get on his legs and proceed on his way! Then I heard him shouting. I set off at once on my ski, tied fast to my feet as they were, and soon came up to him, when I found him lying in an open crack in the ice, which had been filled with drifting snow. He also had his ski tied on to his feet, and so could not move, while he was sinking deeper and deeper into the slush every moment. The sledge and the kayak were behind him, so he could not see them, and did not know whether they were over or under the water. The drag-rope was fastened to the harness across his back, which also prevented him from turning round. I placed myself carefully on the edge of the crack, got a good hold of his Iceland jersey, and pulled him up on to the ice. He must have been waiting a long time for help, and he must have shouted several times before I heard him. This was a lesson to us not to proceed across such ice with the ski tied to our feet. We had to proceed carefully for the rest of the way, and at last we found a tolerably good place for encamping, upon a narrow streak of shore-ice by the island, close to a large crevice. Nansen got into the bag, and his wet clothes were hung up to dry.

On Wednesday, May 27th, we were still weather-bound on this island by wind, snow, and rain. There were large numbers of walruses here; they lay in groups on the ice, and sometimes appeared in the cracks to have a look round. We went for a walk along the coast in a northerly direction, where we found a number of nasty cracks and slushy ice; here and there appeared heads of walruses, and some of them even followed us, putting up their heads now and then, or butting against the ice under our feet, to show us they were keeping an eye on us. We also made an excursion to the south of the island. It blew hard, but we saw a good deal of open water, and only wished we were out by the edge of the ice in fine weather and with a fair wind. A bear must have passed our encampment during the night.

The month of May was over, and we were not getting on at all. Unfortunately, we had more bad weather, and were still weather-bound at the south end of this island, which we had called "Goose Island," because we had found some remains of geese here. On Thursday, June 17th, we left the place at the north end where we had encamped, and managed to drag ourselves to our present pitch, where we had gone through two more snowstorms, after which it cleared up and we had fine weather for a little while. We hoped we should be able to avail ourselves of this to reach the open water, but we got another storm instead. This storm was the worst, and we hoped it would be the last. To be weather-bound for two weeks at the very outset of our journey was indeed sad! Our stock of flesh was nearly finished; we had only a little boiled meat left.

It is bad enough to have to lie in a wet sleeping-bag night after night in a wretched tent, while the snow melts under you so that you sink deeper and deeper into it, and have to turn round from time to time, when the side you have been lying on has got thoroughly soaked, and while the storm forces the snow in through the smallest crevices, creating white sprays of foam over the bag, so that you are obliged to get up from time to time and stop up the chinks. All this, I say, is bad enough; but to know that you are making no progress at all, while the time is passing fast, and the summer is waning—the summer of our joy—to feel that you are shut up in unknown regions, while your longing for home makes the heart throb within your breast—all this, after having lived in this desert of ice for a year and a half, like animals rather than like human beings, depresses the mind terribly.

On our way here on Thursday, 17th, we saw many herds of walruses lying on the ice. Nansen wanted to photograph one of them, so he stole cautiously up to the monsters and hid himself behind a heap of broken ice. As he raised himself to use the apparatus, a she-walrus with her young suddenly dashed through a hole in the ice close to him. He need not have been afraid that the others would get away, for they settled down quite at their ease to sleep. I went over to him and bombarded the beasts with lumps of ice, so that Nansen might get some more "life" into his photograph. We were now no longer afraid to frighten them; on the contrary, we tried to frighten them as much as we could. Nansen struck them across the snout with his ski-staff, and took one plate after another of them. They only lifted their heads now and then, dug their tusks into the ice, and stared at us in anger and surprise.

On the morning of the 3rd of June, we both went up to the top of "Stormy Island," to see the best way to get on by water. But we were terribly disappointed; there was no sign of open water—the south-west storm had driven all the ice against the shore.

At last we decided to set out across the ice towards a steep mountain in the south, the last new promontory we had discovered of this strange land. The wind was fair, and we hoisted the sails on the sledges, but the ice was thin and in a bad condition for travelling over.

Our ski cut through the wet layer of snow, leaving behind them deep furrows, which at once filled with water. After a good day's march we were glad to reach land and encamp, which we did near a glacier between "Bratfjeldet"[1] and the promontory. Our stock of meat was now exhausted. There were plenty of auks, which flew to and from the "Bratfjeldet," but they were all too high up in the air. We had shot a brace of fulmars on the way, but they did not go very far; and we therefore went over to a herd of walruses, which were lying near the encampment, and shot one of them. It was with the greatest difficulty that we were able to chase the others away, so that we could cut some flesh off the one we had shot. We intended to prepare a meal of blood-porridge in the evening. We made this by boiling together walrus blood, fish-meal, maize-meal and train-oil, and thought it would turn out quite a fine dish; but when it was ready, and we began to tuck into it, we found the taste anything but agreeable.

The next day and night were occupied in reaching the promontory. The wind had increased, and we proceeded on our journey at a swinging pace. When we got in under the promontory we found open water,

[1] Mr. Jackson has given the same mountain the name of "Cape Fisher."

IN THE NEIGHBOURHOOD OF JACKSON'S DEPÔT.
*With Nansen in the North.*] [*Page* 312.

the north wind having sent the ice out to sea again. For the first time on this journey we now launched our kayaks. It was a great treat to be able to use the paddles again and to feel the salt water splashing over us. Birds were flying about and diving; the little auks lay in great flocks on the water, and the kittiwakes sailed gracefully about in the air. Presently two other strange birds passed rapidly over our heads. "Eider-ducks, by Jove!" exclaimed Nansen. Near the shore we noticed two wild geese. In a moment we felt as if we had got on far towards the south. We paddled on before a fair wind for some distance along the coast, until we were stopped by the shore-ice, and then we encamped.

On June 6th we made greater and better progress than on any other day. We could not follow the open water any longer, it led to the north-west; but it might still bend in towards the land somewhere farther south, as some islands, situated far out, were probably keeping back the ice. We left the open water and set out across the ice for some low islands to the south. The weather was hazy, so we could not see our surroundings. Nansen lashed an oar and I a bamboo-pole to the stem of our kayaks to serve as steering poles, and to these we held fast as we stood on our ski in front of the kayaks, while the wind filled our sails and carried us rapidly along—sledges, kayaks and all! After a good day's travelling we pitched our camp by the most westerly of the islands, hungry and tired, but happy in mind. It is strange how long we could go without eating: twelve to fourteen hours between each meal was not unusual; but then we toiled and struggled hard, and consequently we could dispose of a good deal. The blood-porridge which we made went a long way; we ate some of it at every meal, but it never seemed to come to an end.

We could not very well throw it away, but had to try to get through it, although it was anything but appetising. An observation at noon showed that we were in 86° 45′ north latitude. It seemed now pretty certain that we were not on Franz Josef Land, but on some land farther west, consisting of innumerable islands. If so, our road to Spitzbergen would be all the shorter.

During the two following days we sailed before a stiff breeze over the ice. To the west we had a great glacier-land, and on the east we passed two low promontories with sounds and islands between. We sailed at a rattling pace. I was generally some distance ahead, as I, being lighter than Nansen, flew more easily along on ski than he. Sometimes our ski cut into the ice, so that we had great difficulty in keeping them on, while now and then our short sledges were capsized by the wind.

On June 8th we were stopped by a snowstorm; we buried ourselves in a snowdrift in the forenoon, after having marched all the night through. Next day we were able to proceed, and we sailed along merrily; the snow was becoming rather wet, but still we got on all right. I was very near sailing right through the ice in one place close to land; the ski and the sledge cut through the melting ice, and it was with the greatest difficulty that I managed to pull myself out and push the sledge back from the snow-slush on to the firm ice. Nansen, who was following behind, just managed to turn to one side in time. We had to take down our sails and make a long detour before we could start again. Under date June 9th, I wrote: "We are getting on well just now. We are sailing rapidly southwards along the coast before a fresh breeze. The land still trends in this direction, but we are not sure how it is with the land to the south.

To-day we have been fearing that we are sailing into a fjord, but we think it must be a sound after all. Our stock of flesh is again exhausted; we have only some boiled meat left. To-night we are going to have a fish-meal 'dænge.'"

From Wednesday to Friday we had been sailing over the ice, and at times we went at such a rate that we had some difficulty in keeping on our ski. On Friday we said farewell to the land east of us, and then followed that to the west. A sound divided this land from the other. On the south side of this we discovered from a hummock open water; we could even hear the noise of the breakers against the edge of the ice. We set out for the open water across a different kind of ice from that we had had hitherto; it was our old friend, the uneven drift-ice.

The wind freshened as we reached the water; the kayaks were lashed together, and we rigged up the sail and crept into our craft, Nansen taking a ski to steer with, and off we went along the shore before a fresh breeze. We were now on the south side of the land, but had no idea where we were. Nansen said it might be Franz Josef Land after all; he seemed to think it agreed with Leigh Smith's map of the south side of this land, while I thought it could not be, according to Payer's map. In the meantime we made good progress, and towards the evening, when the wind went down, we put in to the edge of the ice. Nansen climbed up on a hummock to have a look at the water ahead. After he came back we thought we would both of us go back to the hummock and have another survey of our surroundings. The kayaks were tied with a strap to the ski-staff, which we had rammed into the ice.

We had no sooner got on the top of the hummock than I saw, quite by chance, that the kayaks had got loose from their moorings, and were drifting away from the ice. "Look, look!" I cried, and both of us ran down from the hummock. Nansen threw off some of his clothes and shouted, "Take the watch," which he handed to me; he looked anxiously after the kayaks and then jumped into the cold, icy water.

All our possessions were drifting away from us— food, clothes, ammunition, guns, and all. Our lives depended upon recovering the kayaks; my clothes-bag was the only thing left upon the ice. I had been changing my foot-gear while Nansen was on the top of the hummock the first time. I saw Nansen swimming rapidly ahead, but the kayaks were drifting farther and farther away; the situation was becoming more and more critical, for it was doubtful whether he could manage to stay long in the cold water. I could not keep quiet; I walked up and down the ice and could do nothing—absolutely nothing—to help him. He now and then rested by swimming on his back. I was afraid he might be seized with cramp and sink before my eyes. It would have been of no use if I also had thrown myself into the water. Nansen got farther and farther away, the strokes became more and more feeble, and soon he would not be able to keep himself afloat. At last I saw him with great difficulty seize hold of one of the kayaks and attempt to pull himself up. At first he did not succeed; he tried once more and succeeded, and the next moment I saw him sitting right on top of the kayak. My mind was once again at ease. Nansen took one of the paddles and began to paddle on both sides of the united kayaks towards the edge of the ice again. This part of the trip he told me afterwards was the worst of all. He felt terribly cold in his thin, wet clothes, with the wind blowing right at him. Suddenly I saw him stop paddling,—he seized his gun and shot two auks, which were lying on the water in front of the bow. This made me feel sure he must be all right, after all. He picked up the birds and paddled on again. At last he reached the edge of the ice, some distance to the east of the place from which the kayaks had drifted away. I jumped into the empty kayak, and we were soon back at our former landing-place. "How do you feel now?" I asked. "So cold, so cold," he answered, with some difficulty. I helped him to pull off his wet clothes and to put on the few poor dry ones we had left. I took off my trousers and put them on him, got the sleeping-bag ashore, packed him well up in it and spread the sails on the top. He really looked terribly ill when he got ashore,—his face was pale, his long hair and beard were soaking wet, while he foamed at the mouth and had great difficulty in speaking. He trembled all over, and was scarcely able to stand on his legs. As soon as he was comfortably settled in the bag, I had to get all our possessions up on to the ice, to get proper quarters for the night arranged, wring out the wet clothes, cook our food, etc., etc. I went about attending to all this in my scanty apparel, but fortunately the weather was fine. Now and then I went over to the sleeping-bag, in which I could see Nansen lying trembling, and listened. In a while he fell asleep. I let him sleep till everything was ready, and when he awoke and I asked him how he was, he replied in his natural voice, and was otherwise quite himself again.

We now ate the auks which had been shot under such unusual circumstances, after which we discussed the serious event of the day, and agreed that we were most fortunate in still being in possession of all our things.

# CHAPTER XXVII

*Hunting Young Walruses—A Walrus cuts a Hole in Nansen's Kayak—We hear Dogs Barking—Nansen does not Return from his Reconnoitring—Six Strangers on the Ice—The Norwegian Flag Hoisted—Soap and Civilization*

NEXT evening we set out again on our voyage along the edge of the ice. On Sunday, June 14th, we landed at a place where we saw two large herds of walruses lying on the ice, and farther out in the open water there were large numbers diving and blowing. We scented them a long way off; we had never seen such a large number before; there must have been several hundreds of them. We were in want of meat and blubber, and here was plenty of both. Nansen shot two young ones—we had had enough of old ones—from among the herds, but when we ran forward to secure them, their mothers seized their young dead ones with their flippers and disappeared with them into the water; the rest followed, and there we stood looking like fools.

We then approached the other herd and shot both a young one and its mother, in order not to be disappointed again. We took the blubber from the mother and the flesh of the young one, filled our kayaks with it, boiled a good big pot of flesh and dined in grand style on fresh meat; the ribs of the young walrus were excellent and tasted like mutton. Earlier in the day we had shot a number of auks; the whole deck of the kayaks were

## ATTACK BY A WALRUS

now full, and we were well supplied with food again. We had of late been longing for a bear; but, as usual, when we were in need of one, not one was to be seen. Now it did not matter, since we discovered that young walrus was so nice.

After having slept and taken another meal, we proceeded on our way. We generally arranged to paddle only when we had the current with us. The kayaks we lashed together in order to be more secure against any attack by walruses, which swarmed in the water and on the ice on all sides. We could even hear them puffing and blowing just under our kayaks, without coming to the surface. After a while we separated the kayaks, but from time to time we were obliged to lash them together again whenever the walruses became too aggressive.

In this way we kept going during the night before the 15th in quiet, beautiful weather; and little by little the creatures disappeared, till finally we got rid of them altogether. Towards morning, while I was paddling ahead of Nansen, a solitary walrus appeared all at once a short distance in front of us, but it vanished again as soon as it caught sight of us. "It would be great fun to see where it comes up again," I said; "here is a fine place for resting a bit." An ice-foot[1] projected at this point a yard or so into the water, the edge of the ice itself being lower than usual. No sooner had we come to a standstill than the walrus suddenly appeared close beside Nansen's kayak, which was lying outside of mine. It put one of its flippers on the frail craft, hissing and shaking its long tusks, evidently intent upon capsizing Nansen; but the latter threw himself over to the opposite side of the kayak and gave the walrus a blow on the head with his paddle. The creature turned its head a

[1] An ice-foot is that part of a floe which sometimes projects from it under the surface of the water, the upper part having thawed.

little on one side as it raised itself higher in the water, evidently with the intention to attack me, as I stood ready with my paddle to receive it. But suddenly it changed its mind and threw itself back into the water with a big splash and disappeared. The whole thing was over in a moment, and we thought ourselves well out of it, when Nansen suddenly exclaimed, "Let me get ashore quickly; it has cut a hole in my kayak." Fortunately, we were just above the ice-foot, and the kayak was soon aground. Nansen went ashore, and I brought the sinking kayak into a small bay close by where the edge of the ice was very low. There was a big rent in the side of the kayak near the stern through which the water rushed in, so that I had to tilt it over on one side with one hand, keeping the rent above the edge of the water, while with the paddle in the other hand I rowed both the kayaks into the bay. Nansen was standing on the ice-floe with his gun ready to receive the walrus if it should appear again. Some auks which we shot on the way fell into the water and drifted away, but afterwards I paddled out and picked them up. Fortunately, the weather was fine, and the ice where we encamped in good condition; it was only near the water that it was nasty and soft. Nansen got his feet wet, of course, and all his things in the kayak were soaked through. We took them out and placed them on the ground to dry. The sleeping-bag we took hold of, one at each end, and wrung it fairly dry, after which we crept into it and went to sleep, and forgot all about our troubles with the walruses.

On Wednesday, June 17th, great things happened. In the morning we heard dogs barking. After having mended the hole in Nansen's kayak and caulked the seams of both of them with melted stearine, we intended to set out again. It was Nansen's turn to cook, and after having filled the pot with young walrus flesh and salt water, and lighted the fire, he went up on a hummock close by which we had been using as a look-out; and in a little while he called out to me as I lay half asleep in the bag, "Johansen, I hear dogs barking inland!" I lost no time in getting out of the bag and on to the top of the hummock, where I stood listening for a time, while Nansen looked after the cooking. I was not quite sure whether it was dogs that I heard two or three times, or whether it was only the noise made by the thousands of birds which were hatching among the neighbouring rocks. Nansen decided, however, to make an excursion inland and inquire into the matter, while I was to remain behind and look after our things, so that they should not drift away with the ice, for that part of the floe on which our encampment was pitched might easily get loose and drift out to sea. While we were having our breakfast we made all sorts of guesses as to who the people could be, if there really were human beings in these parts. Perhaps they belonged to the English expedition of which we had heard just before the *Fram* left Norway; or perhaps it was Eckeroll, the Norwegian Arctic traveller. As long as we met some people, no matter who they were, we should at least be able to get a proper outfit from them, and find out where we were.

As soon as we had finished our meal, Nansen prepared to start; he took my gun, as his had no shoulder-strap. As we only had a ski and a half each left he took mine, which was whole, so as to make up a perfect pair, and the aluminium glasses he strapped to his back. He also took a good supply of cartridges with him, and thus equipped he set out, after having arranged with me that I should hang a shirt on a bamboo pole, so that he could see where I was.

After Nansen left I went up on the hummock again and listened. I still heard the noisy chatter of the birds, but this surely could not be what Nansen had taken for the barking of dogs! Then, suddenly, borne upon the wind from the interior of the land, came the barking of several dogs, some with hoarse, others with shrill voices; several times, and quite plainly, did it reach my ears, as if it were close at hand on the ice, not more than a mile away, and not from the interior. By this time I was quite sure that it could not be anything but the barking of dogs, so that there must be people about also. How strange to meet with civilized people now, after having lived so long as savages! It seemed almost incredible! I went up and down by the hummock, listening in eager expectation. I hoped Nansen would find the people and soon be back again!

I was becoming more and more anxious about the solution of it all; my shirt was waving high on a long pole fixed on the top of the hummock, and could be seen a good way off, black as it was, against the white snow. At last I saw a black spot appearing now and then among the uneven ice in the direction of the interior. I thought at first it was Nansen coming back, but I soon discovered that the person who was approaching me had no ski, and when he came nearer I saw the long barrel of a gun over his shoulder. He was a stranger—the first strange man I had seen for three years. I hastened to fetch one of our small flags, which I fixed up beside the pole with the shirt, so that he could see what nationality I belonged to.

I next noticed that he had clean, modern clothes, and that his face, too, was clean and washed. I could hear him breathing heavily, and see him sink through the snow now and then; his long boots reached high up over his thighs. I ran towards him; he waved his cap and I my old greasy hat, and soon we were shaking each other by the hand.

"English?" he asked.

## A WELCOME MEETING

"No," I answered; unfortunately, I could not speak his language. I tried German and French; but no, we could not make ourselves understood to each other. Yet there was already an understanding—that which comes from the heart. Mr. Child—that was his name—had set out at once, when he heard from Nansen that he had left his comrade out by the edge of the ice. Nansen had not time to tell him that I did not understand English.

I conducted him to our encampment, and when he saw our sledges and kayaks, our miserable tent, our cooking utensils, with bear's flesh and blubber, I saw his fine, dark eyes wander from me to all these things, while he seemed to be struck with surprise. I used the "finger-language" as best I could, and when we had both done our best to explain ourselves to each other, I saw two more persons approaching. They were Mr. Burgess and Mr. Fisher, the botanist, both of the Jackson Expedition. The same hearty greetings and the same expression of surprise followed; one of them spoke a little German and French, but there were so many questions and so many things they wanted information about, that I was far from being able to satisfy them; but they were expecting a Finlander by the name of Blomkvist, whom they thought would, no doubt, be able to understand me. At last he arrived, together with two other members of the expedition, Mr. Koettlitz, the doctor, and Mr. Armitage, the second in command, as I was informed later. They had taken two fine sledges with them, which at once attracted my attention; they must have been made in Norway, I thought. Blomkvist was a powerfully built fellow, with clearly cut features, which reminded me of the characters described by Runeberg, the Finnish poet. I told him rapidly in rough outlines the history of the expedition: how Nansen and I had left the *Fram* and had penetrated as far as 86° 14′ and wintered in the north without knowing where we were, as our watches had stopped, etc., etc. "Now tell this to the others," I said. "I do not understand you," he replied in Swedish. He had been so long abroad among foreigners that he had almost forgotten his native tongue, and as I spoke to him in Norwegian he had some difficulty in understanding me. I managed, however, to get on very well in German with the doctor, who is of German descent, and he now became our interpreter. Mr. Armitage took out his pocket-flask and filled a cup with port wine, which he offered me. All took off their caps, and with uncovered heads they gave a cheer for Norway, while they looked up at our little flag. My feelings at this moment may be more easily imagined than described; there I stood, in the midst of these brave men, a horrible, blackened savage in rags, and with long hair, suddenly restored to civilization; among a crowd of strange people, who brought with them the fragrance of soap and clean clothes, surrounded by the ice with which we had been struggling for the last three years, while above my head waved the flag which I felt I represented; never have I felt as I did then, that I had a "fatherland," and with uplifted head I drank the cup of welcome, while the Englishmen's cheers rang out across the icefields.

We now broke up the encampment; it was with a feeling of the keenest satisfaction that I took our store of blubber and bear's flesh and threw it away. It was not now worth while to transport this any farther; there would no doubt be some food for us where we were now going. The auks which Nansen and I had shot lay in a heap on the ice. The Englishmen took them and cut off the heads and feet, which they took home with them in remembrance of our meeting. I was not allowed to do anything; I had only to say how I wanted our things packed and transported. I did not forget any of our unpretentious things; I did not want to leave behind anything of what had been of so much use to us.

Dr. Koettlitz had at once put a pipe into my mouth, and Mr. Child gave me a well-filled tobacco-pouch. We then set off inland, three to each sledge; I went along quite free and easy on what remained of my ski, smoking my pipe now and then when we made a halt. I had to tell Dr. Koettlitz about our journey. Before long I could see the Englishmen's houses, one large and four small, just above the shore, and when we got nearer I saw Nansen standing outside the biggest house, black and dirty, and with his long hair, being photographed. I waved my hat, and he waved with his in return. As soon as I came up to him I told him that of all our various methods of travelling over the ice, that by which I had traversed this last part of our journey was the most agreeable, and with this he also agreed.

Mr. Jackson, the chief of the English expedition, now came up to me, and Nansen acted as interpreter between us. I did not take much notice of what was said, but the grasp of the hand which he gave me, and his merry, pleasant face, told me that the well-known English hospitality had in him a splendid representative. I was also introduced to Mr. Hayward, the cook, who set to work to get some hot water ready for the two wild men who had just arrived.

After Nansen had left me to look after the sledges, he again heard the barking of dogs, and before long he met a man with a dog. It was Mr. Jackson. The meeting was a cordial one. Both fired their guns, but, strange to say, I did not hear the shots. Probably the wind was blowing right inland just then.

Nansen had already been inside the house and had some food. Now it was my turn to sit down to the well-spread table; I was sitting in a real chair, eating with a knife and fork. There was bread and butter, sugar, tea, chocolate, and other kinds of civilized food. I looked at my dirty, greasy hands, and did not quite know what I should do with them. Then some one put a looking-glass just before my face. Gracious goodness, what a sight! I had to laugh,—I scarcely recognised my own features. We then had a warm bath with soap and towels; that was the best of all. How comforting to be able to say good-bye to our more than a year old dirt! And then to get clean, soft, woollen clothes on our bodies again, which we had so often spoken about!

And now began the never-to-be-forgotten days at "Elmwood," on Cape Flora. The Englishmen expected a ship from London, which might arrive any day. She would first have to make a trip along the western coast, and then shape her course homeward.

Nansen was quartered with Mr. Jackson in his room, while Dr. Koettlitz moved out of his comrade's, Mr. Armitage, and gave up his place to me. The others lay on the floor in the large common room, with a splendid stove in the middle of it. The shelves on the walls up to the roof were filled with books. The guns had their place in a corner of the room, where a large musical-box was also to be found. There were photographs and pictures everywhere,— yes, this was indeed something quite different from the hut in the far north! And then we got clean, splendid night-shirts of wool, and soap and water before every meal!

## CHAPTER XXVIII

*English Hospitality—A New Life—Post from Norway—Visit from a Bear—Excursions—Waiting for the Ship—Home-sick*

THE time passed quickly and pleasantly; we received the greatest possible attention from these kind people with whom it had been our fortune to meet; they vied with one another in making life as pleasant as possible for us, interested as they all were in Arctic research. I began to learn English, Nansen and Dr. Koettlitz kindly assisting me in my studies. The latter brought out a number of illustrated English comic papers, and was indefatigable in translating the text into German for me. Blomkvist had an old English-Swedish dictionary, which helped me a good deal, and in the library I found all Cooper's novels, which I knew well, having read them in Norwegian. Before long Nansen said that in the future he would speak nothing but English to me.

It seemed quite strange to us to get so many meals a day, we who had been so long accustomed to one or two only during the twenty-four hours; but we ate just as much at each meal as we did formerly, and did not think we ate too often, but looked forward with pleasure to every meal-time. Strange to say, Nansen and I had grown much stouter since we left the *Fram*; the inactive life in the hut, and our diet of bear's flesh and blubber, were no doubt the cause of it. Nor did it look as if we should get any thinner, considering the way we were now living.

When Mr. Jackson and his expedition left Europe, he took with him from Norway letters for Nansen and others on board the *Fram*, in case it should happen that the two expeditions met. The tin box containing the letters was given to Nansen as soon as we arrived at Cape Flora. There were letters for him and two or three members of the expedition, but none for me. The letters were two years old, but in Nansen's there was nothing but good news.

We were now able to ascertain the correctness of our observations. Mr. Armitage compared Nansen's watch for some time with the chronometer at "Elmwood." We then found that we had not been so far out, after all, with regard to our observations for longitude, and that the watches had gone fairly well; we were now able to solve all the problems which had been occupying our minds, with the exception of the discrepancy between Payer's map and the coast-line as we had found it in the course of our journey. Nansen began at once to prepare a new map of Franz Josef Land in accordance with our observations, and with the map which Mr. Jackson had made from his journeys in these islands.

I began to collect and copy our meteorological observations from Nansen's journal since we left the *Fram*, a piece of work which was difficult enough, on account of all the grease and dirt, which had made most of the figures almost unintelligible.

One day a bear came walking up from the shore towards the house. Nansen and Mr. Jackson rushed out, the first with a gun, and the second with a camera; he wanted to get as near as possible to the bear in order to get a good picture of the animal in its wild state, but the bear turned round and walked quietly away from them. Nansen fired a couple of shots after it; it fell to the ground and began digging into the snow. The rest of us stood on the shore watching the bear's efforts to get away. Now and then it sprang at the two dogs, which it evidently thought too forward; one of the dogs was seized and flung some distance off, while the other, the best bear dog, had an artery in one of its paws torn by the bear's claws. Mr. Jackson wanted to put an end to the bear with a revolver, after he had taken the photographs he wanted, so he fired two shots into its head, but this made the bear quite furious; it hissed and snapped, and struck about with its paws, while the snow round about was coloured red with its blood. A ball in its skull at length put an end to its sufferings.

Behind the house a long, steep slope stretched up towards the basalt mountain, which then rose perpendicularly aloft, its summit being crowned with a mantle of ice. A variety of birds—auks and different kinds of sea-gulls—hatched in this mountain; we always heard their noisy chatter whenever we came outside the house. It was fine sport to sit up there in the talus and shoot auks, which flew to and fro quick as lightning between the mountain and the open water in the ice, and there was scarcely a day that we did not have roasted auk's breast. Mr. Jackson was also busy with long ladders up in the steep, loose basalt mountain, gathering eggs from the birds' nests. We had these eggs every morning for breakfast, and found them most palatable.

Mr. Armitage or Dr. Koettlitz and I were generally out for a walk every forenoon in the neighbourhood of the station. On Sunday, June 28th, a small expedition set off for Cape Gertrude. It consisted of Mr.

Armitage, the doctor, the botanist, Mr. Fisher, and myself. We started in the morning and came back in the evening. It did us good to make an excursion during these quiet days. We used ski for the greater part of the way across a glacier; the ski, which had been ordered in Norway for the English expedition by Nansen's brother, were excellent. I found the Englishmen delightful company. At Cape Gertrude we found walrus teeth, petrified wood, whales' bones and skeletons, sandstone in the basalt mountain, and many other things of interest.

One day I went out for a walk by myself; I wanted to get up to the glacier on the top of the mountain, cross it, and get down on the other side of the island. I had no sooner got to the top than I found myself enveloped in a thick fog; I could scarcely see a step before me and hardly dared move from the spot, as I might easily have walked over a precipice. I had then to descend zigzag on my ski down the same way I had come up, and in this manner I managed to get out of the fog. I came across a moraine, where I collected a number of fossils in a bag which I had brought with me, and handed them over to Nansen. He and the doctor occasionally went out hunting for fossils, and when they returned home after such an expedition, and placed their finds on the table, they generally got into a heated discussion as to which had found the most remarkable. One day Mr. Armitage brought home a large snow-owl which he had shot. Some days before we had just been discussing whether this bird existed in these regions. Neither Nansen nor Mr. Jackson had believed it did, but here Mr. Armitage came forward with the best proof regarding the matter; he had shot the owl with a rifle at a somewhat long range.

On July 5th a bear was shot out on an ice-mountain

near the shore. It was Nansen and Mr. Armitage who brought it down; a number of shots were fired before it succumbed, when it was found it had been hit by five bullets. It was photographed several times while the hunt was going on. This time also the rest of us stood as spectators on the shore, and anxiously followed the events of the chase. Mr. Jackson, who had been out shooting auks, arrived on the scene with his camera before the bear was killed. This was the last specimen we saw of these animals, which, for such a long time, had been indispensable to Nansen and myself. The Englishmen only ate the heart and the sirloin of the bears.

One day Mr. Jackson and I set off along the shore, some distance west of the station, to collect whales' bones and skeletons into heaps, in order that it should be easier to get them on board the ship, when it should arrive. We also found a number of mussel shells at this spot. Almost every day we heard the blowing and puffing of walruses out on the ice near the open water. The days passed pleasantly, and in the evenings we often played cards. Our whist-party consisted of Mr. Armitage, Dr. Koettlitz, Mr. Fisher, and myself. On Friday and Saturday evenings the Englishmen were in the habit of drinking a glass of port wine in remembrance of their friends at home. Nansen and I had no objection to assisting on these occasions.

We were now beginning anxiously to expect the ship, which was overdue, and to pay more attention to the state of the ice and the direction of the wind. It might easily happen that the ice prevented the ship from reaching land, and in that case Nansen and I should have to remain where we were for another winter. We talked about a journey across to Spitzbergen, but we were now in the month of July, and we could not be sure of getting there in time to catch the whalers, and we should then have to winter on Spitzbergen; the only chance of getting home this year was that the English ship should arrive within the next few days. It was a great treat to be back among civilized people again, and to have got away from our severe life on the ice. It was pleasant to be among these amiable Englishmen, who did all they could to make us as comfortable as possible after our long fifteen months in the Arctic ice-fields. But we wanted to get home this year.

There cannot be many who have longed more than we to set foot on their own native soil. Our life up in the eternal ice had caused this longing. We had suffered a good many hardships, and more than once we found comfort in recalling to our minds life at home. And although we both firmly believed that we should live to experience the joys of seeing our friends and beloved ones again, there were many occasions which reminded us that human life is but a fragile thing; that man, who calls himself the "lord of creation," is but a poor transitory being—the smallest atom compared with that Power which has produced everything we see and everything we do not see; that Power which, through all eternity, has ruled everything, and through all eternity will guide everything, according to its own—to us inscrutable—laws; that Power which so often has saved us from destruction on this journey! In human eyes, the last winter we spent in our hut, far away from the world, was terrible. It was gruesome with its darkness and its cold, its privations and its longings! But how insignificant is everything when we think of that incomprehensible, eternal law, which places man and millions of lives in the world, and lets them live there the fraction of a second, for we cannot call it longer, compared with the time-measure of the eternal law! How insignificant are the sorrows and troubles of mankind when one's thoughts turn to this! An Arctic night, like that which we have lived through, possibly enables one to learn and understand better than anything else could the nothingness of human sorrows and troubles.

DR. NANSEN ON SKI.

# CHAPTER XXIX

*The "Windward" Arrives—Farewell to Franz Josef Land—The Last of the Ice—Norwegian Soil under our Feet—"Otaria"—The "Fram" has Arrived—We Meet our Comrades Again—Andrée—A Month of Festivities*

WE now began in earnest to watch for the ship. Four of the members of the English expedition—Blomkvist, the Finlander, Mr. Fisher, Mr. Child, and Mr. Burgess—were also going home this year. Day by day passed without any sign of the ship; on the contrary, the wind brought more ice towards the land, and before long we saw nothing but the interminable white expanse again. At night when we turned in to go to sleep, after having cast a last look out over the ice to see if we could not discover the long-expected masts of the ship, Blomkvist would always remark in English, "No ship, no home!" This fellow also longed for home after the roving life he had led. He had been so long abroad that he had almost forgotten his own language.

Another important event in our life during this remarkable journey occurred on Sunday, July 28th. Early in the morning I was awakened by hearing my companions busily talking; they were all running about in their night-shirts. The ship from London had arrived! She lay by the edge of the ice, looking enormously big, with her hull and three masts! And how near land she had got! In the course of the night the north wind had swept the loose ice, which had been lying outside the edge of the shore-ice, out to sea. The name of the ship was the *Windward*; she had found her way from the largest city in the world up among the eternal ice, and was bringing tidings from the busy world from which we had been so long away.

THE *WINDWARD*.

Mr. Jackson and Blomkvist were the first to go on board, and the latter came back with the information that the *Fram* had not returned to Norway, and that nobody had heard anything about her. Nansen afterwards went on board, while Mr. Armitage and I went to bed again after having enjoyed the sight of the *Windward* for some time. But before long the room was filled with people from the ship; they were all speaking at once, questioning and answering each other. I had heard that there used to be Norwegians among the crew of the *Windward*. Perhaps, thought I, some of those in the other room might be my countrymen! I went into the room in my night-shirt, and asked in Norwegian: "Is there anybody here from Norway?" "Yes, I!" said one voice. "I, also!" said another. "Here is one!" came from a corner of the room; there seemed to be plenty of them. I was now thoroughly awake; I began asking questions, and the three all answered at once. They belonged to that class of Norwegian sailors who always sail in foreign ships, very rarely visit their native country, and seldom speak any other language but English. I then got to hear all the news. In Norway everything was much the same as when we left. China and Japan had been pitching into each other, and the great celestial empire had got a licking. Russia had got a new Emperor, and France a new President. I was also told that in Norway they had received information that the *Fram* had been wrecked in the ice, but that the members of the expedition had been to the North Pole, and had got back to the New Siberian Islands. In this respect I was afraid that Nansen and I would disappoint our countrymen, as we had not got as far as the Pole. In any case, however, we had the satisfaction of knowing that we had done what we could.

We were received with open arms by the whole of the crew on board the *Windward*. The able and excellent Captain Brown did all he could to make us as comfortable as possible. He had brought with him two new Arctic explorers, Dr. Bruce and Mr. Wilton, who both were to winter and take part in Mr. Jackson's expedition. Nansen and I were daily guests on board, where the cook dished up the best things the ship possessed, while Captain Brown and others were busy telling us what had happened during the last three years. There was a party every evening with singing and merriment in the pleasant saloon of the vessel.

Every one was now busy unloading the things which the ship had brought; amongst them were four reindeer, which were to be used on the sledge expedition next year. But the reindeer did not seem to like the place; one had died on the voyage, and the remaining four also died before we left, although there was sufficient reindeer moss for them on board the *Windward*. Some fine sheep, however, which they had brought with them, seemed to thrive very well. The landing of the cargo was quickly accomplished, although it had to be drawn on sledges for a considerable distance from the ship to the shore; and in a week the *Windward* was ready to depart, but she had to wait a few days longer for the homeward letters.

One morning, when we awoke and looked out of the window, the ship had disappeared. A gale, blowing inshore, had driven the ice in against the shore-ice, and the *Windward* had gone adrift, and was obliged to seek a harbour farther west in very shallow water. But the ice began closing in upon her, and at one time it seemed as if she would be wedged in against the land. Fortunately, in a couple of days, she got clear, and now there was a busy time getting ready in earnest for the ship's departure. On the 7th of August the *Windward* was lying with steam up, some distance out to sea, as there was a good deal of loose ice outside the shore-ice, which made it somewhat difficult to get on board. Captain Brown sat in the crow's-nest watching the treacherous ice, and giving his orders in a loud voice; he kept the ship going backwards and forwards, incessantly blowing the ship's whistle. The boat, which had come to fetch Nansen and myself, only just escaped being crushed between two floes. We saw them approaching each other some distance off, but it was the only opening which we could get through for the moment, and the men rowed with all their might; things looked critical, but we just managed to get through, and the moment the stern of the boat was clear of the ice, the heavy floes clashed together with such a force that their edges were crushed to bits. Outside lay the ship in open water, and before long we found ourselves on her deck. But Mr. Fisher, who was going back in her, and the post-bag had not yet arrived; while Dr. Koettlitz, who was not going with us, was still on board. Some distance westwards there was a bay in the ice, for which Captain Brown steered, still sitting in the crow's-nest, and a boat was launched to put Dr. Koettlitz ashore. Partly by rowing and partly by dragging the boat across the floes, Mr. Fisher, with the post-bag and some boxes of fossils, got on board at last. It was with a sigh of relief that we saw the boat hoisted up to its place under the davits, while the farewell cheers resounded across the ice-fields, where we could see Dr. Koettlitz struggling to get ashore to his five comrades.

It was not long before we met with the ice. Captain Brown sat in the crow's-nest and directed the course with that rare ability which he has acquired in his Arctic voyages during many years. He sat there day and night, only going down now and then to get something to eat; he slept no more than was absolutely necessary. The *Windward* broke through the ice at last, on the 11th of August, and then we said farewell to the ice, in which Nansen and I had spent three years of our life. On the same day we saw the first sail on the horizon, and afterwards we saw several more; we felt that we were approaching our goal; the moment which had so often stood before us as the highest of all our desires, the goal of our longings, could not now be far off!

The next day we caught sight of land on the horizon;

# AN EYE-OPENER

it was Norway, our native country! We were only just able to distinguish it in the evening twilight, but still there it was. Next morning we saw its rocky coast; we had got in under land too far north, and had now to shape our course southwards to Vardö. We now saw many ships, with which we exchanged greetings, and before long we had the pilot-boat alongside. The pilot

WATCHING THE FIRST SAIL IN SIGHT.

came on board with his son, and after having exchanged a few words with Captain Brown, the latter asked him, pointing to Nansen, whether he knew that man. The pilot had heard Nansen speaking in Norwegian to me, and was wondering who the Norwegians were who were standing on the bridge of the *Windward*; he evidently seemed to think that we were not properly dressed either. The captain had to tell him it was Nansen, and then he opened his eyes properly. Surprise and joy were to be read in his weather-beaten features; he shook hands with us, and wished us welcome home. Both he, and many with him, had never believed that any of the *Fram's* crew would escape with their lives. But of the *Fram* no tidings had been heard since she left Norway. While we pressed the pilot for news, and he in turn got us to relate some of our adventures, the *Windward* had entered the harbour of Vardö, and the harbour-master came on board. While the anchor was being dropped, Nansen and I got into a boat with the pilot and rowed ashore, in order to get to the telegraph office, to which the pilot showed us the way. No one knew the two strange men, whose dress was the only thing that attracted attention; it was not difficult to see that they were borrowed plumes which we displayed; I myself was wearing the jacket I had made in our winter hut. Some cyclists, whom we passed, looked so obtrusively civilized with their cycling costumes and with their new machines; they glanced at my somewhat original jacket made out of my blanket, but no one had any idea who we were. A cow was walking about by itself in a small street; we could not help looking at her with some curiosity; such animals were not be found where we had been wandering about; we must assuredly be home now. We stamped our feet on the ground, glad to feel the soil of our native country beneath them again. We went into the telegraph office with strange feelings. Nansen put a large bundle of telegrams on the desk before the superintendent, who happened to be present at the moment. "Here are some telegrams," said Nansen, "which I should like to get sent off as soon as possible." The superintendent received the bundle with some hesitation, as he scanned the stranger in the office; but no sooner had he looked at the first telegram than he gave a start, and turned round towards the table, where the lady telegraphists were sitting. He then came back to Nansen and wished him welcome home. He would have to go out and fetch his reserves, he said, and he would keep them at work night and day, in order to get the telegrams off quickly. It was no joke to get so many telegrams handed in at once. Two of Nansen's telegrams to the Press amounted to several thousand words; he had written these out on Franz Josef Land

ARRIVAL AT HAMMERFEST.

in Norwegian and English. We had besides no less than fifty odd telegrams from our comrades on board the *Fram*. These I had all written out during our stay with Mr. Jackson; Scott-Hansen had copied them all in microscopic writing on a small piece of paper, and given us when we left the *Fram*.

Before we left the telegraph office the first telegrams were already sent off. They were to Nansen's wife, my mother, the nearest relatives of the *Fram* crew, and to the King and the Norwegian Government. We then walked over to the hotel, where, according to the telegraph superintendent, Professor Mohn was staying. He had taken special interest in the *Fram* expedition, and we were, of course, most anxious to meet him. In the entrance hall of the hotel we met one of the girls. I thought how long it was since I had seen such a pretty creature, and when Nansen asked for Professor Mohn the young lady scanned us from top to toe, wondering, no doubt, what we wanted with a professor. She told us, however, the number of his room, and Nansen rushed straight in to him. I have never seen any one so surprised as the Professor was, as he jumped up from the sofa on which he was lying, smoking his pipe, and recognised the tall figure before him. "Is it Fridtjof Nansen? Is it possible?" But when he heard Nansen's voice he was no longer in doubt, and, greatly moved, he clasped Nansen in his arms. It took some time before Professor Mohn, during the hubbub of questions and answers which now ensued, could understand what had happened to the expedition; but when he had got to the bottom of it, the jubilation broke loose. Champagne was brought in, and a friend of the Professor turned up and joined the company.

Before long the town had got to know who we were; there were crowds of people outside the hotel, and the ships in the harbour ran up their flags, while a band, called the "Northpole," played the National Anthem outside our windows. We were, indeed, back in Norway! While in Vardö we got fine, new clothes, and I must not forget to mention that we had a Russian bath, which helped us to get rid of the last remnants of the dirt that was left on us after our life in the hut; it was only now that we succeeded in getting thoroughly clean.

After a pleasant time in Vardö, where we met with the greatest hospitality, we went on to Hammerfest, where the whole town turned out on our arrival. In the harbour lay a fine English yacht, the *Otaria*. The owner was on deck, as our steamer came gliding in, and shouted a welcome to Nansen. Nansen recognised in him an English friend, Sir George Baden-Powell, who came on board to us at once, and asked us to be his guests on board his yacht. We accepted his kind offer and moved on board the *Otaria*, the splendid and elegantly furnished saloons of which did not exactly remind us of our poor hut, but still brought us to make a comparison between our life now and then; it seemed an eternity since we were up there in the north.

In Hammerfest Mr. Nansen and Christofersen, Nansen's Secretary, arrived, the latter of whom we had bidden good-bye, in Khabarova, three years ago. It was, indeed, a joyful experience to be home again. Everybody was so kind and amiable—nothing but happy faces were to be seen around us everywhere. The town gave a splendid fête in our honour, amid general jubilation and festivity. There was one drawback in all our joy: where were our comrades on board the *Fram*? We could not be quite happy as long as their fate was unknown. Although we believed they were safe on board their gallant craft, we had as yet no definite assurance of their welfare; and it was getting late in the season. If they did not arrive now, we could not expect them till next year. Perhaps they were just as badly off as we were well off? On the morning of the 20th of August a man came on board the *Otaria* with a telegram for Nansen, who was not yet fully dressed. He must come as he is, said the man—it was the superintendent of the telegraph office himself—the telegram was important! Nansen, evidently suspecting something, came out and tore open the telegram. I heard a great noise in the passage outside my cabin and opened the door a little, when I caught sight of Nansen with the telegram in his hand. There was a peculiar expression, full of emotion, in his face; his eyes were staring at the writing. At last he managed to blurt out, "The *Fram* has arrived!" It was as if a bombshell had burst in our midst; the telegraph superintendent stood quietly watching the effect upon Sir George, Christofersen, and myself. We were thoroughly aroused, and no mistake! "The *Fram* has arrived!" It was the one thing wanting to make all our happiness complete. The telegram ran as follows:—

SKJÆRVÖ, 20-8-96—9 a.m.

DOCTOR NANSEN,—
*Fram* arrived here to-day in good condition. All well on board. Leaving at once for Tromsö. Welcome home.

OTTO SVERDRUP.

So they were not so far away after all, and we should meet them in Tromsö. The news spread like wildfire over the town; the people went almost wild with joy. Everybody seemed suddenly to be rushing about. We on board the *Otaria* longed to be on the way to Tromsö. The *Windward* heaved her anchor before us, and steamed out of the harbour amid jubilant cheers for the *Fram*.

The next day we caught sight of the lofty masts and the crow's-nest of the *Fram*, and soon we glided alongside her, our good, faithful ship. She seemed a little the worse for wear and tear, and well she might; but she had escaped safe and sound from the ice, which was pressing her so hard in its embrace when we left her in the great loneliness of the far north. Now the merry waves played caressingly round the strong

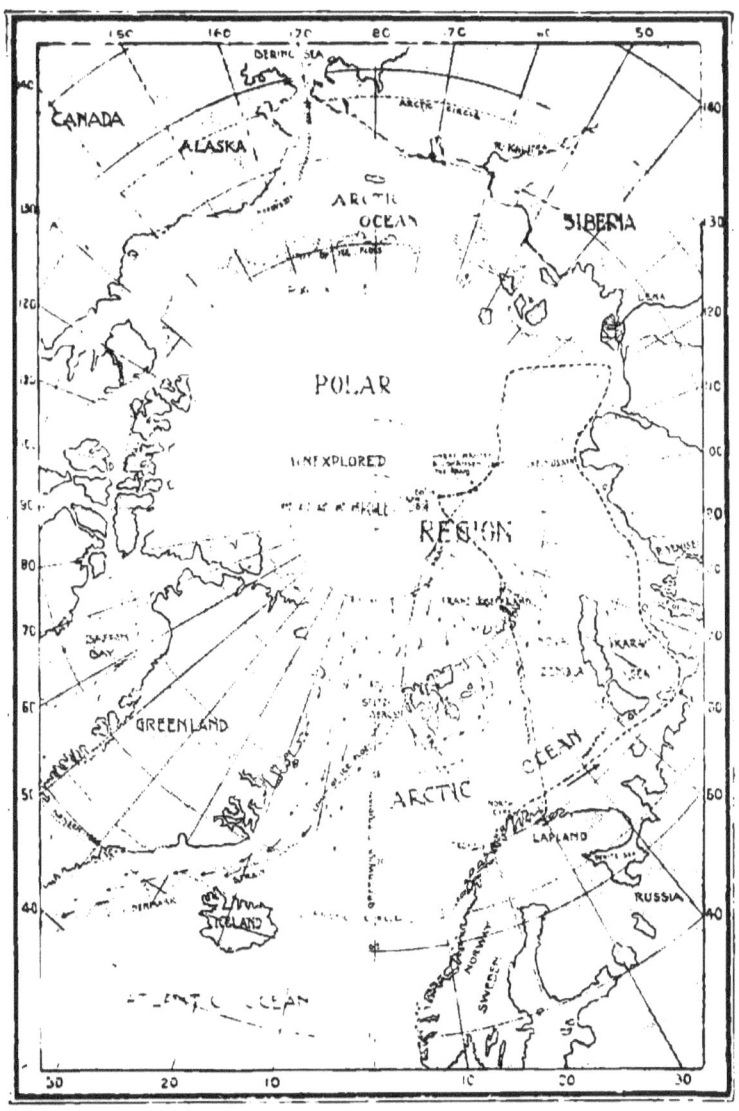

MAP SHOWING DR. NANSEN'S ROUTE.
*With Nansen in the North.*]

hull. "Three cheers for the *Fram*," came from the *Otaria*, as she glided slowly alongside the former and dropped her anchor. "Hurrah!" shouted the boys on

JOHANSEN ON BOARD SIR GEORGE BADEN-POWELL'S YACHT.

the *Fram* in return, as they lowered one of the boats and jumped into it. They now came rowing towards us; most of them were still dressed in their Arctic clothes, and some of them had grown long beards. I saw Bentsen in the bow, and Scott-Hansen in the middle of the boat; he had already provided himself with a new hat and clothes, but he had not shaved off his beard. There, too, was Peder, with an arm in a sling, and all the others beaming with joy and standing in the boat waving their hands. The next moment they were close to the bow of the *Otaria*, where I was standing. I leaned over the railing and shouted: "Welcome, boys!" Bentsen seized my hand and tried to haul me down into the boat; they then jumped over the railing one after the other. "You have done well," said Nansen to them. I cannot describe the moving scenes that followed on the deck of the *Otaria*. It was joy at being together again, after having escaped unscathed the terrors of the ice-desert, which animated us. Sir George Baden-Powell and his wife stood at some distance, enjoying our happiness. "Your comrades seem to be very glad to see you again," said Sir George to me later on. Yes, indeed, our gladness was such as one seldom feels in this life.

We had then to tell one another our adventures since we parted up in the far north. Nansen and I learnt how they had fared during the last and the longest Arctic night; it seemed that they had not had it altogether so comfortable either; but they had all along grown fonder and fonder of the *Fram*. She had carried them right up to 86° north latitude; no finer craft sailed the seas, and she did not disappoint her friends. She bore her name well, and forced her way where it often seemed hopeless; she did not mind if they laid mines, which shattered the heavy ice against her hull; she merely shook herself from truck to keel, but as for betraying us—no, that she never did!

On August 13th, the same day that Nansen and I

set foot on Norwegian soil, the *Fram* forced her way out into open water and shaped her course for

MEETING OF NANSEN AND ANDRÉE.

Spitzbergen, where one morning they fell in with a sailing ship which they hailed and asked after Nansen and Johansen. "Have they come back?" "No," was the answer. "Joy and sorrow wander together," as the old saying runs, the truth of which our comrades, no doubt, felt then. And probably the thought also stole in upon them that we were not likely to return, since no one had heard anything of us, who, they thought, had reached home safely long ago. They felt sure, when we left them, that if we did get home, we should do so the same year.

The name of the ship they met was *The Sisters*. From the Captain they learnt that Mr. Andrée, the Swedish explorer, was at Danes Island with a balloon, in which he intended to start for the Pole. Sad at heart they steered for Danes Island to ascertain if the Swedish expedition there had heard anything further about us. They met with a cordial reception from the Swedes, but they could give no other information than that they had heard nothing. But when our comrades heard about the Jackson Expedition on Franz Josef Land they thought we might be there. If we were not, they knew that if we were alive at all, we should want immediate assistance. They therefore decided to make for Norway, to get certain information as to whether we had been heard of. If not, they intended returning at once to search for us. But when they arrived at Skjærvö one night, and Sverdrup had got the telegraph superintendent roused, he learnt the joyful news that Nansen and I had arrived at Vardö on the 13th. Blessing told me afterwards that he had seen Sverdrup coming running back at a great pace from the telegraph office. They then suspected he was bringing good news, and when their expectations were turned into certainty, the cannons were loaded and a salute of two shots announced in the early morning to the sleeping inhabitants of Skjærvö that something unusual had happened. There was general jubilation, now that their joy was unmingled. They could now give themselves up entirely to the pleasure of being back in Norway. Skjærvö seemed like a paradise to them; there they saw flowers, grass and trees, which their eyes had not looked upon for three years. The whole thirteen of them had come back hale and hearty to their native land, and now all their troubles and cares were at an end.

THE *FRAM* BEING TOWED ALONG THE NORWEGIAN COAST ON THE HOMEWARD JOURNEY.

Soon after the meeting with our comrades in Tromsö, another ship steamed into the harbour; it was Andrée's ship, the *Virgo*, which had returned from Spitzbergen, with the members of the expedition and the balloon on board. Andrée had not been able to make his ascent, on account of the bad state of the weather. Some of us went on board to pay our respects to the members of the expedition, and we were received with the utmost heartiness. Andrée made a speech and cordially wished us welcome home, to which Nansen replied, wishing that Andrée's ingenious plan might be realized the following year, when the conditions might be more favourable. Andrée told me, in the course of the conversation I had with him, that it was with no light heart he was obliged to return; but his resolution and his belief in the possibility of carrying out his plan were as great as ever. It was only a question of patience, and to me he appeared to possess this rare virtue, so indispensable to an Arctic explorer.

We old comrades had a very happy time together as we sailed down the coast of our fatherland. A tugboat, the *Haalogaland*, took the *Fram* in tow, and the *Otaria* followed in her wake as far as Trondhjem. I moved at once from the elegant saloons of the *Otaria* on to the *Fram*, and took up my quarters in "The Grand," which was full of reindeer skins and sleeping-bags, and lived there until we anchored in Christiania.

For a whole month we lived through one continuous series of festivities. We had never dreamt that Norway would receive us in the way she did. Wherever we went, all vied with one another—rich and poor alike—in honouring us and wishing us welcome. And it was a great satisfaction to feel that we had really done something of which our country was proud. It was a splendid reward for all our hardships and privations. The towns competed with each other in entertaining us. At Stavanger, where we arrived in the middle of the night, we were prevented from stopping for any length of time, as we had to proceed at once. When we left the harbour two shots thundered forth from the *Fram*, the like of which we had never heard before while on board her—the whole ship trembled in her timbers. It was Peder who was responsible for this salute. He had, on this occasion, risen from harpooner to gunner. We asked him why he had loaded the cannons so heavily, and whether he did not wish to live any longer, now that he had returned home. But he thought we were all a lot of fools, since we could not understand that he had fired such a loud salute because we had to leave the town without giving the inhabitants an opportunity of getting up any festivities for us. "Well, the least we could do was to give them a proper salute, anyhow," was his opinion.

Our reception in Christiania was most impressive. None of us will ever forget the moment when we landed. The whole of the fjord was filled with vessels in gala attire, and on the shore there was one interminable mass of people. But there was a silence over the people which inspired one with a feeling of solemnity, especially when the large choir intoned: "Praise the Lord, the mighty King, with honour!"

And now we are home; but up among the eternal ice the solitude reigns greater than ever, for no longer does any vessel lie there to disturb the wild play of the ice, and no longer are human beings trying to penetrate its secrets. Or perhaps the ice-desert was now seething with rage, because a handful of men had bidden defiance to the edict that its territory was forbidden ground, and had penetrated into regions hitherto untrodden by human foot.

www.ingramcontent.com/pod-product-compliance
Lightning Source LLC
Chambersburg PA
CBHW030341230426

43664CB00007BA/496